Ecclesiastes

and

Song of Songs

TEACH THE TEXT COMMENTARY SERIES

John H. Walton
Old Testament General Editor

Mark L. Strauss
New Testament General Editor

When complete, the Teach the Text Commentary Series *will include the following volumes:*

Old Testament Volumes

New Testament Volumes

To see which titles are available, visit the series website at www.teachthetextseries.com.

TEACH the TEXT
COMMENTARY SERIES

Ecclesiastes
and
Song of Songs

Edward M. Curtis

Mark L. Strauss and John H. Walton

GENERAL EDITORS

Rosalie de Rosset

ASSOCIATE EDITOR

BakerBooks

a division of Baker Publishing Group
Grand Rapids, Michigan

© 2013 by Edward M. Curtis
Captions and Illustrating the Text sections © 2013 by Baker Publishing Group

Published by Baker Books
a division of Baker Publishing Group
P.O. Box 6287, Grand Rapids, MI 49516-6287
www.bakerbooks.com

Printed in the United States of America

Library of Congress Cataloging-in-Publication Data
Curtis, Edward M.
    Ecclesiastes and Song of Songs / Edward M. Curtis.
        pages cm. — (Teach the text commentary series)
    Includes bibliographical references and index.
    ISBN 978-0-8010-9223-7 (cloth)
    1. Bible. Ecclesiastes—Commentaries. 2. Bible. Song of Solomon—
Commentaries. I. Title.
BS1475.53.C87 2013
223′.807—dc23   2013006733

13   14   15   16   17   18   19   7   6   5   4   3   2   1

This volume is dedicated to my excellent wife, Joy who has patiently encouraged me in ministry and in projects like this one. Her wise insights in reading through the various drafts of this commentary have made it a better volume. Her love for me gives me regular glimpses of what God's *hesed* looks like, and I greatly appreciate her partnership for the last forty-seven years.

The volume is also dedicated to my two grandchildren, Ryken and Aven. They have brought immeasurable delight to their Pop-pop. I pray that they may continue to grow in their love for God and others and have the wisdom and courage to live out God's truth in the world. I trust that they will find meaning and fulfillment in the world that Qoheleth describes as they live in trusting dependence on our sovereign Lord.

Contents

Welcome to the Teach the Text Commentary Series

Why another commentary series? That was the question the general editors posed when Baker Books asked us to produce this series. Is there something that we can offer to pastors and teachers that is not currently being offered by other commentary series, or that can be offered in a more helpful way? After carefully researching the needs of pastors who teach the text on a weekly basis, we concluded that yes, more can be done; this commentary is carefully designed to fill an important gap.

The technicality of modern commentaries often overwhelms readers with details that are tangential to the main purpose of the text. Discussions of source and redaction criticism, as well as detailed surveys of secondary literature, seem far removed from preaching and teaching the Word. Rather than wade through technical discussions, pastors often turn to devotional commentaries, which may contain exegetical weaknesses, misuse the Greek and Hebrew languages, and lack hermeneutical sophistication. There is a need for a commentary that utilizes the best of biblical scholarship but also presents the material in a clear, concise, attractive, and user-friendly format.

This commentary is designed for that purpose—to provide a ready reference for the exposition of the biblical text, giving easy access to information that a pastor needs to communicate the text effectively. To that end, the commentary is divided into carefully selected preaching units, each covered in six pages (with carefully regulated word counts both in the passage as a whole and in each subsection). Pastors and teachers engaged in weekly preparation thus know that they will be reading approximately the same amount of material on a week-by-week basis.

Each passage begins with a concise summary of the central message, or "Big Idea," of the passage and a list of its main themes. This is followed by a more detailed interpretation of the text, including the literary context of the passage, historical background material, and interpretive insights. While drawing on the best of biblical scholarship, this material is clear, concise, and to the point. Technical material is kept to a minimum, with endnotes pointing the reader to more detailed discussion and additional resources.

A second major focus of this commentary is on the preaching and teaching process itself. Few commentaries today help the pastor/teacher move from the meaning of the text to its effective communication. Our goal is to bridge this gap. In addition to interpreting the text in the "Understanding the Text" section, each six-page unit contains a "Teaching the Text" section and an "Illustrating the Text" section. The teaching section points to the key theological themes of the passage and ways to communicate these themes to today's audiences. The illustration section provides ideas and examples for retaining the interest of hearers and connecting the message to daily life.

The creative format of this commentary arises from our belief that the Bible is not just a record of God's dealings in the past but is the living Word of God, "alive and active" and "sharper than any double-edged sword" (Heb. 4:12). Our prayer is that this commentary will help to unleash that transforming power for the glory of God.

The General Editors

Introduction to the Teach the Text Commentary Series

This series is designed to provide a ready reference for teaching the biblical text, giving easy access to information that is needed to communicate a passage effectively. To that end, the commentary is carefully divided into units that are faithful to the biblical authors' ideas and of an appropriate length for teaching or preaching.

The following standard sections are offered in each unit.

1. *Big Idea*. For each unit the commentary identifies the primary theme, or "Big Idea," that drives both the passage and the commentary.
2. *Key Themes*. Together with the Big Idea, the commentary addresses in bullet-point fashion the key ideas presented in the passage.
3. *Understanding the Text*. This section focuses on the exegesis of the text and includes several sections.
   a. The Text in Context. Here the author gives a brief explanation of how the unit fits into the flow of the text around it, including reference to the rhetorical strategy of the book and the unit's contribution to the purpose of the book.
   b. Outline/Structure. For some literary genres (e.g., epistles), a brief exegetical outline may be provided to guide the reader through the structure and flow of the passage.
   c. Historical and Cultural Background. This section addresses historical and cultural background information that may illuminate a verse or passage.
   d. Interpretive Insights. This section provides information needed for a clear understanding of the passage. The intention of the author is to be highly selective and concise rather than exhaustive and expansive.
   e. Theological Insights. In this very brief section the commentary identifies a few carefully selected theological insights about the passage.
4. *Teaching the Text*. Under this second main heading the commentary offers

guidance for teaching the text. In this section the author lays out the main themes and applications of the passage. These are linked carefully to the Big Idea and are represented in the Key Themes.

5. *Illustrating the Text*. Here the commentary provides suggestions of where useful illustrations may be found in fields such as literature, entertainment, history, or biography. They are intended to provide general ideas for illustrating the passage's key themes and so serve as a catalyst for effectively illustrating the text.

Abbreviations

ASV	American Standard Version	NIV	New International Version
b.	born	NLT	New Living Translation
ca.	*circa*, about, approximately	NRSV	New Revised Standard Version
cf.	*confer*, compare	pp.	pages
e.g.	*exempli gratia*, for example	v(v).	verse(s)
ESV	English Standard Version	ZIBBCOT	John H. Walton, ed. *Zondervan*
Heb.	Hebrew		*Illustrated Bible Backgrounds*
KJV	King James Version		*Commentary: Old Testament.* 5
ll.	lines		vols. Grand Rapids: Zondervan,
NAB	New American Bible		2009.
NASB	New American Standard Bible		

Introduction to Ecclesiastes

Qoheleth and the Issues of Life: A Broader Biblical Perspective

Qoheleth[1] (the Hebrew name for the teacher credited with the material in this book; see the commentary on Eccles. 1:1), or the "Teacher" (NIV) or "Preacher" (ESV), describes an imperfect world where things often do not work the way it appears they should. It is a world seemingly characterized by randomness and arbitrariness, abounding in things we cannot understand or control. Inequities of all sorts occur; people sometimes work hard but are unable to enjoy the fruits of their labors, while others who have done little useful work are able to enjoy the pleasures of life. Our knowledge of the patterns that constitute wisdom is always partial, and attempts to discover how the world works in any comprehensive way always end in failure. For Qoheleth these are the realities of life under the sun. There is injustice, there are abuses of power, the potential for success is not evenly distributed among individuals, and people will encounter difficult circumstances, despite the fact that they seem to be doing the right things.

Qoheleth's observations leave us wondering how a person should live in the light of such realities. He obviously sees value in recognizing the realities of life and does not set us up to expect a life free of difficulty

Qoheleth warns that power and achievements will not bring ultimate fulfillment. However, the numerous monuments, steles, and statues erected by rulers in the ancient world highlight the allure of those goals. This stele of King Adad-Nirari III, king of Assyria (810–783 BC), describes his military campaigns into Palestine. The end of the inscription reads, "At that time I had an image of my royal self made. The power of my might, the deeds of my hands, I inscribed thereon."

and trouble. At the same time, he does not conclude that these distressing realities justify disengaging from life, but he tells us to be diligent and proactive as we live. The many proverbs in the book emphasize the importance of living wisely and rejecting the path of folly. Qoheleth emphasizes the importance of living a balanced life and encourages developing significant interpersonal relationships. He also warns against attempts to find meaning and fulfillment in money, power, or achievements. While Qoheleth recognizes that there are inequities in the opportunities that are available for people to enjoy, he affirms the importance of enjoying life and recognizes that opportunities for pleasure and enjoyment exist even in the most difficult circumstances.

Most people today would acknowledge that the world we experience is imperfect and is characterized by randomness and chaos, and many would argue that life as we experience it is all that there is. There is no life after death to which a person might look for hope; there is no supernatural or spiritual realm, and our task as human beings is to make the best of life in this world. There is no meaning to life except what we determine for ourselves. These people would concur with much of Qoheleth's pragmatic advice, but they would also conclude that ultimately we must agree with Macbeth:

> Life's but a walking shadow, a poor
>   player
> That struts and frets his hour upon the
>   stage
> And then is heard no more: it is a tale
> Told by an idiot, full of sound and fury,
> Signifying nothing. (act 5, scene 5)

Such perceived realities lead many to resignation and despair, while others find some satisfaction and fulfillment in useful and productive lives, healthy relationships, and helping others.

The worldview reflected in Ecclesiastes is very different from that of modern secular culture. Qoheleth embraces the view that is normative throughout the Old Testament.[2] He affirms the existence of God and recognizes that God's providence is at work in the world and in human history, though often in ways that we are unable to understand fully. But the fact that God is at work does not alter the way Qoheleth (or anyone else) experiences the world, so given the apparent randomness and the chaotic nature of human experience, what are we to conclude? Is it not the case that the providence of God somehow lies behind all the outcomes that we observe, including the anomalies and inequities? How does this relate to our understanding of who God is and how he works in the world?

For those convinced that God is a part of the broader reality and that his providence plays an active role in human affairs, the issues that Qoheleth points out are significant. How can God be all-powerful, just, and good when life works the way it does? Some attempt to resolve the problem by redefining the nature of God and conclude that the God who governs the world cannot be the loving and compassionate God whom many parts of Scripture describe. An all-powerful god who oversees the kind of world in which we live could only be a capricious and unjust tyrant. Others, like Rabbi Harold Kushner, argue that while God is good and compassionate, the moral governance of the universe is such an immense task that he is unable to address every issue that arises, and some things just fall through the cracks. After years of reflecting on the tragic illness and death of his son, Rabbi Kushner says, "I believe in God. But I do not believe the same things about Him that I did years ago. . . . I recognize His limitations. He is limited in what He can do by laws of nature and by the evolution of human nature and human moral freedom."[3] He goes on to say that despite this discovery, we should continue to love God and forgive him. If you can do this, Kushner says, it is possible "to live fully, bravely, and meaningfully in this less-than-perfect world."[4] Scripture, however, declares that Yahweh is the sovereign and all-powerful Lord who created and upholds all things; Scripture also declares him to be compassionate, good, and just. The struggle of Christian theology has been to understand how these things can be true given the realities that are the common experience of those who live in the world.[5] It is these questions that Qoheleth sets in stark relief, though for the most part without giving his readers clear and explicit answers.

Christians have understood the lack of perfection in the world to be a consequence of human disobedience in the Garden of Eden, and it seems clear that Qoheleth is describing a fallen world. The toil and struggle that he portrays could be viewed as flowing out of the judgment on human beings because of their rebellion against God, and the limits to human understanding stemming from their finitude are further diminished by the fall. Human rebellion and refusal to live according to God's order could be seen as contributing to the chaos that characterizes life under the sun. While these ideas account for some of the lack of congruence between what we see and the way things should be, Qoheleth never does more than obliquely allude to these theological ideas.

A crucial issue that any person of faith must grapple with is the tension between Scripture's numerous unequivocal theological statements about the nature of God and life experiences that seem to contradict those statements, and Qoheleth was not the only person in Israel who dealt with such challenges. Walter Brueggemann notes

Ecclesiastes does not directly address the reason why life is filled with hardship and toil, although Qoheleth would not disagree that it is a result of the fall. Adam and Eve try to hide behind fig leaves after they succumb to temptation in this relief on the sarcophagus of Junius Bassus (d. AD 359).

a pattern of orientation–disorientation–reorientation in the psalms.[6] People are oriented to see the world in ways that reflect the general orderliness, goodness, and reliability of life. Sometimes, though, difficult experiences are disorienting, bringing into question that understanding of the world. Personal tragedies, or threats or disasters that impact a community or nation, may cause people to question the worldview that they comfortably embraced when things were going well. Such circumstances force them to struggle with the dissonance between the way they thought things were and the new realities that seem incongruent with the old worldview. Out of the tension created by such experiences, people come to a reorientation that integrates the previous understanding and the new experience. Unlike most biblical examples, where a personal or corporate crisis is the catalyst that forces the worldview modification, Qoheleth focuses more broadly on realities of life that are in tension with what was probably the typical orientation of many Israelites. He seems determined to challenge his readers and force them to struggle toward new understandings consistent with the realities he observes in the world.

Qoheleth raises questions and challenges us in ways that contribute to disorientation and struggle, but he does not normally answer the questions for us. One could conclude from Qoheleth's evidence that we must embrace an agnostic position where no certain conclusions about God or the meaning of life are possible. Obviously, many of Qoheleth's questions cannot be answered on the basis of the experiences of life, and if any answers are possible, they will have to come from some outside source.

For Israel that outside source was God's self-revelation to his people through the prophets and through his works in creation and history. It is likely that Qoheleth's own answers would include this revelation, since he tells us to "fear God and keep his commandments" (12:13), but how does one live by faith in God's revelation in ways that are consistent with reality? Obviously a naïve faith that flies in the face of reality does not reflect wisdom, but how does a person strike the balance in ways that do?

Gerhard von Rad identifies one aspect of the answer in his comment about Proverbs 21:30–31, which recognizes that outcomes ultimately depend not on human skill and determination but on God's providential oversight. Von Rad translates the verses, "There is no wisdom, no understanding, no counsel against Yahweh; the horse is made ready for the day of battle, but the victory belongs to Yahweh." He recognizes that the point of this proverb is not to discourage a person from diligence and planning.

> If one were to remove [this proverb] from its context one could even perceive in it the expression of a radical, theological agnosticism. But this would be to misunderstand it completely. Its aim is, rather, to put a stop to the erroneous concept that a guarantee of success was to be found simply in practising human wisdom and in making preparations. Man must always keep himself open to the activity of God, an activity which completely escapes all calculation, for between the putting into practice of the most reliable wisdom and that which then actually takes place, there always lies a great unknown. Is that a dangerous doctrine? Must not—we might ask—as a result of this great unknown factor, a veil of resignation lie over all

human knowledge and action? This question can be answered only by the degree of trust which man is capable of placing in that divine activity which surpasses all planning. The double sentence of Proverbs 21.30f. can have a comforting effect, but, with different religious presuppositions, it could have a depressing effect.[7]

The same observation can be made about Ecclesiastes. The way one understands the book depends on the context in which it is set. If it is isolated from the broader biblical context, then its message can be understood in a profoundly negative way; if it is set into the context of Israel's broader religious understanding, then its message can be encouraging and positive. The book's impact on a person will depend largely on whether that individual can be confident about Yahweh's favor. In the light of what Qoheleth points out about life, how can one ever be sure of God's favor or confident of his steadfast love? The answer given throughout the Old Testament is that we know who God is and how he works, because he has revealed himself to his people. Even in the midst of the inequities and chaos of life, indications of his goodness and justice can still be found. The author of Psalm 42 describes the difficulties he is facing as "your [God's] waves and breakers" (v. 7). John Goldingay says about the verse,

At first sight the belief that God is behind the trouble that comes to us is a frightening doctrine: what kind of God is this, whose purpose includes so much distress? But the alternative—a God whose purpose is continually being frustrated by evil—is even more frightening. Better a

Fragments of Ecclesiastes from the Dead Sea Scrolls, manuscript 4Q109

God whose mystery we cannot understand (but who has given us grounds for trusting when we cannot understand) than one whose adequacy we cannot rely on, or whose interest we cannot be sure of.[8]

Throughout the Old Testament, God's people are encouraged to reflect on who God is, to study his works in creation and in history, and to meditate on the truth he has revealed about himself. They are instructed to carefully examine the world for examples of his steadfast love. Such disciplines keep before God's people some of those "grounds for trusting." Qoheleth mentions none of these things, so if his readers are to explicate the message and application of Ecclesiastes the ideas will have to be brought in from outside the book. It does, however, seem legitimate to do so given the book's place in the canon of Scripture.

One's knowledge of God will determine whether one can live in this fallen world with hope and anticipation or be resigned to a life of fear and frustration. Qoheleth makes it clear that life rarely gives unambiguous evidence that God is in control, or that God cares about us, or that his governance of human affairs is beneficent, just, and kind. That knowledge must come from God's self-revelation and must be embraced by faith. It can be substantiated by experience as people live in the fear of the Lord, experience his provision and grace, and grow into a more intimate relationship with him. As the rest of biblical revelation makes clear, such knowledge, informed by Scripture, can penetrate to the depths of a person's soul and provide a basis for hope and confidence in a world characterized by the uncertainties, inequities, and irresolvable conundrums seen by this Old Testament sage.

Two other points need to be made about this book. One has to do with the book's lack of structure and the author's habit of presenting ideas that stand in tension with ideas presented elsewhere in the book. This lack of a linear structure is likely related to the author's purpose and pedagogy. As Craig Bartholomew has noted, this book "calls the reader to engage with Qoheleth's journey and to enter into the dialogue he evokes." The reader should "feel the agony of Qoheleth's journey,"[9] and such journeys are rarely characterized by linear logic and neat structure. Qoheleth's approach is related to wisdom's goal of developing skill in living. Skill does not result from simply receiving correct information from knowledgeable instructors. Qoheleth's method seems designed to provoke the kind of dissonance in the reader that contributes to developing skill in living according to Yahweh's order.

The final point relates to a major theme of Ecclesiastes. Qoheleth presents himself as one who has accomplished far more than most of us could ever imagine, and yet he concludes that it is all vanity and chasing after the wind. The fulfillment and satisfaction that he intuitively had desired has not been found in those accomplishments or things, nor have they brought about the advantage he had hoped to gain. Qoheleth concludes that the appropriate way to live is in the fear of the Lord, and other biblical passages agree that this will lead to peace and well-being. Ecclesiastes warns us of the folly of seeking ultimate satisfaction and fulfillment in anything other than God himself. Qoheleth encourages us to enjoy our lot in life but warns us about expecting life to be more satisfying than it was designed to be. As long as we see our toil for what it is, we can, and should, enjoy it and not be frustrated by it. As John Walton says,

> The message of Ecclesiastes is that the course of life to be pursued is a God-centered life. The pleasures of life are not intrinsically fulfilling and cannot offer lasting satisfaction, but they can be enjoyed as gifts from God. Life offers good times and bad and follows no pattern such as that proposed by the retribution principle. But all comes from the hand of God (7:14). Adversity may not be enjoyable, but it can help make us the people of faith we ought to be.[10]

The New Testament and the teaching of Jesus elaborate on many of the same issues and make it clear that it is possible to live so as to gain a profit that death cannot destroy.

The author of Ecclesiastes concludes that fulfillment is not found in things. Later Jesus would reinforce this view when he spoke about laying up treasures in heaven rather than on earth. This jewelry hoard was found in a ceramic jug buried for safe keeping under the floor of a dwelling in Beth Shemesh from the Late Bronze Age (thirteenth century BC).

Jesus says, "Do not lay up for yourselves treasures on earth, where moth and rust destroy and where thieves break in and steal, but lay up for yourselves treasures in heaven, where neither moth nor rust destroys and where thieves do not break in and steal" (Matt. 6:19–20 ESV). Jesus also tells us that the key to this outcome is found in a life of faith or trusting dependence on God and obedience to his truth. Thus Qoheleth points his readers to a path of God-centered living that the fuller revelation of the New Testament will affirm is the way to life as it was meant to be. It leads to a life that brings glory to God and brings blessing to the person who lives by faith; it is also the key to a life that generates a profit that death cannot erase.

Where All Is *Hebel*, Can Life Have Meaning?

Big Idea *Does life have meaning and lasting value?*

Understanding the Text

The Text in Context

Ecclesiastes reflects the perspective of Old Testament wisdom literature in affirming that God created all things and that there is order because of God's design and oversight. Wisdom teachings affirm that people, though limited by their finitude and fallenness, can discover elements of that order by observing the world, and a major goal of wisdom is to develop an understanding of God's order. Ecclesiastes focuses on aspects of life that seem incongruent with the general order reflected in books like Proverbs; the author, Qoheleth, focuses on what he sees and experiences in the world, with little resort to special revelation. He describes a fallen world that no longer works the way God designed it. Qoheleth never specifically relates his observations to the fall, although allusions to the early chapters of Genesis suggest that these ideas remain in the background. His later references to the fear of the Lord show that he was writing in a context that presupposed Israel's traditional religious

values, and many of Qoheleth's questions can be answered on the basis of only those values and ideas.

These introductory verses include a brief statement about Qoheleth (1:1), a declaration of the book's overarching theme (1:2), the programmatic question of the book (1:3), and a poem (1:4–11) reiterating the themes and connecting readers emotionally to his assertions and questions.

Historical and Cultural Background

Qoheleth was perplexed by questions that confounded many in the ancient Near East: why pious people suffer, the mystery of the divine, the way things work in the world, whether life has meaning, and so on. The Epic of Gilgamesh relates how Gilgamesh, renowned for his superhuman abilities and accomplishments, found little fulfillment and satisfaction in them. The story "tells of one man's heroic struggle against death—first for immortal renown through glorious deeds, then for eternal life itself; of his despair when confronted with inevitable failure, and of his eventual realization that the only immortality he may expect is the enduring name afforded by leaving behind some lasting achievement."[1]

Gilgamesh develops these themes "in a distinctly Mesopotamian idiom,"[2] while Qoheleth develops them in ways consistent with Israel's Yahwistic perspective. However, as van der Toorn points out, the parallels between Gilgamesh and Ecclesiastes involve themes that are too common to require Mesopotamian influence: "Reflections on human mortality, the value of friendship, and the advantage of wisdom are the bread and butter of the sage all over the ancient Near East—and elsewhere."[3]

Interpretive Insights

1:1 *the Teacher, son of David, king in Jerusalem.* The source of the book's wisdom is identified as Qoheleth (Heb. *qohelet*), but the meaning of this term is unknown. The traditional translations, "Teacher" or "Preacher" (both of which will be used throughout this commentary), understand Qoheleth as one who convenes a group for worship or teaching.

1:2 *Meaningless!* The book begins with the assertion that everything is *hebel* (often translated "vanity" [KJV, ESV] or "meaningless" [NIV]) and ends with almost identical words (12:8), thus establishing a central theme of the book. The word *hebel*, which

Key Themes of Ecclesiastes 1:1–11

- Everything under the sun is *hebel*.
- Can people live so as to gain a (lasting) profit?
- The world is characterized by constant motion that appears to lead nowhere.

Ecclesiastes and the Epic of Gilgamesh share many of the questions that wisdom literature in the ancient Near East tries to address. This tablet of the Epic of Gilgamesh contains the story of Gilgamesh's search for immortality (1800 BC).

occurs almost forty times in Ecclesiastes, concretely refers to a puff of air, breath, or wind. It is often used as a metaphor, and the question becomes which aspect of *hebel* is intended in these uses (see the sidebar "*Hebel*"). Many understand the term as describing that which lacks meaning or value, that which has no substance, or that which is temporal and short lived.

1:3 *What do people gain . . . ?* Throughout the book Qoheleth reflects on the idea of people's gain or advantage as they live life.[4] The primary word translated "gain" or "profit" (*yitron*) comes from a root that means "to be left over" or "remain." The other words, *motar* and *yoter*, come from the same Hebrew root and, in Ecclesiastes, appear to have meanings generally similar to *yitron*. Commercially, profit is what remains after all the expenses have been paid. Qoheleth seeks a way to live to secure a gain or profit in life, and here his concern seems to involve the broad question of the meaning of life. Occasionally he asks the question in a way that

Solomon and Qoheleth

From 1:16 and 2:4–9 some have concluded that Solomon was the author and suggest that he wrote Ecclesiastes in his old age as he reflected on his failures in life. It seems unlikely that Solomon would complain about situations that he could correct (inept government bureaucracy, incompetent officials, etc.), and the Hebrew in the book seems later than that used by Solomon. Uncertainty remains about date and authorship, but the message of the book is unaffected by these matters.

suggests he is seeking a profit that death cannot eliminate, but this is never explicit, and the reader is left to consider the exact nature and extent of the profit Qoheleth is seeking.

1:4–11 *The sun rises and the sun sets.* The poem in 1:4–11 engages readers to consider whether their lives are any different from these repetitive cycles of nature and whether a person can gain a lasting profit in life. It also prepares the reader for Qoheleth's subsequent examples and may provide additional insight on the meaning of *hebel*. Poems work by drawing readers into the poet's experience and impacting them holistically. According to Leland Ryken, ideas presented in this way "achieve wholeness of expression by appealing to the full range of human experience, not simply to the rational intellect."[5] The poem emphasizes the transitory nature of human life (one aspect of *hebel*) by comparing

human activity with natural phenomena that are always in motion but that show little evidence of purpose or movement toward a predetermined goal (another aspect of *hebel*). The sun rises, sets, and returns to do the same thing over and over. Rivers run into seas, which are never filled. The wind blows, first one way and then another, only to do the same thing again and again. For all the motion and activity, the earth never seems to be significantly impacted or changed. Similarly, generations come and go (1:4), and people are seldom remembered by those who follow them (1:11). The brevity of a person's life and the recurrent patterns of human experience make it hard to imagine that one person can impact the

One example of the meaninglessness of life given by Qoheleth is that no one remembers former generations. The huge statues and monuments erected by the powerful eventually deteriorate, fall, and are forgotten. Shown here are the crumbling statues of Pharaoh Amenhotep III known as the Colossi of Memnon because of their size (sixty feet high; fourteenth century BC). They guarded the entrance to his mortuary temple, which is now gone.

world in a truly significant way. Does the life of a single individual mean any more than a river rushing toward the sea or the constant movement of the wind? Kidner says, "The poem . . . sets the tone of the book by its motto-theme and by its picture of a world endlessly busy and hopelessly inconclusive."[6]

All things are wearisome. Ecclesiastes 1:8 likely emphasizes humankind's limited ability to understand the way things work in the world (another aspect of *hebel*). Garrett says, "No one can explain, influence or control [the world]. Humanity, for all its intellectual investigations, must accept life and death and the coming and going of generations in this world as an unexplained and inexplicable given. . . . The resources of human reason leave humanity facing a blank wall."[7] The poem describes the tedious and tiring nature of life and personalizes the problem for the reader. It brings readers to acknowledge, both logically and experientially, the reality of the problem.

Theological Insights

Qoheleth emphasizes that life is characterized by difficulty and struggle; it is *hebel*—it is like a puff of air or wind. He raises the question of whether a person can secure a profit or advantage in life, and this question raises a more basic one: does human life even have meaning? When set against long-lived and unchanging phenomena like the sun, wind, rivers, and the sea, whose impact is not always readily apparent, how can one suppose that an individual life has significance in the larger framework of history? These examples make it difficult to imagine that life has

Hebel

In 1:14–15 *hebel* describes things people lack the ability to change or control. Ecclesiastes 2:1 describes the pursuit of pleasure as *hebel*, while 2:11 describes major human accomplishments (building projects, the accumulation of wealth, pleasure, etc.) in the same way, probably because these endeavors do not bring the satisfaction that those who pursue them desire. In 2:15 Qoheleth acknowledges that wisdom provides significant advantages over folly but concludes that it is *hebel* because it cannot deliver a person from death. It is *hebel* when a person works hard and accumulates much but is unable to enjoy the benefits of labor (2:18–21, 26; 6:1–2). Work motivated by envy or obsession with work and the accumulation of wealth to the neglect of relationships and pleasure (4:7–8) are *hebel*, as are the changing fortunes of politics (4:13–16). Talk not backed up by deeds, dreams not matched by diligence (6:9, 11), and the laughter of fools (7:6) are *hebel* because they lack substance and do not accomplish any useful outcome. Anomalies, such as righteous people experiencing what wicked people deserve and vice versa (3:16–19; 8:14), are examples of *hebel*. Finally, youth and the dawn of life are *hebel*, presumably because they last such a short time (11:10).

It is unlikely that the semantic range of *hebel* can be captured by a single English word. Ogden concludes, "Qoheleth does not mean to claim that life is empty, vain, and meaningless. . . . Life is replete with situations to which even the sage, the philosopher theologian, has no answer. It is the word *hebel* that Qoheleth applies to describe these situations."[a] Provan adds that *hebel* refers "to the fragile, fleeting nature of existence," stressing "the ephemerality of existence or its elusiveness and resistance to intellectual and physical control."[b] This understanding of *hebel* is also consistent with the phrase "chasing after the wind," with which it is often paired.[c] That metaphor describes attempting to accomplish something impossible—catching or controlling the wind. Both phrases emphasize that life is filled with situations beyond our ability to fully understand or control and that people cannot discover that which gives meaning to life.

[a] Ogden, *Qoheleth*, 25.
[b] Provan, *Ecclesiastes, Song of Songs*, 57.
[c] Eccles. 1:14; 2:11, 17, 26; 4:4, 16; 6:9.

meaning and is moving toward some glorious conclusion.

These verses illustrate Qoheleth's propensity for asking questions that he does not answer and for asking them in ways

Qoheleth asks if life has meaning when it is just part of the wearisome cycle of nature, like the rising and setting of the sun. This relief from the ceiling of the Nut Chapel at Dendera, Egypt, shows the Egyptian view of the movement of the sun at night. The sun is swallowed by the sky god, Nut, travels through her body, and is reborn as a new day begins.

that provoke reflection and frustration on the part of his readers. He shows where the path will lead if one attempts to answer such ultimate questions from the limited perspective of human experience and sets in clear relief the tension that often exists between the way we experience the world and what special revelation tells us about how things work.

Teaching the Text

Qoheleth wants us to understand the realities of life "under the sun" (1:3), and his perspective is deliberately limited to what one sees and experiences in the world, with little appeal to God, faith, or special revelation. When teaching this section, one needs to affirm the difficulty and complexity of life and its enigmatic character. There are many things that we cannot understand and many things that we cannot control. Our lives are but a breath, and in the whole scope of creation and history, what does a single life matter? How does one even begin to answer the questions that Qoheleth

raises here? Ecclesiastes makes it clear that questions about the meaning of life or how a person can live so as to make a significant and lasting impact cannot be answered on the basis of the experiences of life. The data of life are far too ambiguous and unclear for that.

Our culture constantly proclaims the message that everything that matters revolves around us, and that through education, hard work, and creative insight people can find meaning and make a lasting impact. We suppose that advances in technology will lead to new heights of human advancement. Qoheleth, however, raises serious questions about whether we are building something that is always advancing. His assertion that all is *hebel* highlights our limited understanding and control as human beings and suggests that our accomplishments rarely make the impact we would like. His observations cast a dark shadow over the idea that we can, through human effort, create an ideal world. The realities of life preclude that, and our obsessive effort to bring about those outcomes is as futile as pursuing the wind.

Qoheleth, though, saw value in struggling with these issues and grappling with the tension that his examples create. It is helpful to provide some answers and direction while teaching this book, but it is also important to teach in ways that keep aspiring sages engaged in the struggle rather than simply delivering "right answers" to them. Qoheleth's teaching methods reflect wisdom's goal of helping people develop skill in living according to Yahweh's order. Such skill is never developed apart from practice and struggle, including the kind of intellectual struggles that the conundrums of Qoheleth provoke in those who choose to travel the path of wisdom.

Illustrating the Text

Human perspective, experience, and effort cannot answer the dilemmas of life.

Personal Testimony: In preparation for a class on Ecclesiastes, I (Edward) asked my students to read Ecclesiastes 1:1–11 at least five times before our first session and to reflect on it. A few students concluded that this was a good description of the life of a non-Christian but did not think it had much relevance for a believer. Others vigorously disagreed with this assessment and said they felt that the author was describing their own lives. Several said that they frantically move from one activity to another, wondering if all the pursuits lead to anything or if they really matter. One girl said she often feels like the gerbil on the wheel—frantically running but never getting anywhere. Another said that he resonates with the puff-of-smoke metaphor and sometimes wonders if anything in his life has any more substance than a puff of smoke that disappears into the sky.

One generation fades into another, and little is remembered of most individuals.

Personal Testimony: We have little difficulty understanding that generations come and go, and our generation too is passing away. Qoheleth tells us that there will be no remembrance of former things; anyone who has tinkered with family genealogies can relate to his point. My (Edward's) efforts to trace my family tree have had limited success. Two women in my history are fascinating precisely because I can find so little about them. I know they existed, and their names appear on birth records and marriage certificates, but I know nothing about them or their legacy. I am here because of them, but I know little else. I often wonder what part of my efforts at life and ministry will remain—precisely the kinds of questions that Qoheleth's words are meant to provoke in us.

Many of the repetitive activities in life leave little record of their significance.

Human Experience: Many duties, like dusting or weeding or home maintenance, take up our time, only to become necessary again and again. The next generation, or even the next person who owns the house, will see little to indicate the huge amounts of time we have expended to keep things looking just right.

Qoheleth's Futile Search for Meaning in a World Where All Is *Hebel*

Big Idea *Human accomplishments are as insubstantial and fleeting as a puff of air; trying to find ultimate meaning in them is as futile as trying to catch the wind.*

Understanding the Text

The Text in Context

The next major section in Ecclesiastes consists of 1:12–2:26, which we will discuss in two parts (1:12–2:11 and 2:12–26). Qoheleth began in 1:2 by declaring that all is *hebel* and asked whether a person can live in the world so as to gain some profit or advantage (1:3). The poem in 1:4–11 emphasized the repetitive, difficult, and short-lived nature of life and implied negative answers to the question of profit and to whether life has meaning. In 1:12–2:11 Qoheleth, using the methods of wisdom, describes his attempts to find answers and presents his conclusions. Qoheleth's experience supports his initial conclusion in 1:2, and the smaller subsections of the unit regularly conclude with the judgment of *hebel* / "chasing after the wind."[1]

Historical and Cultural Background

Kings in the ancient Near East often promoted their greatness by celebrating their deeds in royal inscriptions. Seow notes that these texts were meant "to enhance respect for the king and memorialize his achievements forever."[2] Some kings also left autobiographies,[3] and this section in Ecclesiastes begins in much the same way

In 2:4 Qoheleth recounts how he "undertook great projects" and discovered that everything was meaningless (2:11). This royal inscription describes the founding of Dur-Sharrukin (Khorsabad), the capital city of King Sargon II. In it he describes some of his building projects, "Palaces of ivory, mulberry, cedar, cypress, juniper, and pistachio-wood I built at their lofty command for my royal dwelling-place."

as these compositions. Solomon comes to mind as we read these verses, but rather than his accomplishments proving his unsurpassed greatness, Qoheleth concludes that they do not really matter as far as satisfaction, fulfillment, and the meaning of life are concerned. He finds that they are all *hebel*. Solomon was the example par excellence of wisdom, success, and accomplishment, though here, Solomon is probably a paradigm for humanity and represents any person who tries to find meaning and fulfillment in a life that is not centered in God.

Interpretive Insights

1:13 *by wisdom.* Proverbs 1:7 says that "the fear of the LORD" is the first principle of wisdom, and throughout the biblical tradition it stands as an essential element in knowing truth. References to the fear of God later in Ecclesiastes (3:14; 5:7; 7:18; 12:13) show that Qoheleth understands the importance of this idea, but it plays a limited role in his explorations. Kidner says, "We can assume that the wisdom he speaks of is . . . the best thinking that man can do on his own. . . . Yet it has no answer to our misgivings about life. It only sharpens them by its clarity."[4] Qoheleth's search for knowledge proceeds independently of the insights of special revelation (note the numerous references to "I," "me," "my," etc.), and this is perhaps meant to show the limits of such an approach. As Goldingay points out, "The occupational hazard of the wise man is to walk by calculation rather than by faith,"[5] and when faced with ultimate questions like the ones raised by Qoheleth, wisdom's limits become painfully apparent.

- Qoheleth has searched relentlessly for ultimate meaning in the world.
- Nothing he has pursued—wisdom, pleasure, building projects, wealth—has given him the satisfaction he desires or the meaning of life he seeks.
- All his accomplishments have led to the same conclusion—they are *hebel*.

What a heavy burden God has laid on mankind! "Burden" occurs in the Hebrew Bible only in Ecclesiastes. It refers to a business or task with which a person is occupied. "Heavy" can refer to moral evil or to what is difficult or tragic. "Heavy burden" likely describes the frustration and difficulty of trying to understand life and explain the things people experience in the world. Bartholomew says that the "heavy burden" relates to the fact that life "is filled with enigmas that [a person] cannot resolve so that the quest for meaning is like trying to get hold of the wind. . . . Meaning may be there but it cannot be grasped—it is like trying to shepherd the wind—and the enigmas cannot be reconciled."[6]

Verse 13 contains the book's first reference to God. Qoheleth affirms the sovereignty of God over the affairs of life, even as he recognizes human limits in understanding and controlling life. Some infer from the verse that the "heavy burden" is designed and imposed by God and conclude that "Qohelet's God [is] distant, occasionally indifferent, and sometimes cruel."[7] However, much of the "heavy burden" stems from human rebellion against God and the disruption and dysfunction to the created order that it produces. Thus what "God has laid on mankind" may reflect not so much his design and desire but rather what he

Ecclesiastes 1:12–2:11

allows as he works to redeem and restore the creation that was originally very good.

1:15 *What is crooked cannot be straightened.* Some things in life are impossible to do or change, and such limits are part of the "heavy burden" (1:13) that characterizes life in the world. Human goals and aspirations must be set in ways that take into account these limits. As Provan says, "The fundamental human problem resides in a lack of harmony between common human aspirations and the very nature of reality itself, [and] the futility . . . of human refusal to accept things as they are. There is a human insistence that the impossible can in fact be achieved—that what God has made 'crooked' or 'twisted' can indeed be made straight by human, mortal effort. . . . Refusing to accept reality can only result in unhappiness and weariness."[8]

1:17 *madness and folly.* Qoheleth has sought knowledge about the meaning of life by understanding wisdom and its antithesis, "madness and folly." Despite discoveries and accomplishments unmatched by any who have preceded him, Qoheleth's efforts have not succeeded. The task was like pursuing the wind; it simply could not be done.

1:18 *with much wisdom comes much sorrow.* The Hebrew word translated "sorrow" usually involves anger, vexation, and frustration, and Qoheleth's quest has confirmed the truth of this proverb. Trying to understand how the world works, why things happen as they do, and how one might change these realities often produces

One of Qoheleth's projects that gained nothing was the creation of luxurious gardens filled with fruit trees and water reservoirs. This stone relief from the palace of Ashurbanipal at Nineveh shows a well-watered park filled with trees (645 BC).

pain and agitation, because the more one understands the enormity and complexity of the problems, the more apparent human limits become. Despite these limits, Qoheleth continues his pursuit of wisdom.

2:1–3 *pleasure.* The Teacher tries to find meaning in pleasure by cheering himself with wine while still being guided by wisdom. Presumably he wants to indulge so as to experience pleasure but not to the point where he loses rational control. Qoheleth also recognizes that while his impressive building projects, lush gardens, and lavish lifestyle may provide welcome distraction from the realities of life, they cannot provide the answers he is seeking.

2:10 *delight . . . reward.* Qoheleth's quest has not brought him the profit or advantage he seeks, but he has found reward in his toil. The Hebrew word for "reward" often means "portion" or "lot,"[9] and Fox says the word refers to "something one gets, irrespective of whether it is adequate or satisfying or deserved or durable."[10] In Ecclesiastes "reward" or "lot" (see 3:22; 5:18–19; 9:9) involves both resources and opportunity. A person's lot may include few resources or abundant resources but little opportunity to enjoy, and one's lot in life may change over time. Just as a person's lot in life is related in some inexplicable way to God's providence (1:13), it is also related to choices that we make throughout life. Trying to understand this is one of the unfathomable mysteries that perplexed Qoheleth.

2:11 *nothing was gained under the sun.* Qoheleth has searched for the meaning of life in wisdom, pleasure, and great accomplishments and has done it to a degree rarely possible for people. He has discovered that all of this is like chasing the wind. He tried to find a way to live that will enable him to gain a lasting profit, but he has found nothing that can secure the advantage he desires.

Theological Insights

Crenshaw says, "God embedded truth within all of reality. The human responsibility is to search for that insight and thus to learn to live in harmony with the cosmos."[11] He further notes that throughout biblical wisdom, "being wise meant a search for and maintenance of order,"[12] and this is the task on which Qoheleth has embarked. Qoheleth's interest is not just the pragmatic aspects of wisdom that enable people to accomplish certain tasks; he is interested in ultimate questions, such as the meaning of life and whether one can live so that life really matters. As Qoheleth observes the world, he recognizes that life is an unhappy business (cf. 1:13 ESV), in part because of human limits that constrain people and prevent them from achieving the understanding of and mastery over life for which they strive. He does not explain these limits but sees them as falling under the broad rubric of God's providence.

A key point of this section is that the meaning of life is not to be found in human accomplishments, pleasure, or any human endeavor. Verheij has argued that Ecclesiastes 2:4–6 "is a paraphrase of the planting of the Garden of Eden, with indeed Qohelet himself as subject, instead of God."[13] In this case Qoheleth's efforts to re-create paradise have not led to something that is "very good" (Gen. 1:31) but to *hebel* and the discovery that there is nothing to be gained under the sun (Eccles. 2:11). The accomplishments described here are consistent with those attributed to Solomon, and as Whybray has observed, "The moral is obvious: what was true of the life of the world's most privileged person is bound [all the more so] to be true of the lives of us all. This is a warning not to treat the acquisition of wealth and power as the most important goal in life."[14]

Teaching the Text

Humans feel that there should be meaning and significance to life. When nothing gives them a sense that their lives really matter, the feeling of emptiness leaves them perplexed and troubled. Qoheleth's search proceeds with the unlimited resources of Solomon, and he discovers that all his wisdom, accomplishments, wealth, and pleasures fail to produce the fulfillment and satisfaction he desires. The clear implication is that every attempt at self-fulfillment will lead only to *hebel* and chasing after the wind. Despite Qoheleth's testimony, the pursuit continues today. People pursue education, wealth, pleasure, and accomplishments of all kinds in their search for happiness and meaning, and those who succeed, even at the highest levels, regularly affirm that their achievements have not given them what they have sought. The hope, though, remains that "just a little more" will finally bring the satisfaction and meaning they crave.

Our culture has bombarded us with the idea that happiness and fulfillment are just out of reach but can be found if we just get into this school or accumulate this much wealth or marry that person or become a partner in the business or any number of other possibilities. We have embraced a lie and are consumed by all sorts of pursuits that, according to Qoheleth, by their very nature lack the power to satisfy and to give meaning to life. Ecclesiastes describes the experience of a man who had it all: wisdom/education, wealth, power, remarkable accomplishments, and pleasures of every imaginable kind, but who found that these things did not satisfy what Kushner calls "that unnameable hunger in the soul"[15] that human beings yearn to have satisfied. The siren songs of materialism and success call out loudly in our culture, and few can resist them. Those who respond to the melody always run aground on the rocks of *hebel* and find themselves chasing after the wind.

There are problems that can be understood and solved; there are enormous benefits to education; there are injustices and

Is wealth the key to happiness? In 2:8 the Teacher recounts how he has "amassed silver and gold" but found that it was meaningless. These gold earrings and bracelets are from ancient Egypt.

difficulties that can be rectified; and wisdom encourages us to do all we can to accomplish these things. At the same time, we must recognize our limits and live life within these constraints rather than constantly trying to straighten the intrinsically crooked or count what is lacking. An essential part of living well is learning to live within the limits that God and life under the sun impose on us. When we see our toil for what it is, we can find pleasure in it and not be frustrated by it, but the "difficult business" of life (2:17, author's translation) will be even worse if we obsessively persist in trying to straighten the irreversibly crooked elements in life.

Illustrating the Text

No human pursuit or success can produce the fulfillment people desire.

Quote: Leonard Woolf. Woolf (1880–1969), the husband of novelist Virginia Woolf, was a British publisher and political theorist who wrote over twenty books on literature, politics, and economics. He reflects about his life and work:

> I see clearly that I have achieved practically nothing. The world today and the history of the human anthill during the past five to seven years would be exactly the same as it is if I had played Ping-Pong instead of sitting on committees and writing books and memoranda. I have therefore to make a rather ignominious confession that I must have, in a long life, ground through between 150,000 and 200,000 hours of perfectly useless work.[16]

Film: *Citizen Kane*. This classic movie (1941) shows a man, Charles Foster Kane, rising from humble beginnings to a position of immense power and wealth, enabling him to acquire anything he desires. He builds a huge mansion on top of a hill to house his possessions, rivaling those of kings. Still, he finds little fulfillment in life and is angry and frustrated because of what his money and power cannot accomplish. His obsession with wealth and power drives his family and friends away, and he dies miserable and alone, surrounded by his things. His reflection on life as he nears death reveals that the closest he ever came to satisfaction and fulfillment was in childhood when he was poor and with his family. The movie's final scenes show workers in the basement of Kane's house throwing his things into the furnace. The camera slowly pulls away from the dwelling sitting high above the valley, black smoke rising from the chimney. It is hard to imagine a more graphic way of declaring that the life of Charles Kane was *hebel*.

Lyrics: "Is That All There Is?," by Peggy Lee. This tune (1969) is the signature song of enduring vocal legend Peggy Lee (1920–2002). The song hauntingly poses a number of life's supposed delights, such as a child's first visit to the circus or a person's first love, and, in the light of the lack of fulfillment those things often bring, asks the question, "Is that all there is?" The song's chorus ends in resignation by concluding that if that is all there is, "Let's bring out the booze and have a ball."

Enjoy Life Despite Its Difficulties and the Reality That All Will Die

Big Idea *Death destroys every human gain; how can life have ultimate meaning?*

Understanding the Text

The Text in Context

The themes of the previous section (1:12–2:11) continue, as evidenced by the repetition of *hebel* and "chasing after the wind" (1:14, 17; 2:11, 17, 26), with *hebel* occurring six additional times in 2:12–26 (vv. 15, 17, 19, 21, 23, 26). The Hebrew terms for toil/labor/struggle (all related to the Hebrew root *'amal*) occur eleven times in these verses and establish a major emphasis in the section. "Toil" describes Qoheleth's search for meaning, fulfillment, and advantage as he ponders wisdom and its antithesis—madness and folly. Wisdom provides a significant advantage over folly, but it is eliminated by death, the ultimate testimony to human finitude; this relative advantage does not constitute the profit for which Qoheleth is searching. He affirms many harsh realities about life and concludes that there is nothing better for a person than to eat, drink, and find enjoyment in toil when God makes that possible.

Historical and Cultural Background

Questions about the meaning of life, the reality of death, and the endurance of one's legacy reflect universal themes in literature. The Epic of Gilgamesh recounts its hero's lack of personal fulfillment from his building projects and accomplishments, and the death of his close friend sets him on a quest to find the secret of immortality. Gilgamesh returns home from all his adventures without having obtained his goal—immortality. The story ends where it began, with Gilgamesh back in his home city of Uruk, echoing the words with which the epic began.[1] In a passage that closely parallels Ecclesiastes, Gilgamesh is given advice about how to live in the light of this reality:

> When the gods created mankind
> they fixed Death for mankind,
> and held back Life in their own hands.
> Now you, Gilgamesh, let your belly be
>   full!
> Be happy day and night,
> of each day make a party,
> dance in circles day and night!

Let your clothes be sparkling clean,
let your head be clean, wash yourself
with water!
Attend to the little one who holds onto
your hand,
Let a wife delight in your embrace.
This is the (true) task of *mankind*(?).[2]

Interpretive Insights

2:12 *What more can the king's successor do . . . ?* In 1:13–17 Qoheleth claims
that his search has been done in a thorough
and comprehensive way, and he is confident
that those who later pursue these questions
cannot surpass what he has already done.
Despite great advances, questions about
the meaning of life, the mysteries surrounding death and
the afterlife, or the way God
works in the world remain
as impenetrable for us as
they were for Qoheleth.

2:13 *just as light is
better than darkness.*
The wise person lives in
broad daylight, while the
foolish person stumbles
through life in the dark,
but the metaphor may
imply more. Wisdom is

In the Epic of Gilgamesh,
Gilgamesh tries to leave
a legacy by slaying the
monster/god Huwawa. But
even this great deed cannot
help him avoid the ultimate
destiny of humankind
decreed by the gods,
which is death. In the end
Gilgamesh receives advice
similar to that in Ecclesiastes
2:24. This plaque may show
Gilgamesh standing on the
head of Huwawa.

- Wisdom's advantage over folly is like the difference between night and day.
- Death eliminates every apparent advantage; it leaves
no survivors, and nothing can be taken to the grave.
- It is good for a person to eat, drink, and find pleasure
as God gives opportunity.

characterized by order, which is often represented by light, whereas darkness represents
disorder and the antithesis of wisdom.

2:14–16 *the same fate . . . not be long
remembered.* Death, the "fate" to which
Qoheleth is referring, affects everyone and
makes no distinction between wise and
foolish, rich and poor, powerful and help-
less. Not only does death rob individuals of
gain that might result from wisdom, hard
work, skill, or good fortune, but also their
accomplishments will largely be forgotten.
Sometimes the only evidence of a person's
existence is found in a census record. Details
of who a person was, what that individual
was like, and the impact he or she had on
others are often difficult to find.

2:17–23 *What do people get for all the
toil and anxious striving . . . ?* Qoheleth's
frustration stems from his inability to find
anything that gives meaning or results in
fulfillment; everything turns out to be
hebel. Frustration comes from things he
can neither understand nor control; death
indiscriminately, and with apparent finality,
wipes out any profit one might generate;
and this is amplified by having to leave everything a person has built and saved to
others, who may be wasteful fools. If these
are seen as the only realities, it is no wonder
that Qoheleth reacts with such harshness. If
death is the end, the choices that we make
about good and evil, the meaning of life,

and so on appear to have no lasting significance. As Kidner says, "If . . . every card in our hand will be trumped, does it matter how we play?"[3]

2:24 *to eat and drink and find satisfaction . . . is from the hand of God.* Trying to find meaning and fulfillment through one's own effort is futile, but there are also things in the world that provide pleasure and encouragement. Qoheleth exhorts us to receive these things as gifts from God and tells us that, on this basis, they can be enjoyed and bring meaning and satisfaction to life. Rather than "secular resignation," Qoheleth affirms God's sovereign providence in determining outcomes in life (vv. 24–26), and this makes it clear that there is more to his perspective than the empirically based epistemology that characterizes the experiment of 1:12–2:26.

2:26 *the person who pleases [God] . . . the sinner.* These terms likely designate the wise person and the fool (one who misses the mark or offends) rather than the moral and the immoral person. The terms are not entirely devoid of moral connotations but likely have fewer moralistic implications than the translations "person who pleases God" and "sinner" suggest. The verse is not about retribution (people reap what they sow); rather, "the import of the verse is to claim sovereign freedom for God in imparting gifts."[4]

It is *hebel* to try to understand or control the mysterious distribution of gifts that come from God. According to Ogden this verse is "another reminder of the unpredictable nature of things, and of the fact that we can never fully understand the complexities of life in this world."[5] Wisdom dictates that we simply receive whatever comes rather than anxiously expend energy trying to anticipate or control what God might do.

Theological Insights

Qoheleth affirms the profit (*yitron*) of wisdom, but his hope for a positive answer to the question "What do people gain from all their labors?" (1:3) is dashed by the realization that death will erase any advantage of wisdom. No matter how much people accumulate, how much wisdom they acquire, or how high they rise on the ladder of success, death comes to them just as it does to the poor, struggling beggar and robs them of everything they have gained. Nothing can be taken to the grave, and even the little control that people have over their accomplishments and possessions is lost when a person dies. As Crenshaw says, "Utter futility characterizes the human endeavor to gain happiness by means of wisdom, pleasure, or achievements. Death cancels the supposed advantages. . . . The refrain glances ironically at persons busily engaged in storing up earthly possessions without realizing that they cannot hold onto them."[6]

Qoheleth's remarks about death are limited to observation and self-discovery, and he describes life as we experience it. We cannot see past death's temporal finality, and apart from special revelation we have no way to answer questions about what lies beyond the grave. Goldingay says that "Qoheleth takes the wisdom approach to its logical conclusion and proves this to be actually a dead end. He too shows that there is no escape from the theological impasse within the wisdom tradition itself."[7] This impasse is evident when one tries to answer the questions Qoheleth is exploring, and one of the author's goals may be to prod

interact with Ecclesiastes. Some explication is perhaps appropriate, but it is important to understand where the road ends if there is no revelation beyond what we can know from observation or empirical inquiry.

Teaching the Text

Our culture is dominated by the idea that personal fulfillment and satisfaction can be realized through achievement or the accumulation of things. Often the key is assumed to be wealth, appearance, education, awards, or great accomplishments; sometimes the key is seen in philanthropy or service to others. Qoheleth makes it clear that such things do not hold the key to meaning and fulfillment in life, nor can they satisfy the deep longing of the human soul for significance and a sense that one's life makes a difference. Relentlessly seeking these things as the ultimate goal of life is as futile as trying to capture the wind.

Such things may bring temporary pleasure and satisfaction (though often they do not), but Qoheleth insists that death will rob us of all such gain. In the light of such realities it is useless to struggle obsessively for gain or accomplishments; death will eliminate them. Seow says, "Death will put an end to every aspiration for which one has striven. Qohelet is not just saying that 'you can't take it with you,' however. Rather he is also pointing out that one cannot beat the

the reader to consider whether there might be *some profit* after death. Whatever Qoheleth knew/believed about these matters[8] is irrelevant to the point he is making here. Death destroys everything that people pursue in the hope of finding the meaning of life or an enduring profit. It is likely that Qoheleth's inability—or refusal—to suggest answers is part of the pedagogy by which he engages his readers in the struggle of living under the sun.

Many answers to the concerns raised by Qoheleth's observations about death will have to await the further revelation of the New Testament. It is difficult for a Christian to teach this material without moving too quickly to the answers we know are coming, but that temptation should be avoided as we system by passing on one's accumulation to posterity either."[9]

Qoheleth does provide some positive advice for living in the world. He concludes that there is nothing better for a person than to eat, drink, and find enjoyment in toil and to recognize these opportunities as coming from God. Qoheleth's view is that satisfaction comes not as a result of what we secure through work and self-effort but as a gift that comes from God's hand. Brown says, "Neither achieved nor planned, neither grasped nor produced, the gifts of true pleasure are simply received from God," and they are to be "received in gratitude and savored for their own sake."[10]

The fulfillment and satisfaction for which humans long are not the result of self-effort, even in the religious realm—more sacrificial ministry, more involvement in religious activities, more "successful" ministry, and so on. The deep longing of the human soul for satisfaction must be found in one's relationship with God and received as a gift from him. Buchanan says, "The portrait of the faithful [in Scripture] is not a portrait of the fulfilled. What defines them . . . is hope. . . . What defines them is a yearning: knowing in their bones, in spite of loss or sorrow or aloneness, that there is Something more, Something else, Something better."[11] As Buchanan recognizes, "fulfillment is heaven's business,"[12] though Qoheleth could not see the answer in such clear terms.

Finally, Qoheleth's observations raise questions about the nature of God. He says in 2:24 that opportunities for pleasure and enjoyment come from God, but he also asserts that God has assigned to humanity the heavy burden of life under the sun (1:13). He indicates that God both distributes to and withholds from people the gift of pleasure (2:26), and based on our observation and experience of life, the distribution seems random and beyond any rational pattern. This tension between providence and the human experience of life regularly creates existential and philosophical difficulties for people as they live in the world. As Brown puts it, this tension heightens "the impenetrable mystery of life granted by an inscrutable God."[13] Qoheleth does little to resolve the tension, and the ambiguity constitutes a significant part of this author's efforts to develop skill in living according to Yahweh's order.

Illustrating the Text

It is good to eat, drink, and find pleasure as God gives opportunity.

Biography: Flannery O'Connor. O'Connor, the great American author, was a devout Christian who wrote stories at once full of the reality of the violence of life and the presence of grace. Her characters are often wryly funny in the midst of sometimes horrific situations. She believed that God has called us to endure life while delighting in it, the tension described in this passage. Her own life reflected that tension; she maintained an unquenchable humor (shown liberally in her letters) and took enormous pleasure in raising animals and visiting with and writing to friends, all while suffering from the horrors of degenerative lupus, which finally took her life when she was only thirty-nine.

Death eliminates every apparent advantage; nothing can be taken to the grave.

Anecdote: One of Qoheleth's points is illustrated by comparing two different attitudes toward possessions as reflected upon death. The first is seen in a funeral for an individual who had worked hard all his life and had been very successful in terms of material prosperity. The pastor spent almost forty-five minutes recounting the accomplishments and acquisitions of the deceased: the houses he had all over the country, the expensive automobiles he owned, the custom-made shirts that were the only ones he would wear, the impressive addresses of his children, and so forth. The man obviously valued his wife and children, but nothing was said at the funeral to suggest that this individual valued much besides money and things or that he and his family thought in any other terms insofar as evaluating his life and legacy was concerned. A different attitude was reflected upon the death of a woman whose means were much more limited. She lived frugally but accumulated a number of things that she truly enjoyed. After friends and family members took what they wanted of her possessions, they put several boxes of things on the curb for the trash. They did so knowing that she would have no regrets at all. She never lost sight of the fact that these were just things. She enjoyed them for what they were: things that came to her from the hand of God. She took delight in them but never saw them as giving meaning to her life or defining the value of her life. She lived life the way Qoheleth commends.

In 2:19 Qoheleth laments leaving behind the fruits of his labor to those who may only squander it, making the toil to amass it meaningless. In 1877 Cornelius Vanderbilt, shown here, died, leaving a fortune approximated at $100 million. His heirs spent freely as they built grand homes and adopted extravagant lifestyles. Today the mansions have been sold and the fortune is much diminished (Anne Chisholm, "More Money Than Anyone Else," nytimes.com).

Personal Testimony: I (Edward) recently used an article by American humorist Erma Bombeck (1927–96) in an undergraduate class. Reflecting on life, Bombeck talked about three women: Bo Derek, Farah Fawcett, and Bette Midler. Few of my students knew who these women were, yet only a few years ago, they were popular icons. Having to explain a joke or story quickly erodes its effectiveness in making a point, but the experience illustrates how quickly fame fades. Such examples illustrate the futility of seeking the meaning of life in fame and accomplishment. The reality is that there will likely be no enduring remembrance (2:16).

Anecdote: A wealthy baron in Scotland was known for his frugality and shrewd investing. When he died, he left all his money to his son, who had always been fascinated by Loch Ness and the elusive monster reputed to live there. The son pursued the search, spending almost all his inheritance to buy a small submarine and sophisticated electronic gear designed to detect whatever might live in Loch Ness. One wonders how his father would have viewed such use of the money he had so carefully accumulated, protected, and bequeathed.

Ecclesiastes 2:12–26

Everything Is Beautiful in Its Time, but We Cannot Understand God's Work and Timing

Big Idea *God is the sovereign Lord; people are his finite creatures.*

Understanding the Text

The Text in Context

Qoheleth reflects on time and timing and contrasts finite, mortal, and time-bound human beings with the infinite and eternal God, whose work lasts forever. Ecclesiastes 3:1–8 affirms that timing is essential for success. Bad timing can prevent a person from capturing the potential of the moment, and it is rarely possible to recover what has been lost by inappropriate timing. The primary point of the section, though, is to present a contrast between humankind's inability to get timing right and God's creation of everything as beautiful or appropriate in its time. People cannot discover either the timing or the patterns that reflect God's purposes and work in the world, nor can they see how God's creation coheres. The result is frustration as people experience life they do not fully understand and cannot control, and Qoheleth sees this frustration as one mechanism that can draw people to God and a life centered in him.

Historical and Cultural Background

The importance of words or actions appropriate for a specific situation was emphasized by sages throughout the ancient Near Eastern world. People struggled with knowing the propitious time for actions and sought to know enough about the future to avoid disaster. People in Mesopotamia regularly pursued this knowledge through omens, such as by examining the livers of sacrificial animals or observing the stars, and they attempted to change the

> When people in Mesopotamia needed to make an important decision or wanted to know the best action to take, they often turned to divination. A question would be posed, an animal sacrificed, and its entrails examined. This clay model of a liver was used to help diviners interpret what the gods were communicating when a liver was inspected (1900–1600 BC).

fortunes suggested by the omens through magic. Israel's law and her prophets condemned such practices.

Interpretive Insights

3:1–8 *everything . . . every activity.* These words indicate that this is a comprehensive picture of life in the world. The author uses a literary device known as "merism," in which two opposites (e.g., birth/death; seeking/losing) imply all the activities that lie between the two poles. The number seven sometimes symbolizes completion, and the fourteen pairs of opposites (2×7) suggest that the poem covers the spectrum of what ordinarily occurs in life. The list describes what people do rather than what they should do, and each individual will not necessarily experience every activity. Some endeavors can be understood either concretely or metaphorically, and the author likely intended to leave these possibilities open for the reader.

3:9 *What do workers gain from their toil?* Qoheleth's emphasis on human inability to determine the proper time for acting further reinforces his conclusion that people cannot secure lasting gain through their own efforts, as he again raises the

- Timing is critical, but humans cannot fully understand timing—either theirs or God's.
- God sees the whole picture; people see only a tiny part.
- God's work lasts forever; nothing can be added to it or taken from it.
- People desire more than life under the sun but cannot discover the larger story that unlocks the mystery.
- The human desire to move beyond their time-bound nature is designed by God to prompt people to revere him.

question that was previously asked in 1:3 and 2:22.

3:10 *burden God has laid.* This "burden" (cf. 1:13) reflects both human finitude and the fact that it is a fallen world, and these limits do not operate independently of the providence of God. Inability to understand time and timing or to understand how things cohere in the world adds significantly to the burden of life. Provan says, "What is 'evil' [heavy] about life . . . is that it cannot be controlled and manipulated so as to render the rewards sought after."[1] The burden is amplified when people refuse to acknowledge their limits and live, strive, and plan as if these limits do not exist.

3:11 *everything beautiful in its time.* Despite what Qoheleth observes, he affirms order and coherence in the world God has created. The Hebrew word *yapeh* usually means "beautiful," but here it means "fitting" or "appropriate" and implies that creation fits together in a coherent way. The order includes patterns that suggest purpose and goals. As Krüger observes, Qoheleth's conclusion "cannot be 'empirically verified.' It cannot be derived from experience but rather formulates a perspective—taken from tradition (Genesis 1)—that makes the interpretation of experience possible."[2]

This is another of the sage's confessional or "faith statements," which seem to be at variance with the world that Ecclesiastes describes and that we experience.

what God has done. While it is often possible to understand bits and pieces of what God is doing, people cannot put it all together and understand what God is doing from beginning to end. Kidner says, "We are like the desperately nearsighted, inching their way along some great tapestry or fresco in an attempt to take it in. We see enough to recognize something of its quality, but the grand design escapes us, for we can never stand back far enough to view it as its Creator does, whole and entire, *from the beginning to the end.*"[3]

3:12–13 *nothing better . . . than to be happy and to do good.* Qoheleth exhorts his readers to enjoy life and to understand that the ability to enjoy is a gift from God. He sees the negative aspects of life, but he also sees the good. Qoheleth does not address the question of why some people are born into great wealth and privilege while others are born into abject poverty and circumstances that allow few opportunities for pleasure. He simply urges people, whatever their circumstances in life, to find opportunities and ways to enjoy. Qoheleth adds to his earlier advice by encouraging his readers to "be happy" or "enjoy" (cf. NLT, NRSV) and to "do good." Focusing our attention on doing good and enjoying the good things around us can help us to see the bitter realities of life in more balanced ways that make it easier to enjoy life.

3:14 *everything God does will endure forever.* People cannot secure lasting profit or gain through self-effort. In contrast to humans, whatever God does is eternal (that is, it transcends time), complete, and comprehensive.

Time-bound, mortal human beings intuitively sense that there must be more than life as they experience it, but they cannot understand enough of the work of God to know how to resolve the tension. Garrett says, "We feel like aliens in the world of time and yearn to be a part of eternity. We feel the need for ourselves and our work to be eternal and yet are grieved to be trapped in time. We also desire to understand our place in the universe against the backdrop of eternity."[4] This yearning, this unease, is designed to draw people to reverence for God.

so that people will fear him. The "fear of the Lord" is a common term for the life of faith throughout the Old Testament, but many argue for a different meaning in Ecclesiastes. Longman maintains that Qoheleth's view is "that God acts the way he does to frighten people into submission, not to arouse a sense of respectful awe of his power and might."[5] Seow's conclusion is more likely correct: "The concept of the fear of God here, as elsewhere in Israelite wisdom literature, stresses the distance between divinity and humanity. It is the recognition that God is God and people are human."[6]

3:15 *God will call the past to account.* This obscure verse comes at the end of a section contrasting the work of God and the work of humankind. The ESV translation reads, "God seeks what has been driven away." According to Seow the phrase "seems to suggest that it is God who will take care of what is pursued [driven away], namely, all those matters that are beyond human grasp."[7]

As Qoheleth talks about the cycles of life, he includes "a time to plant and a time to uproot" (3:2). In agrarian societies, life's rhythm revolved around the seasons and the weather. This small tablet describes the months for various agricultural activities such as planting, reaping, pruning, and harvesting for the nation of Israel (tenth century BC).

Theological Insights

Ecclesiastes 3:1–8 emphasizes the importance of time and timing and describes many things that seem largely within our control (when to plant or to uproot plants; when to keep something or to discard it). The list also includes activities over which we generally exercise no control (when to be born or when to die), and then there are activities, such as laughing or weeping, where our responses are largely determined by circumstances over which we have minimal control. Even as wisdom emphasizes the importance of our decisions and the necessity for living according to Yahweh's order, this poem focuses on human limits in getting things right and controlling outcomes in life.

The section asserts that God has made everything appropriate in its time (3:11) and sustains the world so that his purposes are accomplished. The incongruity between such faith assertions and the lack of coherence that we experience in a fallen world creates obvious tension for the person of faith. This epistemological tension is a significant part of the dilemma Qoheleth sets before his students as he challenges them to forge out their own answers.

Qoheleth claims that while humans do have some control over their lives, they have less than many suppose—and far less than most people desire. God's providence is at work in ways that can be neither predicted nor resisted, and his providence sometimes impacts outcomes that ordinarily seem to fall within our control. When this occurs, it is God's purpose that will prevail. Qoheleth makes it clear that human independence and autonomy are not the final determiners of outcomes—certainly not ultimate ones. This serves as a reminder that the goal of biblical wisdom is not to provide full knowledge that allows us to control our

Ecclesiastes 3:1–15

circumstances and outcomes, but rather to enable us to live in harmony with the purposes of God and the order he has designed into the universe.

Teaching the Text

Teaching the text should draw those we are teaching into the tension that Qoheleth presents and affirm the realities that he points out, disquieting as they may be. We are creatures, limited in our ability to understand the world and the work of God in it. We do not have the control over our lives that many people imagine we do, and living wisely means accepting these realities. Qoheleth also affirms that God has designed a world where things cohere and are appropriate, even beautiful, in their time. Bartholomew says, "[Qoheleth] cannot access the larger *story* that will make sense of the order he observes in time. Humans need a grand story or metanarrative from which to make sense of life, but they are limited and thus live in the terrible epistemological tension between what they need and the realities of life."[8] Qoheleth shows

us that if a person seeks to answer these ultimate questions solely on the basis of human reason and experience, the result will likely be agnosticism and despair. It is also important to recognize that sin obscures our ability to see how things cohere in the world. What we see of God's work is only part of a process that is moving creation, impacted by the fall, toward the new heavens and the new earth, which reflect God's ultimate purposes in creation.

Qoheleth asserts that we should enjoy life and the blessings it brings us; we should see them as coming from the hand of God and as indications of his goodness. Qoheleth tells us in 3:14 that the dissonance people experience as they struggle with these disquieting realities is an important mechanism for bringing people back into the trusting dependence on God for which human beings were designed. Provan says that we should give up on the quest for profit and full understanding through our own efforts and

Life brings times of laughing and dancing, and Qoheleth declares that we should enjoy those times as gifts from God. This beautiful figurine shows a woman gracefully dancing (Sicily, second century BC).

"reorient life toward the Creator. . . . To struggle for anything other than harmony with this reality is to act insanely and with utmost futility. Instead, the only rational response is to 'revere him [God],'" which means "acknowledging that he is Creator and that we are only creatures."[9]

One final lesson is suggested by the poem on time with which the section begins (3:1–8). As Murphy points out, "One of the ideals of the sage was to have the right word at the right time,"[10] and a significant part of wisdom's teaching was directed toward developing the skill of right words and right actions at the right time. A diligent commitment to wisdom and persistent practice are essential for progress toward that important goal. Practice will never make perfect, but it will make us better.

Illustrating the Text

We must use wisdom in our decisions, but we cannot fully control the outcomes.

Personal Testimony: On a recent trip to teach in Europe, my wife and I (Edward) were impeded by flight disruptions resulting from a volcano erupting in Iceland, an event we had not factored into our travel plans. We struggled for days trying to decide when to stop rescheduling our flight from Edinburgh to Amsterdam. We kept hoping the flight ban would lift. Finally, we made a decision to take the twenty-four-hour bus trip to Holland, where I was scheduled to teach.

In hindsight it appears that our decision was *good*, but it is impossible to know if it was *best*. The experience was frustrating, with so many contingencies lying outside our knowledge and control. The whole affair was further complicated by the rapidly changing availability of bus, train, and ferry and the difficulty in making arrangements with long lines, jammed phone lines, and thousands of others trying to do the same thing.

Personal Testimony: My (Edward's) wife's grandmother (according to an unverified family story) was traveling from her hometown of Marieham, in what is now Finland, back to the United States. A friend had made it possible for her to upgrade her journey to a new ship making its maiden voyage across the Atlantic. Circumstances caused her to be late for the ferry from Marieham to Stockholm, delaying her journey sufficiently for her to miss the connection in England with the *Titanic*. Stories abound of people who were supposed to be in the World Trade Center on September 11 or on a flight or in a train station where a terrorist bomb exploded, causing them to miss a disastrous connection. Timing can be critical, yet God's providence oversees timing, even that which we are unable to understand or control.

God's Providence and the Limits of Human Understanding

Many commentators have noted parallels between Ecclesiastes 3:1–15 and the early chapters of Genesis. The creation account makes it clear that people—while made in the image of God, with value and worth—are created beings. They are finite; they are not God. Implicit in this is the fact that they are dependent on the Creator and are accountable to him. They are not autonomous beings but were designed to live in dependence on the Creator. The story of the fall in Genesis 2–3 is set in this context, and a central issue in the account has to do with the response of the creature to the Creator's instruction. In Genesis 2 the man and woman are confronted with God's will and given the opportunity to acknowledge God's authority over them by obeying his instruction. As Kidner says, "As [the tree] stood, prohibited, it presented the alternative to discipleship: to be self-made, wresting one's knowledge, satisfactions, and values from the created world in defiance of the Creator."[1] Von Rad says, "What the serpent's insinuation means is the possibility of an extension of human existence beyond the limits set for it at creation."[2] He further describes the result of their disobedience: "Man has stepped outside the state of dependence, he has refused obedience and willed to make himself independent. The guiding principle of his life is no longer obedience but his autonomous knowing and willing, and thus he has really ceased to understand himself as creature."[3] The human refusal to stand as a creature before the Creator brought great disruption to the created order and to human function in the world. What Qoheleth describes is consistent with these consequences.

Qoheleth's observations about human limits make it clear that humans have less control over their lives than they often

When Adam disobeyed God's command, it resulted in the meaningless toil about which Qoheleth speaks. The temptation and fall of Adam and Eve is depicted on this statue pedestal (AD 1210–20) at the Cathedral of Notre Dame, Paris.

imagine is the case. The unfathomable work and purposes of God sometimes intersect with areas of life where we imagine our freedom prevails, further eroding the degree of freedom that we imagine we possess, and we are left with a considerably deflated view of our mastery over life. Such realities can be depressing and frustrating. Qoheleth also makes important points about God. He is the Creator, and everything he made is beautiful in its time. God's work and purposes are not time bound; they are eternal; they are both coherent and complete. God is sovereign over history and the affairs of his creatures, and despite the distressing realities that Qoheleth points out, evidence of God's goodness can be seen in the blessings he bestows on his creatures.

The same work of God that we do not fully understand and cannot change, and the providence that appears to thwart human freedom and independence by its random intrusion into life, can, if we know God's purposes and intentions are good, be a basis for hope, optimism, and confidence. It is also clear that God's desire is for people to fear him and live in trusting dependence on him. One can plausibly infer that this is what determines whether these realities are a source of hope or distress.

Allen says,

Not long ago I heard a short story read aloud. Virtually every word of the story seemed to grip the audience and afterwards I wondered why. It was not simply because it was a good story that was read with great artistry; rather, the audience heard it unfold without knowing which part of the story would be important. For someone to come out of a house, get into a car, and slowly drive away is a prosaic event. But when this action is part of a story it can, as it did, hold our attention because it just might turn out to be significant.

In a well-constructed short story everything makes a contribution to the overall effect, just as every detail in a great painting is important. But we do not experience everything in our actual lives this way: only some of our life is interesting. As our life unfolds, most of it is utterly prosaic. Well-constructed stories appeal to us because all the events make a contribution to the whole. Perhaps we wish that all the events in our lives were as interesting or at least contributed to some overall meaning.[4]

Books like Qoheleth or Ruth suggest that because of God's providence, each detail in our lives, even the seemingly prosaic ones, may prove to be significant, and do, in fact, make a contribution to the whole, whether we understand it or not. A more complete explication of God's purposes for his people and for history will have to await the additional revelation of the New Testament, but in the meantime Qoheleth's advice is to fear God.

Tension between the Experiences of Life and the Assertions of Faith

Big Idea *Tension between the harsh realities of life and the claims of faith highlights humanity's limited ability to answer life's ultimate questions and understand God's order.*

Understanding the Text

The Text in Context

The next major unit consists of Ecclesiastes 3:16–4:16; we will discuss the section in two parts (3:16–4:3 and 4:4–16). Qoheleth has affirmed that God's work is complete and enduring and that he has "made everything beautiful in its time" (3:11). He continues to point out much that is not congruent with the way things should be and that stands in tension with the sweeping confessional assertions of 3:11 and 15. Unchecked injustice and oppression make it difficult to see the beauty and coherence in God's design, and such realities raise questions about God's moral governance of the universe. These tensions make it difficult to see how God can be sovereign and also good and just. Delays in God's response to such situations are inexplicable and defy our sense of how things should be. The section connects back to earlier material[1] and confronts us with the tensions for which Qoheleth is well known, as he presents ideas that seem to stand in hopeless conflict.

Historical and Cultural Background

Justice was a value widely affirmed throughout the ancient Near East. A reform edict of Urukagina of Lagash (ca. 2400 BC) freed the inhabitants

Administration of justice was an important role of kings in the ancient Near East. This cuneiform cone (2350 BC) records the reforms of the Sumerian king of Lagash, Urukagina. He reduced taxes and curbed the abuses of the powerful over the citizens of Lagash.

of Lagash from usury, burdensome controls, hunger, theft, murder, the seizure of their property, and slavery. As a result "the widow and the orphan were no longer at the mercy of the powerful man."[2] Similar comments can be found in other Mesopotamian law codes. The oppression of the weak and poor is also recognized as evil in several Egyptian wisdom compositions.[3]

Interpretive Insights

3:16 *in the place of justice—wickedness.* This verse puts the focus on the public administration of justice, normally decided by the elders at the city gates. Justice, an essential part of God's order, was to characterize God's chosen people, and it was to be based on truth—as opposed to social status, wealth, political connections, and so on (see Exod. 23:6; Lev. 19:15). Israel's history reveals that justice was regularly ignored, and this often came under prophetic condemnation. The idea of corrupt leaders and judges is universally repugnant, even if such individuals seem to be an ever-present reality in society.

3:17 *God will bring into judgment both the righteous and the wicked.* This statement seems to fly in the face of what Qoheleth says elsewhere in the book (e.g., 3:16; 4:1–3), which creates a problematic tension. This likely reflects the author's teaching method, which involves presenting an idea and then following it with a contrasting one to force readers to think through the issues he is raising. He is probably not presenting the ideas with the expectation that the student must choose one or the other of his options but rather is seeking to stimulate his readers to forge solutions to the dilemmas he has presented. There

- How do we resolve the tensions between experience and faith?
- How far should we trust the experiences of life in answering life's ultimate questions?
- Can we know that human beings and animals are fundamentally different?
- Can we know that there is life after death?
- A person's worldview must be solidly rooted in reality and take full account of both general and special revelation.

are more pieces to the puzzle than the two options that Qoheleth presents.

3:18–21 *no advantage over animals.* Qoheleth's observations about death raise questions about whether humans are any different from animals. Both have breath, and when it is gone there is no more life. Based on what Qoheleth sees, there is no basis for concluding that humans have any advantage over animals. As Provan says, "For all that they like to think of themselves as gods, human beings are mortal, just like the beasts."[4] Qoheleth's observations again expose our human limits as we recognize our inability to answer such questions.

Who knows if the human spirit rises . . . the spirit of the animal goes down . . . ? While Qoheleth observes that both humans and animals go to the same place (the grave), he raises the possibility of a different destination for human spirits. He asks the question in a form that makes it clear that the answer is "No one knows." Observation and experience provide no way to answer this question definitively, and it appears that Qoheleth has no confessional basis for answering it either (although, see 12:7).

3:22 *who can bring them to see what will happen after them?* Obviously, no one knows what will happen in the future, and

Bartholomew notes that there are two possible inferences from the question. He says, "Like vv. 20–21 it could enhance the sense of meaninglessness and enigma. Alternatively, and especially in the light of v. 17, it could imply that even this enigma is under God's control."[5] God alone knows the future and controls it, and no amount of human effort will unlock the mystery. Given this reality, Qoheleth's advice is to live in the present and to enjoy the possibilities for enjoyment that one's circumstances allow.

4:1 *I looked and saw all the oppression.* Few things call the moral governance of the universe into question like oppression, an idea emphasized through repetition ("oppression . . . oppressed . . . oppressors"). The mistreatment of others raises questions about how such things can be allowed to happen and why nothing is done to stop the evil. Whether this involves the economic oppression in a Dickens novel, slavery in the American South, or the genocides in Africa or the Balkans, such acts epitomize evil and things that ordinary moral sensibilities recognize should never be. The egregious nature of such acts calls into question the nature of humankind and the evil of which humans are capable. Oppression also raises questions about the moral governance of the universe in

that many who are oppressed have done nothing to deserve the treatment they are receiving. Another aspect of the tragedy is emphasized by the repetition of the phrase "no comforter." Some people demonstrate their contempt for fellow human beings made in God's image by oppressing them; others show their lack of compassion by failing to show suffering people the basic kindness and respect they deserve.

power was on the side of their oppressors. Oppressors often have sufficient

Qoheleth says in 4:1, "I saw the tears of the oppressed—and they have no comforter; power was on the side of their oppressors—and they have no comforter." This relief pictures three women with their hands over their heads in mourning, as a soldier, part of the powerful invading Assyrian army, leads them into captivity (Nimrud palace relief, 865–860 BC).

power to make it virtually impossible to end the oppression. When uprisings are successful, often power simply shifts to a different group, and the only real change is in the identity of the oppressed and the oppressors. Such revolutions do not produce the fundamental respect for others or the just treatment that is consistent with seeing every human being as made in the image of God.

4:2–3 *dead . . . happier than the living . . . better [yet] . . . one who has never been born.* Qoheleth's shocking statement reflects what oppressive suffering can do to people. Such declarations are not positive statements about death but reflect the reality that suffering under an evil system can be so terrible that death is a welcome relief. Seow says, "The point is that the living still have to witness [and perhaps suffer from] the injustices of life, whereas the dead . . . no longer have to do so."[6] The person who has never been born escapes all the suffering and misery that is often a part of life. On the other hand, she or he also misses all of life's pleasures and opportunities.

Theological Insights

Qoheleth's observations and experiences stand in tension with other assertions that are clearly faith based. He says God has made the world so that everything is appropriate in its time. At the same time, he describes life experiences that seem to contradict this received tradition. He declares that God will judge the righteous and the wicked, but he observes ongoing injustice and oppression. The person of faith struggles with how to deal with the dissonance between biblical affirmations and the injustice and oppression that persist in the

world. Old Testament authors uniformly express their confidence about the certainty of future retribution and things being set right through God's judgment, but since Israel's understanding of eschatology was limited, the focus of that teaching is largely on this life rather than on judgment after death. Job recognizes that wicked people sometimes "spend their days in prosperity, and in peace they go down to Sheol" (Job 21:13 ESV), and Qoheleth seems convinced of the same thing. It is these kinds of issues that Qoheleth sets before his readers.

Given Qoheleth's pedagogy, it is difficult to determine what he believes about life after death or whether he is a person of faith or a skeptic, but these are not the central issues in the book. The tension likely reflects Qoheleth's goal of developing skills for living in a world filled with significant tensions. He sees struggling with these questions as an important mechanism by which people are equipped for experiences different from those the textbook told them they would encounter. Qoheleth understands that the requisite skills for living do not result from wise sages delivering right answers to their disciples. Rather, the students must struggle with these issues and questions for themselves as they move toward wisdom and spiritual maturity.

Teaching the Text

Qoheleth believes that a worldview must be based on the way things really are, and he recognizes that both tradition/revelation and knowledge derived from observation and experience should contribute to one's worldview. Those who live in the fear of the Lord and accept that the Lord's special revelation is true often face tensions between faith affirmations and the experiences of life. Psalmists often struggled as they experienced life in ways that seemed incongruent with the promises of God to which they were committed, as did Job, and their human limitations prevented them from fully understanding the work of God. Qoheleth sets these tensions before us to make us aware of the enigmatic nature of life in the world and of our limited ability to understand it. Even though the New Testament provides us with answers to some of Qoheleth's specific questions about ultimate gain and the afterlife, the process of struggling with questions we cannot answer with certainty remains a basic characteristic of life under the sun.

Qoheleth's tensions illustrate the struggle that is a central feature of the life of faith. We live in the dissonance between what ought to be and what we experience in the world; we live in the interim between promise and fulfillment. Qoheleth also affirms the importance of avoiding a naïve faith that operates in denial of the realities and complexities that are an innate part of life. He draws us into the struggle through the questions he asks and the issues he raises, but he leaves many of those questions unanswered, because we must resolve them for ourselves. The life of faith sometimes requires us to hold on to two apparently contradictory propositions as

Qoheleth affirms that God will judge the wicked, but he also observes that in the world, "in the place of justice—wickedness was there" (3:16). In the ancient Near East, the city gate was the place where citizens brought their pleas for justice to the leadership. At the ancient city of Dan, the excavations shown here reveal a platform between the outer and inner gates where a king or judge would sit to hear judicial cases.

we wait for clarification that will resolve the tension. Attempting to live life on the basis of human discovery and accomplishment will leave us unable to answer many of the basic questions of human existence, and such questions can be answered only if God reveals those answers to his people. Attempting to answer them through human effort will lead to dead ends, uncertainty, and frustration.

Teaching this text will require us to forthrightly acknowledge our limits and the reality of the struggle that living under the sun entails. It is important to draw those we are teaching into the dissonance and remind them that the kinds of experiences reported by Qoheleth are a regular part of living in the world. It is also important to emphasize that the tensions and struggles do not catch God by surprise or have the power to thwart his ultimate purposes. Finally, it is important to recognize that the world with all its enigmas and struggles is the context in which sanctification takes place. It is also in this fallen world that God's redemptive activity takes place, and that task is one in which he graciously allows us to participate, both personally and in ministry to others.

Illustrating the Text

What our eyes see may differ from the promises of God that our ears have heard.

Anecdote: A joke relates the story of a man who rushes into the emergency room of a hospital and says, "I need help right away. I need to see a doctor who is an expert in eye problems and ear problems immediately." The admitting nurse explains that doctors specialize in either ear problems or eye problems, but no doctor specializes in both. Growing more upset, the man says, "I have to find someone who deals with both." "Why is that so important?" asks the nurse. The man replies, "Because the things I see with my eyes are so different from the things I keep hearing with my ears, I know there must be something seriously wrong with me."

Qoheleth makes it clear that the person of faith lives in the interim between promise and fulfillment. As we live in the light of truth that God has revealed about himself yet also experience the realities of life in a fallen world, what we see with our eyes will sometimes be very different from what we hear regarding the promises of God and Scripture. Often such tensions and struggles are at the center of the life of faith.

News Story: John F. Kennedy Jr. (1961–99) and his wife, Carolyn Bessette, along with her sister Lauren Bessette, were all killed on July 16, 1999, when the small plane he was piloting fell into the Atlantic near the coast of Martha's Vineyard in Massachusetts. Kennedy had taken off in the early evening, which meant he would be descending over water after dark. He became disoriented in what was a haze over the horizon (a phenomenon called "spatial disorientation"), and the plane spiraled out of control, nose-diving into the water. According to many reports, Kennedy had insufficient experience flying by instruments at night, and he took risks too many amateur pilots have taken.[7] In flying, pilots must learn to depend on their instruments instead of their own sense of direction. Trusting the compass, altitude indicator, and gyroscope are essential to safe flight, especially when disoriented.

Ecclesiastes 3:16–4:3

Justice after Death | The Dignity of Humans

The sage sets before us the tension between the experiences of life and the claims of faith, and his statement that God will judge the righteous and the wicked (3:17) is consistent with the frequent assertions of the Bible that God is both sovereign and just and that he will deal with evil. The reality, however, is that wicked people do sometimes prevail and go to the grave with no clear indication that justice has been meted out in their case. Likewise, there are victims of injustice and oppression who die without ever seeing relief from the evil they have experienced. Many psalms deal with this issue, as does the book of Job, and the prophets regularly declare that, despite present appearances, God will judge the wicked. As Murphy says, Qoheleth is affirming "the biblical belief that God is somehow just and that God does judge, however contrary the evidence may appear to be." At the same time, he recognizes that "judgment belongs to God's time, not to human time."[1] As other biblical authors struggle with this tension they simply relegate this judgment to the future and emphasize things like the suddenness and

The Israelites expected that the righteous would be rewarded and the wicked punished during their lifetime. But that was not reality, and so Qoheleth recognized that God would bring judgment in God's time. Unlike the Egyptians, who had built a time of judgment into their view of the afterlife by the weighing of the deceased's heart, the Israelites had little revelation about how God's judgment would be accomplished. This papyrus drawing shows the Egyptian gods Anubis (jackal-headed figure) and Re (falcon-headed figure) weighing a heart, in a container on the left scale pan, against a figurine of Maat, wearing the feather of truth (right scale pan), while Thoth (ibis-headed god) records the results (fourth to first century BC).

unexpected nature of the judgment. There are occasional hints of the possibility of vindication after death, but no unequivocal affirmations of judgment after death occur in the Old Testament. The common assumption in Israel seems to have been that justice would prevail in this life rather than beyond the grave. Farmer suggests that this passage raises the possibility that since God is not bound by time, perhaps the judgment could come after death. She says, "The orthodox [expectation] . . . was that God would set things right 'under the sun.' But here Qohelet is suggesting that the discrepancies which can be observed when one compares orthodox expectations with human experiences can be explained only if the 'appropriate time' for judgment is not limited to our lives 'under the sun.'"[2]

Qoheleth's reflection on death not only raises questions about the possibility of a person gaining a profit that death cannot take away but also leads him to ask whether people are any different from animals (3:16–21). A negative answer to his question would lead to a conclusion about human worth that is very different from what is found in Psalm 8 or in the "image of God" passages in Genesis (Gen. 1:26–28; 9:6). These passages affirm that human beings, made in the image of God, are set apart from the animals and given dominion over them. Genesis 9:6 indicates that the image of God gives humans value and worth above that of animals. The New

Testament extends the idea of human value based on the image of God to the way we view others and talk about them (e.g., James 3:9–10). To view others with contempt is wrong, because they are human beings made in God's image.

While there is no clear indication in the text that Qoheleth is thinking along these lines, it is interesting to note that the image of God in people also provides the fundamental basis for human rights, and it is this recognition that should make injustice and oppression of others an unthinkable practice. Job, though without relating it to the image of God, denies that he has ever rejected the cause of servants who brought a complaint against him. His basis for treating them fairly is their common humanity, as he makes clear in Job 31:15: "Did not he who made me in the womb make them? Did not the same one form us both within our mothers?" Such thinking is obviously absent when people deny others justice or oppress them.

Qoheleth does make it clear that attempts to answer questions about what happens after death or even about whether there is a difference between people and animals based solely on empiricism and human observation will not succeed. The uncertainty that necessarily results opens the door for oppression of others and abuse of human rights, and limits our horizon to life under the sun. It also leaves little basis for a positive conclusion about the meaning of life.

On Achieving the Balance That Reflects God's Order

Big Idea *Living contrary to Yahweh's order increases the dissonance and frustration that characterize life under the sun.*

Understanding the Text

The Text in Context

These verses continue the larger section that began in 3:16. Ecclesiastes 4:1–3 and 3:16–17 are related by the theme of injustice, while 4:1–3 is related to 4:4–16 by the "better than" proverbs in both sections. Verses 7–8 constitute the central section of the unit and describe people who have no significant relationships with others.[1] Qoheleth describes problematic human behaviors that contribute significantly to the heavy burden of life under the sun (cf. 1:13–14), and these examples make it clear that human dysfunction plays a significant role in the struggles that characterize life.

Historical and Cultural Background

"Better than" proverbs were common in both Israel and Egypt. As sages attempted to discover and describe the patterns they detected in the world, they recognized that some things were better than others and expressed these observations in proverbial form. As Krüger shows, many of the ideas in the proverbs that Qoheleth cites here are also found in Greek, Egyptian, and Mesopotamian literature.[2]

Interpretive Insights

4:4 *toil . . . spring[s] from one person's envy of another.* Rivalry can be a strong motivation for achieving one's potential, but it can easily escalate into injustice and oppression of others. It feeds the compulsive behavior of the workaholic who neglects relationships in order to get more (v. 8), and it contributes to the human misery in the world. It dehumanizes both the one against whom the behavior is directed and the perpetrator of the abuse. While gain may result from such behavior, it does not bring satisfaction or give meaning to life, and death will erase all of it.

4:5 *Fools fold their hands and ruin themselves.* People who refuse to work destroy themselves. Proverbs often uses the metaphor of being attacked by an armed bandit to describe the inescapable consequences of idleness. While the main focus of these proverbs is on the damage people do to themselves, such behavior also brings suffering and misery to family members, neighbors, and the broader community.

4:6 *Better one handful with tranquility than two handfuls with toil.* Qoheleth sees an appropriate balance between work and rest as reflecting wisdom and God's order. The balance he commends is likely one between compulsive work driven by envy (v. 4) and the idleness described in 4:5. The Hebrew word translated "tranquility" means "quietness" or "rest" rather than inactivity.

4:8 *a man all alone.* No reason is given for this man's being alone. Perhaps his obsession with acquiring more and more left him insufficient time to cultivate relationships. Perhaps he was so engrossed in gaining more that he did not do what was necessary for relationships to flourish. "One person who has no other" (ESV) more precisely reflects the Hebrew, and the Jewish commentator Rashbam understands "the 'other' as another person who would share the wealth: the miser is alone but refuses to take a partner who would share the earnings."[3] Wisdom texts often leave such things unspecified to encourage thinking about why such a situation might occur.

no end to his toil . . . not content with his wealth. Two aspects of this person's behavior are emphasized. The first is external: he never stops working. The second is internal: he never finds satisfaction in what he has.[4]

For whom am I toiling . . . and why am I depriving myself of enjoyment? The man realizes that his obsessive attempts to gain

Key Themes of Ecclesiastes 4:4–16

- Human achievement motivated by envy disrupts community and secures nothing of lasting value.
- Balance between work and rest reflects wisdom and God's order.
- Human achievement isolated from relationships deprives one of pleasure and accomplishes nothing of lasting value.
- Humans are made for relationships, which generate many benefits.

more and more have deprived him of enjoyment, because he has no one with whom he can share and enjoy.

meaningless—a miserable business! This situation is *hebel* because it is doomed to failure from the beginning; by the nature of things it cannot work the way this person desires. It simply will not bring the satisfaction and fulfillment he desires. In addition, such obsessions often cause people to neglect the things that can bring pleasure and fulfillment. Brown says that "the vanity of it all is that unremitting determination and single-minded diligence reap not self-fulfillment but self-deprivation," and he adds that "the toiler has only himself or herself to blame."[5] The business of life is often more frustrating than it needs to be, because people pursue a course that makes it that way.

4:9 *Two are better than one.* For all the difficulties that relationships involve, Qoheleth recognizes them as an essential part of life and sees the hard work of relationships as worth the effort. Benefits come both from the help we receive from others and from the opportunities that relationships provide for helping others. Human beings are designed to function in community rather than in independence and autonomy, and the benefits that relationships provide are many.

4:12 *A cord of three strands.* It is important to have people to help us when we encounter difficulties. This proverb is not about marriage (though marriage may be one example of its truth), nor is God the third strand, as is often suggested when the verse is used at weddings (though it is true that God-centered marriages are important). Farmer says that this section in the context of 3:16–4:16 suggests that "some activities are less *hebel* than others. . . . Working to achieve community seems to promise more lasting rewards than simply working to become rich."[6]

4:13 *Better a poor but wise youth than an old but foolish king.* This example describes the rise to power of a king who was born in poverty and whose background also included prison (perhaps because of his poverty). The king stopped listening to advice from others, his popularity waned, and he was replaced by a young and poor, but wise, ruler. The example overturns normal expectations as Qoheleth concludes that youth and poverty (not characteristics highly valued by wisdom) with wisdom are preferable to age and kingship (highly desired by wisdom) with folly.

no longer knows how to heed a warning. The wise person is open to instruction and correction, while the fool resists advice. Since the old king apparently once behaved wisely, this suggests that a person's commitment to wisdom must be persisted in and practiced throughout life. This commitment, like many other things in the life of faith, requires a "long obedience in the same direction."[7] The arrogance of the king made him ineffective and likely contributed

to his being replaced by the younger and wiser man.

4:14 *may have come from prison . . . may have been born in poverty.* The details of this example are not certain, because of pronouns in the Hebrew text whose antecedents are unclear. The NIV, along with several other translations, and many commentators understand verse 14 to refer to the young man who replaced the old, foolish king. I feel, along with many other commentators, that the coherence of the story is best maintained by taking the verse to refer to the old king who was deposed. Qoheleth's point here seems unaffected by which noun one takes to be the antecedent of the pronouns "he" and "his" in v. 14.

4:16 *those who came later were not pleased with the successor.* Even kings rarely impact the future in significant ways, and the acclaim they receive from their subjects is often short lived. This illustrates Ecclesiastes 1:11's claim that "there is no remembrance of former things" (ESV).

meaningless, a chasing after the wind. Fame and accolades do not produce lasting advantage, so they are *hebel*. The fame fades, and today's popular figure becomes a forgotten artifact. Kidner says about the king described here, "He has reached a pinnacle of human glory, only to be stranded there. It is yet another of our human anticlimaxes and ultimately empty achievements."[8]

Theological Insights

People who refuse to function according to God's order cause pain and distress to others and diminish their own personalities. Qoheleth's examples reflect well-known wisdom topics.[9] What he describes is consistent with the early chapters of Genesis, which portray the human desire to be like God, humankind's decision to reject the Creator's authority and function independently of him, and the subsequent dysfunction, rivalry, and violence that resulted from abandoning Yahweh's order.

Genesis 2:18–25 likely provides a theological backdrop for Qoheleth's observations. The passage affirms that people are designed for relationships in which individuals help others and receive help from others. While Genesis 2:18–25 focuses on the relationship between a man and a woman in marriage, the human need for relationships goes beyond that specific relationship and is part of God's design. Hoekema says,

> What is being said . . . is that the human person is not an isolated being who is complete in himself or herself, but that he or she is a being who needs the fellowship of others, who is not complete apart from others. . . .
>
> Man cannot be truly human apart from others. This is true even in a psychological and social sense. . . .
>
> It is only through contacts with others that we come to know who we are and what our strengths and weaknesses are. It is only in fellowship with others that we grow and mature. It is only in partnership with others that we can fully develop our potentialities. This holds for all the human relationships in which we find ourselves: family, school, church, vocation or profession, recreational organizations, and the like.[10]

The effect of the fall on human relationships is seen in the envy that prompts Cain to kill his brother (Gen. 4:3–8), the

Envy is not a part of God's order, and the negative results can be illustrated by Genesis 4:8, where Cain kills his brother Abel. This carved ivory panel illustrates the entire story and shows God's response to their sacrifices, the murder of Abel by Cain, and Cain leaving God's presence (eleventh century AD).

vindictiveness and violence of Lamech (Gen. 4:23–24), or the corruption of the generation of Noah (Gen. 6:11–13). Qoheleth's examples of oppression and abuse showcase the ongoing nature of the problem and the harmful impact of life lived apart from God's order.

Scripture provides insight into how relationships should function, and values like love, respect, justice, and kindness allow relationships and community to flourish. The application of wisdom principles, such as avoiding anger, rash words, and arrogance, contributes to the same outcomes. Paul's description of the church as the body of Christ (Rom. 12:5–21; 1 Cor. 12:12–27) indicates the potential for unity, healing, and mutual edification as God's people function according to his order.

Teaching the Text

Scripture abounds with warnings about the dangers of God's people assimilating the values of the world,[11] though because we are immersed in the culture, those influences

The accumulation of wealth was a universal pursuit for the kings of the ancient Near East. Reliefs and tomb paintings show the tribute brought from conquered lands or the plunder gathered after a military victory, all to increase the king's treasury. But Qoheleth says that the gathering of wealth just to have it is meaningless. Shown here is a painting from the tomb of Sebekhotep (ca. 1400 BC); gold nuggets and gold rings are being brought before the Egyptian king.

are often subtle and difficult to identify. Peterson says,

> It is nearly as hard for a sinner to recognize the world's temptations as it is for a fish to discover impurities in the water. There is a sense, a feeling, that things aren't right, that the environment is not whole, but just what it is escapes analysis. We know that the spiritual atmosphere in which we live erodes faith, dissipates hope and corrupts love, but it is hard to put our finger on what is wrong.[12]

Kidner has observed that "a fault may be hidden not because it is too small to see, but because it is too characteristic to register."[13] Both observations reflect the subtle influence the world has on us, and our culture promotes many of the values that Qoheleth finds problematic. His descriptions of foolish behaviors and attitudes should prompt us to carefully consider the degree to which we have been influenced by such values.

Qoheleth sees an obsession with money and human accomplishments to the neglect of developing human relationships and enjoying life as corrosive and harmful. The person who works endlessly in an effort to find fulfillment and satisfaction is a tragic figure and reflects a futile and miserable way to live. Often such toil in pursuit of more wealth prohibits the person from "enjoyment" of life, and it is a futile goal that has no more chance of succeeding than does trying to catch the wind.[14]

Other appropriate teaching points might include the importance of balance in living, or the value of quietness/tranquility and how that can be a priority in the fast-paced, stress-filled world most of us experience. One might also encourage reflection about our motives and the degree to which we are driven by envy. It could also be beneficial to consider wisdom's teaching about successful relationships, as well as the role of relationships in moving us toward maturity and godliness.

Qoheleth raises significant questions about what constitutes success and wise living. Our culture rewards those who are driven to do more and to acquire more. Corporate culture often has little patience with those who strive for balance between work, family, and other worthwhile pursuits, and unfortunately many are eager to sacrifice everything else in order to make it to the top in a career. Christian thinking about success may well require a modification of goals and a revised definition of success. The downside of that kind of thinking is that it can be costly in terms of job opportunities and advancement, but one must ask with Ecclesiastes, "What is better?" and "What does God's order require?"

While Qoheleth's focus on reversals of fortune comes later in the book, it is perhaps appropriate to consider here how a significant economic downturn, with its attendant job loss, foreclosure, bankruptcy, and so on, changes one's perspective. How do Qoheleth's questions about the meaning of life, balance, and the importance of relationships, and his exhortations to enjoy and find pleasure in the world express themselves in a world where financial goals and aspirations have been shattered and have given way to a focus on surviving?

Illustrating the Text

Focusing on achievement at the expense of relationships diminishes life's delights.

News Story: A syndicated column by Dr. Howard Halpern in the *Los Angeles Times* presented observations from women about success. One woman, advancing to the top of a Fortune 500 company, said, "Despite all this, there was a certain sense of emptiness and loneliness in my life. . . . Gradually I realized that I had forfeited outside interests and relationships in favor of my career—I had chosen a corporate culture that demanded that of me." After losing her job, she thought about life and happiness and described her present situation: "My life is very different today. I have a job that I enjoy very much, but I also take time for myself—my outside interests, relationships, etc. I guess I could sum it up in a word—balance." Another woman, having achieved success and power by her midtwenties, recognized some disconcerting things about herself: "One is that I was not happy . . . the other was that I was losing important parts of my personality." She proceeded to keep her life and personality balanced while staying active in the business world, a hard task. For all people, both men and women, pursuit of meaning through career achievement can be destructive.[15]

Balance includes character and decisions not ruled by human definitions of success.

Literature: *The Pearl*, by John Steinbeck. In this American novella (1947), Steinbeck (1902–68) presents the story of Kino, his wife, Juana, and their baby, Coyotito. Though they live in dire poverty, they love each other and have a basic contentment. A fisherman, Kino one night finds in an oyster the "pearl of great price," otherwise called "the pearl of the world."[16] He is overcome with happiness at the potential success and relief this will bring his family. However, the pearl precipitates a "curious dark residue . . . every man suddenly became related to Kino's pearl. . . . He became curiously every man's enemy." His home is invaded, even burned, and his marital happiness is threatened, as are his and his family's lives. Not until he has lost his child does Kino become aware of what true success is; he renounces greed and throws the pearl into the sea.

Anecdote: A student considering a career in academia took note of the different lifestyle choices of two of his mentors. Both professors were in their thirties. One was divorced and spent close to eighty hours a week researching and writing. The other was married, had recently adopted a child, and spent half the time her colleague spent on academic research in order to be with her family. The student concluded that the first woman would likely get tenure (she did) and have a productive life at a prestigious university. He thought it unlikely that the other would succeed at that level. His observations made him rethink what constitutes a well-lived life.

Ecclesiastes 4:4–16

Wisdom and Propriety in Dealing with God

Big Idea *Proper worship and prayer must reflect who God is and who we are.*

Understanding the Text

The Text in Context

Ecclesiastes 5:1–7 deals with proper decorum and attitude as one comes before God, while 5:8–9 deals with injustice, oppression of others, and political corruption. Qoheleth presents typical wisdom advice about interpersonal relationships and argues that those same values are important in a person's relationship with God. Listening to others rather than just spouting words, openness to instruction (especially from those who are wise), and the avoidance of rash promises are important in dealing with others; the same values should characterize a person's demeanor before God.

Historical and Cultural Background

Ecclesiastes 5:8–9 describes oppressive and corrupt government practices, which were common in antiquity.[1] The abuses took many forms, and in Persian, Greek, and Roman times[2] central governments levied taxes on a local official, who then collected them from his subjects. The governor could keep any amount above that required by his superiors. Such practices gave rise to significant abuse. Tax collectors would often demand more money from the people

> During Roman times, the tax system oppressed the poor and was an example of corruption, as tax collectors levied an amount that would both pay the government and create a profit for themselves. This relief depicts a tax collecting scene (Gallo-Roman, second century AD).

than was required and pocket any excess. In a system where each bureaucratic layer is demanding payment, the person who is struggling just to make a living can easily be bled dry.

Interpretive Insights

5:1 *Guard your steps.* A proper attitude is essential as a person approaches God, and one must recognize who God is and who we are as worshipers. Many of the specific faults about which Qoheleth warns appear elsewhere in the wisdom literature as examples of foolish behavior to be avoided in interpersonal relationships.

A proper approach to God requires obedience, not just listening to his instruction, and this exhortation regularly occurs in Deuteronomy (e.g., 5:1; 6:3; 27:10; 31:12). The remainder of the section deals with the propensity of fools to make promises they do not keep—the likely meaning of "sacrifice of fools."

do not know that they do wrong. The Hebrew says, "They [the fools] do not know to do evil," an idea that makes little sense in the context since they are being criticized for doing evil. Seow argues that this idiom can be translated "do not acknowledge or recognize doing evil." He says, "Qoheleth . . . speaks of fools who are so stupid that they do not even recognize [or refuse to acknowledge] that they are doing wrong."[3]

5:2 *Do not be quick with your mouth.* Words uttered thoughtlessly or in haste typify the rash behavior that characterizes foolish people. Qoheleth commends prudence in worship and in one's relationship with God, as well as in relationships with others. Promises made to God but not followed by action, rash words spoken to

- One's relationship with God should be characterized by wisdom, not folly.
- God desires obedience rather than empty words and promises.
- People should come to God with respect and openness to his instruction.
- Corrupt leaders are common; leadership that promotes the people's well-being is a blessing.

God, or words reflecting a foolish person's agenda constitute folly.

God is in heaven and you are on earth. Qoheleth's statement likely emphasizes the great difference between human beings and God. It is the knowledge of who God is (the all-wise Creator and Sovereign Lord) and who we are (creatures and subjects) that is the basis for the reverential awe that the Old Testament calls "fear of the Lord" (cf. v. 7).

5:3 *A dream comes when there are many cares.* The first part of the verse is unclear, though often both parts of a proverb communicate similar ideas. In this case dreams would represent ideas and intentions that, like the foolish person's words, are never translated into deeds (see below). In the Hebrew Bible there is no other example of "dream" being used in this way. Dreams in the ancient world were thought to be a means by which the divine communicated with people,[4] and a dream with a negative or unclear meaning could be a cause for great concern. On this basis the verse could be translated, "As a dream is accompanied by many worries, so a fool's speech comes with many words."[5]

many words mark the speech of a fool. The second half of this proverb identifies a basic characteristic of a fool: many words but no substance. A person boasts about what he or she is able to do, only to disappoint when it actually comes to doing it; someone promises to pay what is owed but always has some excuse to delay payment. Foolish people are well known for their verbosity, and few of their promises are backed up with action.

5:4–5 *When you make a vow to God, do not delay to fulfill it.* Qoheleth's language is similar to Deuteronomy 23:21–23. People were not obligated to make vows to God, but when they chose to do so, they were required to do what they promised. Failure to fulfill a vow in a relationship constituted foolish behavior, and Qoheleth makes it clear that wise and judicious behavior before God is both God's due and what he expects from those who come before him.

5:6 *do not protest to the temple messenger, "My vow was a mistake."* The Hebrew says "messenger," and suggested identities for the messenger include God, an angel (a common meaning for the Hebrew word), or a priest. This was probably a messenger sent

Qoheleth cautions his readers that when they make a vow to God, they must fulfill it. Shown here is a votive stele that a person named Nebmen is presenting to the god Ptah. Vows in the ancient world involved giving a gift to the gods, generally in the form of an offering. This stele portrays such an offering and would have been presented in the temple to remind the god that the vow had been fulfilled (Memphis, Egypt, Eighteenth Dynasty, 1500 BC).

by the temple (so NIV) to collect what the foolish person promised to give when the vow was made. The word "mistake" probably indicates a failure to think through the implications of the promise made to God. The situation may be like that described in Proverbs 20:25, where a person declares something to be holy or set apart exclusively for the Lord's use and thus no longer available to the one who dedicated it. Only after the rash vow has been made does the person begin to consider the implications of the loss of the item that was vowed.

5:7 *Therefore fear God.* Qoheleth is likely reflecting on religious practice that he sees around him and is making the point that God is not pleased by insincere ritual or empty words. Instead, God desires the sincere obedience that comes from trusting dependence on him. According to Walton, fearing God is "taking God seriously—just as we might take a parent seriously or the police seriously when we are convinced that they will act on what they say and follow through."[6]

5:8 *do not be surprised.* Qoheleth again makes the point that one should not be surprised at injustice and oppression. It flows naturally from the realities of life and human nature that he has observed.

one official is eyed by a higher one. It is uncertain whether "official" refers specifically to government officials or to haughty and arrogant people in general. Bartholomew argues that government officials had a particular responsibility for upholding justice and righteousness in society, so it is appropriate to understand the verse as focusing on political corruption.[7] Longman calls the section "The Network of Oppression," and says, "Government officials all the way up to the king use their position for their own advantage, with the result that the people suffer."[8] The verse describes systemic corruption in which government officials (or corporate executives, or union bosses, or policemen, or the military, or elected officials, or rich and powerful people of various sorts) oppress others or are complicit in the activities by protecting those under them who engage in these activities. The prophets regularly condemned leaders in Judah and Israel for this sort of behavior, and history is replete with examples of such abuse. Typically those harmed the most by such corruption are the ones least able to bear the losses.

5:9 *The increase from the land is taken by all; the king himself profits from the fields.* The translation of this proverb is difficult. In contrast to the situation described in verse 8, where corrupt government structures work to the disadvantage of the people, verse 9 likely describes the way things should work. A king should rule in ways that protect the interests of the people

and that allow them to gain appropriate benefit from their work. A just government will protect citizens from corrupt and unfair practices that rob them of legitimate compensation for their efforts. As Garrett points out,

> The example that makes this point is agriculture. In an anarchic society no boundaries or property rights can be maintained, access to wells and other common resources cannot be fairly regulated, aqueducts and dikes will not be kept in good repair, and no organized resistance to ravaging armies can be offered. In short, the agricultural economy will collapse. Government may be evil, but it is a necessary evil.[9]

I suggest that an appropriate translation for the verse would be: "A benefit for the land in every way is a king committed to cultivated fields."

Theological Insights

Many passages in the Pentateuch emphasize the importance of listening to God's instruction and obeying it (Deut. 5:1; 6:3; 27:10; 31:12), and the prophets regularly describe the people of Judah as deaf (Isa. 42:18–20; 43:8–10; Jer. 5:21; 6:10) or as refusing to listen to Yahweh's word (Jer. 11:10; 13:10; Zech. 7:11–13). Isaiah says, in contrast, that God's ideal servant will be characterized by careful attention to God's instruction and a persistent obedience to what he hears (Isa. 50:4–7).

People in the Old Testament might make a vow to God in connection with a request for deliverance from some difficult situation, and their prayer might include the promise that they would bring a thanksgiving offering to the temple. It is possible that some people came to understand these vows as a means of manipulating God into granting their requests or perhaps impressing God with their piety so that he would bless them in special ways. It is also possible that such promises reflected the casual way in which God was viewed by some and were made more for the benefit of observers than as acts of genuine devotion to Yahweh.

"One official is eyed by a higher one, and over them both are others higher still" (5:8). This relief from the throne room at Khorsabad shows the crown prince, Sennacherib, on the far left, with a row of courtiers following behind him. Not pictured here, but in authority over them all, is King Sargon II.

Teaching the Text

This section has implications for the way we approach God in prayer and worship. Proper worship must reflect who God is and who we are as creatures. Proper respect for the sovereign Lord means that we come before him to listen to his instruction and obey it. It is the epitome of arrogance and folly to suppose that we can instruct God or manipulate him with our clever words. It is appropriate to emphasize our intimate relationship with God in Christ and the access and boldness that this involves, but it is still important to recognize who God is and to treat him with the respect he deserves. Teaching this text might involve exploring what this looks like and how one achieves the balance between intimacy and respect in different worship settings and with different worship styles.

The text also makes it clear that God desires a commitment characterized by wisdom rather than folly. While extravagant promises and rash vows may appear to reflect deep piety and personal sacrifice,

they do not please God. Qoheleth's teaching raises questions about evangelism that encourages high-pressure techniques to "close the deal" and force a decision. One wonders about the wisdom of using highly emotional appeals to get young people to make decisions about missionary service or other ministry commitments. This text also has implications for the way churches and Christian organizations raise money and appeal to potential donors for funds. There is often a fine line between motivating people to do God's will and manipulating them into making the kinds of rash, emotion-driven promises that Ecclesiastes tells us are unwise and dishonoring to God.

Finally, 5:8–9 reminds us that God hates injustice and oppression, and God's people honor him when they live in ways that demonstrate integrity and God's truth. Teaching this text might involve reflecting on what justice means for us and how this applies to various issues that confront our society. The text also reminds us that government institutions often promote injustice and oppression by protecting people in high places who are the perpetrators of such evils, and such realities illustrate the folly of putting our trust in governments or political parties to bring about an ideal world. It is essential that we allow Scripture to be the final authority on issues of justice and right dealing rather than allowing our commitment to a political party or other agenda group to determine how we think. Failure to listen to God and to do what he says can result in our becoming the ones who watch over the perpetrators of injustice and contribute to the continuation of the oppressive practices.

Illustrating the Text

God deserves the same respect offered in our best interpersonal relationships.

Bible: **Malachi.** The prophet Malachi speaks the words of the Lord, faulting the people of Judah for behaving toward God in ways that would be unacceptable in relating to other human beings. In Malachi 1:6 the Lord says, "A son honors his father, and a slave his master. If I am a father, where is the honor due me? If I am a master, where is the respect due me?" Again he says, "When you offer blind animals for sacrifice, is that not wrong? When you sacrifice lame or diseased animals, is that not wrong? Try offering them to your governor! Would he be pleased with you? Would he accept you?" (Mal. 1:8). The Great King deserves the kind of respect people would show to important persons with whom they interact.

Anecdote: An African traveler tells the story of being among one of the most vicious tribes known; while he was there, his attention was drawn to their idol stuck high on a pole, seeming to convey the idea that the god could see around the country and into every one of the people. The tribe's superstitious faith caused them to believe that every act of dishonesty would be seen by their god and that they would be punished accordingly. The effect of this faith was that no dishonest act occurred within sight of this idol, and the property closest to the idol was perfectly secure. On some level, this tribe understood respect.

God's people must live in ways that demonstrate integrity and God's truth.

News Story: The kinds of oppressive practices condemned by the biblical prophets exist in every time and culture and include depriving people through robbery and injustice, unfair taxes, and economic systems designed to make it impossible for people to improve their economic situations. The current relevance of this is evident in an article in the *New York Times* that reports on the Stolen Asset Recovery Initiative run by the World Bank and the United Nations. It estimates that "$20 to $40 billion is stolen annually from developing countries through bribery, misappropriation and corruption . . . a figure represent[ing] about 15 to 30 percent of aid to the developing world."[10] The destructive power of greed is transcultural and transhistorical. While this problem is likely one that reflects things that are crooked and cannot be straightened, as Ecclesiastes 1:15 puts it, it is imperative that God's people, in ministering to others, demonstrate a depth of integrity that sets them apart from the prevailing culture. Certainly, it is essential to bring wisdom and the forces of justice to bear in trying to minimize things like graft and corruption.

The Folly of Greed: Be Content with What God Provides

Big Idea *The relentless pursuit of wealth does not give life meaning or bring satisfaction.*

Understanding the Text

The Text in Context

This section's focus on wealth and enjoyment sets it apart from what precedes and follows it. Earlier themes also recur as the author insists that wealth will not bring fulfillment and ultimate satisfaction to anyone. He again emphasizes the importance of pleasure and warns of the tragedy of failing to take advantage of opportunities to enjoy. He reminds us of the uncertainty of wealth and that death will rob us of any accumulated gain. While the proverbs cited by Qoheleth do not give a comprehensive picture of wealth—individual proverbs never do that—he does identify certain negative aspects of wealth that are not always evident to people, especially those who are intent on gaining more and more.

Historical and Cultural Background

The problem of greed and the supposition that the thirst for wealth and possessions can be satisfied by acquiring more appears to be innate in human beings. Warnings about it abound in literature; museums and opulent palaces around the world testify to the extent to which people throughout history have gone in their efforts to accumulate wealth, often by oppressing others. Despite their efforts, people who pursue wealth consistently fail to find the fulfillment and satisfaction they are seeking.

A text from Emar in Syria provides interesting parallels to this section of Ecclesiastes.[1] A son listens to his father's advice about living wisely and reminds his father of the futility of accumulating wealth that will be left behind at death. The son concludes that "what really matters is what one can enjoy in the world of the living, because . . . what happens in the afterlife is beyond human understanding."[2]

Ecclesiastes 6:3 speaks of a rich person who was not buried properly. Throughout the ancient Near East people believed that the way a person was buried impacted how the deceased experienced the afterlife. In Mesopotamia it was thought that those who had not been buried properly were condemned to wander the earth aimlessly and to bother the living. Such ideas are not found in the Old Testament, though many passages affirm the importance of a proper burial.

Interpretive Insights

5:10 *Whoever loves money never has enough.* According to Harvard psychologist Daniel Gilbert, "Economists and psychologists have spent decades studying the relation between wealth and happiness, and have generally concluded that wealth increases human happiness when it lifts people out of abject poverty and into the middle class but that it does little to increase happiness thereafter."[3]

5:11–12 *As goods increase, so do those who consume them.* The proverbs in these two verses (along with the other proverbs in this section and throughout Ecclesiastes) are typical wisdom sayings, each of which captures a tiny cross section of truth. The sage is not providing comprehensive teaching about wealth but is simply pointing out that disadvantages sometimes come with wealth. Such sayings are designed to dissuade people from seeking wealth as a central focus in life. Qoheleth cites these sayings in a context that encourages finding contentment and enjoyment in one's lot rather than constantly focusing on what one does not have and always striving for more. His point is that making the accumulation of wealth the central priority in life is both futile and unwise.

- The desire for wealth and possessions is unquenchable and can never be satisfied.
- Wealth has benefits but significant downsides as well.
- Seeking meaning and fulfillment from wealth is futile; it can be lost in an instant, and death will take all of it.
- Wise people take advantage of opportunities to enjoy, because they do not know what the future holds.
- Wise people look for examples of God's goodness in every circumstance and enjoy all of God's gifts.

what benefit are they . . . ? Increased wealth often produces far less benefit than most people imagine as they relentlessly work to get more and more. Qoheleth points out that in certain respects the poor person even has an advantage over the rich in that he is able to sleep better than the rich man. Hard work and few worries about his "empire" allow him to sleep well, while the rich man's fullness keeps him awake. Whether this results from too much food or from worries about his wealth is not clear. While many today would respond that Qoheleth's sayings are insensitive and perhaps absurd, it is important to remember that proverbial sayings regularly make their point through hyperbole. His point is not to promote the benefits of poverty but to emphasize the importance of being content with one's lot rather than obsessively focusing on gaining more in the

Qoheleth observes that once death comes humankind can carry nothing with them into the afterlife (5:15). This funerary bust of a wealthy female shows the elegant jewelry she may have enjoyed wearing during her lifetime but which she must leave behind upon death (Palmyra, third century AD).

vain hope that it will give meaning and contentment to one's life.

5:17 *in darkness, with great frustration, affliction and anger.* This description of the rich person after the loss of wealth is often true of the person whose thirst for more is insatiable. People obsessed with the pursuit of wealth frequently fail to avail themselves of opportunities to enjoy. Kamano says, "The appetite which can never be filled prevents humanity from experiencing enjoyment."[4] People who live this way often become bitter, frustrated, and cynical. One would think that the financial disaster described in verse 14 would prompt a person to pursue a different course, but that is rarely the case.

5:18–19 *to eat, to drink and to find satisfaction . . . this is their lot.* Qoheleth repeats the advice given in 2:24–25 and 3:12–13 and emphasizes the importance of accepting our "lot" and finding opportunities for pleasure and delight in our present situation. "Lot" refers to a person's circumstances in life and includes such things as when, where, and to whom one is born; health; abilities; wealth, status, and educational opportunities; and the like. One's lot establishes

Qoheleth says in 5:18, "This is what I have observed to be good: that it is appropriate for a person to eat, to drink and to find satisfaction in their toilsome labor under the sun during the few days of life God has given them—for this is their lot." In this relief Ashurbanipal and his wife are celebrating his military triumphs by relaxing in his beautiful garden with music, food, and drink (North Palace at Nineveh, 645–635 BC).

both opportunities and limits for what that person can do. Qoheleth recognizes that these things do not take place outside the sovereign oversight of God or take him by surprise. Qoheleth is keenly aware of the mystery that is involved here as God's providence plays a significant role in determining our lot in life. At the same time, the way we live and the choices we make contribute to the picture as well—whether we live wisely or foolishly. Qoheleth offers two important principles for living well: the first is to recognize the good things that regularly appear around us as gifts that come from God; the second is to enjoy these gifts when they come rather than postponing enjoyment until some future time. Accepting the good gifts that God gives and finding delight in them is an important aspect of the trusting dependence on God for which humans have been created. This stands in sharp contrast to a life lived independently and autonomously as people attempt to set their own course and seek ultimate fulfillment and meaning in their own accomplishments.

5:20 *occupied with gladness of heart.* To be "occupied with gladness" can distract people from the ugly realities of life that Qoheleth points out and can help them cope with the bad business that life sometimes involves. Eating, drinking, and enjoying one's work reflect the way God has designed the world to work and his intentions for human beings. Qoheleth's call to enjoy the good things that God gives is not just a response of resignation to the harsh realities he has observed. It reflects a perspective that enables a person to recognize the difficult realities of life while still affirming God's goodness and finding delight in his gifts. Regularly seeing the good things around us as gifts of God and receiving them in this way can help immensely in situations where we are overwhelmed by tragedies that call into question the goodness of God.

6:3 *he cannot enjoy his prosperity.* Things like prosperity, children, and long life that are expressions of God's blessing and indications of his favor do not necessarily give meaning to life or guarantee that it will be satisfying and fulfilling. The ultimate meaning, satisfaction, and profit that Qoheleth—and every human being—seeks will have to come from something other than simply possessing these blessings.

a stillborn child is better off than he. Qoheleth's comment is a typical wisdom generalization designed to make a single point, relative to his observations in 5:13–17 and 6:1–6 and his exhortation to enjoy the good things that people regularly experience in life. Neither the rich person he describes

nor the stillborn enjoys these pleasures, and Qoheleth sees that as tragic. The rich man in his example, however, does experience the difficulties that are part of life in the world, while the stillborn is spared them. The stillborn and the rich person come to the same end in death, but the stillborn gets there sooner and without the pain and frustration that characterize life under the sun. In this respect, Qoheleth concludes that the stillborn is better off.

6:8 *the poor . . . knowing how to conduct themselves before others?* While wisdom, wealth, and excellent relational skills provide some protection from the evil resulting from the greed of others, they cannot guarantee that a person will never become the victim of oppression and injustice.

6:9 *This too is meaningless.* The attempt to find lasting satisfaction and meaning in wealth and possessions is *hebel*. There are things in life, like satisfying the deepest needs of the soul, that people cannot achieve on their own, no matter how hard or how persistently they try. Instead people must live with openness to the gifts God wishes to give us.

Theological Insights

Covenant blessing in the Old Testament often takes the form of wealth and material prosperity. At the same time, Israel is warned about the danger of failing to recognize God as the source of its wealth (Deut. 8:7–18). Proverbs 10:15 recognizes the security that wealth provides, but Proverbs 18:10–11 alerts us to how easy it is for a rich person to trust in wealth rather than in God. Paul reminds Timothy that "the love of money is a root of all kinds of evil. Some people, eager for money, have wandered from the faith" (1 Tim. 6:10).

No matter how much one accumulates, wealth cannot give meaning and fulfillment to life. Nevertheless, people continue to nurture the hope that the satisfaction they long for will come when a little more is secured. The benefits of wealth are short lived, and the relentless pursuit of material goods will never result in a lasting profit. Death will ultimately rob a person of every penny that has been so carefully accumulated. Qoheleth does not address the question of why people's lots in life are so different and unequal, though some of the reasons are obvious: human evil and oppression, human folly, and God's sovereign choice. Qoheleth's focus is on how one should live, and he tells us that in whatever circumstances we find ourselves we should accept our situation and look for evidence of God's goodness and faithful love. Such blessings express themselves in loving relationships and in the enjoyment of the simple pleasures of life, such as food, drink, and the like. Receiving such things as gifts from God and finding pleasure in them rather than focusing on the things that are wrong or that we wish were different will contribute to our well-being and delight.

Teaching the Text

Qoheleth confronts our materialistic culture with the message that the acquisition of wealth and possessions can never give meaning to life or fulfill the deepest needs of the human soul. He commends a life that values such things as building relationships, taking time to rest, and enjoying life in the world. God often blesses his people with money and material things, and with that blessing comes the responsibility to use wealth in ways that honor God and that minister to the needs of those around us. Qoheleth affirms it is fully appropriate to embrace the possibilities for enjoyment and pleasure that come to us, as long as we see the blessings as a gift from God and the pleasure takes forms that honor God. Christians also need to remember that there are downsides to wealth and that it has the power to undermine faith and trust in God as well as to destroy relationships and ministries. Christians need to carefully reflect on the futility and folly of expending great amounts of time and energy trying to secure things that in the final analysis will be lost at death and that ultimately do not really matter. This is doubly the case when the pursuit of wealth is done at the expense of other things that bring delight to God and honor him.

Ecclesiastes calls us to accept reality and the limits that are a part of being human and encourages us to find opportunities for pleasure and delight in whatever circumstances we find ourselves. Such opportunities come as gifts from God, and they are to be gratefully received from that perspective. At the same time, Qoheleth raises significant issues for the life of faith as he affirms God's sovereignty in a world that is broken and where inequity and anomalies abound.

Illustrating the Text

Wealth and possessions will never bring lasting satisfaction and fulfillment.

Art: *The Moneylender and His Wife*, **by Quentin Massys.** In this painting (1514) by

The Money Lender and his Wife, 1514 (oil on panel), by Quentin Massys or Metsys (ca. 1466–1530)

Massys (ca. 1466–1530), the moneylender sits at a table with a pile of money and his scales in front of him, looking carefully at a single coin. His wife is sitting next to him with a Bible or religious book open in front of her, appearing to be interrupted in her reading. As she turns the page of her book, her eye is drawn to the money on the table and to the coin her husband so carefully examines. Massys did the painting to show how easily money can distract us from the worship of God.[5]

Poetry: "The Pulley," by George Herbert. Qoheleth insists that money does not bring with it the guarantee of enjoyment;

certainly, it does not bring fulfillment and satisfaction. Qoheleth says clearly that God has withheld the satisfaction that people seek in money and accomplishments so that people may fear him. This idea is captured in a poem by devout British minister and poet George Herbert (1593–1633). This poem (1633) portrays God pouring blessings on humanity but withholding rest and satisfaction so that humans might not adore God's gifts instead of adoring him.

> When God at first made man,
> Having a glass of blessings standing by,
> "Let us," said he, "pour on him all we
>   can.
> Let the world's riches, which dispersèd
>   lie,
> Contract into a span." So strength first
>   made a way;
> Then beauty flowed, then wisdom,
>   honour, pleasure.
> When almost all was out, God made
>   a stay,
> Perceiving that, alone of all his treasure,
> Rest in the bottom lay.
> "For if I should," said he,
> "Bestow this jewel also on my creature,
> He would adore my gifts instead of me,
> And rest in Nature, not the God of
>   Nature;
> So both should losers be.
> "Yet let him keep the rest,
> But keep them with repining
>   restlessness;
> Let him be rich and weary, that at least,
> If goodness lead him not, yet weariness
> May toss him to my breast."[6]

Ecclesiastes 5:10–6:9

The Mystery and Complexity of Life under the Sun

Qoheleth has given us important practical advice about dealing with money and living well in the world. He has warned us about thinking that ultimate meaning and satisfaction can be found in wealth. He has also warned us of the disaster that can result from supposing that money is something that it was never intended to be. He makes it clear that we are to accept our lot in life and rejoice in our toil, because this is the gift of God (5:19). He also makes it clear that we are to identify and enjoy the good things that are part of our present circumstances rather than coveting someone else's situation and constantly wondering why his or her situation is better than ours. He recognizes that each person's lot in life is somehow related to the providence of God but does little to unravel the mystery of why there are such radical differences in people's circumstances.

Qoheleth regularly draws from Israel's proverbial tradition and seems to affirm its value in living life. It is evident that a person's lot in life can be advanced or worsened depending on whether the person makes wise decisions or foolish ones. Wisdom or diligence can commend a person in ways that improve his or her lot and open up opportunities that did not exist before. The mystery lies in this synergism between human effort and the providential activity of God. Qoheleth recognizes both aspects and affirms their importance.

Possibilities for upward economic mobility would have been limited in ancient Israel, since most people farmed small family-owned lands and their career choices were largely determined by family circumstances. Missionaries often report on tribal situations where children have little opportunity for more than a few years of education and where, if they learn to read at all, there are few books available to them. Their lot in life seems to offer very limited possibilities. A person's lot in life is generally fixed by when and where she or he lives, and throughout much of history there has been little chance that a person's lot would change in any significant way.

Some reasons for the uneven distribution of opportunities in terms of a person's lot in life are noted by Qoheleth and elsewhere in Scripture. God presently allows evil to operate in the world, and things like injustice and oppression negatively affect people's circumstances and options in life. Often people choose to live independently of God's order, and negative outcomes attach to such foolish choices. At the same time, Scripture recognizes that God's purposes are moving forward despite these realities and will ultimately be accomplished. Qoheleth does little to resolve the mystery of providence but simply says to live wisely and to live in trusting dependence on God's providential activity in the world. The mystery of providence remains a part of life in the world.

Seeing things that bring pleasure as gifts from God enables a person to enjoy life and to flourish in even the most devastating circumstances. Being able to set difficulty and injustice in a context that affirms the goodness of God and his purposes has the power to transform. This is evident in Lamentations 3 when Jeremiah shifts his focus from the destruction of Jerusalem to the steadfast love of God and his mercy. It is evident as well in Psalm 63 when David shifts his focus from the threat to his life to God's goodness. Many examples of this can be found among God's people in Scripture and throughout history. At the same time, Qoheleth makes it clear that, for all the secondary causes he identifies, ultimately the inequity of the lots of human beings lies under God's general sovereignty, and this again sets in relief the tensions that exist between the assertions of faith and the way people experience life in the world.

Embracing the principles that Qoheleth espouses does not immediately resolve the problems associated with wealth but rather sets in clear relief the complexity of living out these principles in the world. How does one determine how much to save for retirement? How does a person anticipate future needs given the uncertainties of the economy and the impossibility of predicting what the future may hold in terms of educational expenses, job loss, or catastrophic medical expenses? Obviously, the answers will differ depending on many variables. The line between responsible preparation and irresponsible hoarding can sometimes be difficult to identify.

Psalm 63 may reflect the time when David fled for his life in the dry, barren wilderness of Judah, shown here. Even in these difficult circumstances he was able to rejoice in God and praise him for his love and help.

Humanity's Inability to Know What Is Good

Big Idea *Because of God's providence, things are not always what they seem to be, and who knows what is good for a person?*

Understanding the Text

The Text in Context

Ecclesiastes 6:10–12 begins the second half of the book and looks back at important themes, like the meaning of life, satisfaction, fulfillment, *hebel*, and profit/advantage. The verses also introduce important ideas in the second half of the book, such as people's limited ability to know or discern what will happen in the future. The proverbs in chapter 7 are set in a context that emphasizes human limits and the work of God. Qoheleth asks two questions (6:12): "Who knows what is good for a person?" and "Who can tell them what will happen [in the future]?" The proverbs of 7:1–12 then explore the question of what is good. Verses 13–14 conclude the section by affirming that humans cannot fully understand or change the work of God, nor can they know what will happen in the future.

Historical and Cultural Background

Ideas similar to these proverbs are found in individual proverbs from Mesopotamian or Egyptian literature, though there are no direct parallels. Egyptian and Mesopotamian proverbs emphasize the importance of a good reputation, being open to wisdom and instruction from others, avoiding anger, and the importance of patience and self-control.

Interpretive Insights

6:10 *has already been named.* This likely reflects Genesis 1, where God's sovereign authority is demonstrated by naming the things he has made.[1] This affirms both God's sovereignty and Adam's finitude—and the finitude of his descendants. Seow argues that Qoheleth's point goes beyond foreknowledge and affirms "divine predetermination."[2]

what humanity is has been known. This verse likely contrasts the weakness of humans with God's sovereign power; the connection between Adam and *'adamah* (Heb. "ground, earth") further affirms human limits. As humans seek to understand God's order, there are realities from which they cannot escape, and primary among these involves who God is and who human beings are.

someone who is stronger. This phrase probably refers to God, and Qoheleth's point is the futility and absurdity of humans trying to resist God and ignore his order.

6:11 *The more the words, the less the meaning.* The Hebrew says literally, "when words increase, *hebel* increases." Arguing a case with someone whose power makes it unlikely that the case can be won is futile, and wisdom dictates accepting the reality of the situation rather than pursuing the argument. Provan says, "It is one of the great delusions of our time . . . that the exertion of human power can change the shape of reality,"[3] and certainly that is true when the stronger one (v. 10) is the sovereign Creator. Provan adds, "We can insist all we like, with increasingly strident and authoritative words, that reality should be different, but all the words in the world will not make it so."[4]

6:12 *who knows what is good . . . ?* No one but God knows "what is good" in a final and comprehensive way, though Qoheleth has already identified some things that are good, and he will continue to explore the question in 7:1–12. There is more to "good" than meets the eye, and human limits regularly prevent us from knowing what is good in any absolute sense.

meaningless days they pass through like a shadow. "Meaningless" (*hebel*) and

Key Themes of Ecclesiastes 6:10–7:14

- Wise living requires acknowledging human finitude and limits.
- Humans cannot determine what is good for them.
- Humans cannot know what will happen in the future.
- Humans, by their words or actions, cannot change God's purposes.

"shadow" emphasize the short-lived and insubstantial nature of human existence in the world.

Who can tell them what will happen under the sun . . . ? Things are not always as they appear on the surface, and experiences often take on a different appearance in hindsight. Sometimes things that initially seem terrible contribute to good outcomes in the end, and the reverse is true as well. "Under the sun" indicates that Qoheleth is thinking about what happens on earth rather than in the afterlife.

7:1–12 These verses bring together several proverbs dealing with human limits and the work of God, as Qoheleth explores the question "Who knows what is good for a person?" (6:12). The proverbs are characterized by the Hebrew word for "good" (ten times in 7:1–12) and often take the form of "better than" proverbs.

"A good name is better than fine perfume" (7:2), perhaps the perfume that would have been used for burial. This portion of the Book of the Dead of the scribe Nebqed shows his sarcophagus with a perfume cone on its head. While a priest performs the "opening of the mouth" ritual to prepare Nebqed for the afterlife, a woman mourns beside the funerary offerings (Egypt, Eighteenth Dynasty, 1391–1353 BC).

Ecclesiastes 6:10–7:14

7:1 *A good name . . . the day of death.* A "good name" or reputation is an important wisdom value; it is "better than" valuable perfume. Some believe that the connection between a person's reputation and the day of death is that some people's reputations can outlive death. Others have suggested that an individual's reputation remains in doubt until the "day of death" because until that time a person can do something to ruin his or her reputation.

7:2 *better to go to a house of mourning than to go to a house of feasting.* Qoheleth emphasizes the importance of living in the light of one's mortality. It is better to go to a funeral than a party, because the funeral brings one face-to-face with human mortality—something that seldom happens at parties.

7:3 *Frustration is better than laughter.* Qoheleth contends that pleasure and enjoyment are good but also affirms that what is good for a person is complex and cannot be reduced to pleasure. Sometimes things that are good for us may be difficult and distasteful, and positive character traits often result from difficult and painful experiences. Qoheleth commends a serious attitude that accepts the realities of life and lives in the light of them, over a frivolous attitude that lives in denial of uncomfortable realities like human limits and mortality.

7:5–6 *better to heed the rebuke of a wise person.* Wise people welcome discipline and correction because they understand the potential benefits; fools vigorously reject rebuke and prefer to party instead. The songs and laughter of fools are superficial and lack substance. Thornbushes may crackle and blaze spectacularly, but the fire is short lived and provides insufficient heat to accomplish essential tasks.

7:7 *Extortion turns a wise person into a fool, and a bribe corrupts the heart.* It is uncertain whether the "wise person" is the perpetrator or victim of the abuse, though more likely the wise person is the victim.[5] The proverb then describes this person's distress at being victimized. Even wise people lack sufficient wisdom to always escape oppression and its consequences.

7:8–9 *end . . . better than its beginning.* The significance of an experience is not always apparent in the beginning, nor is the impact of a person's life always evident apart from hindsight, as the stories of Joseph and Ruth illustrate. Human perspective is limited by our time-bound nature and our inability to see beyond the horizons of our own experience. God's purposes, however, extend across generations and history, and humans cannot understand how the various pieces fit together. Obviously,

Qohelet compares the "laughter of fools" to the "crackling of thorns under the pot" (7:6). In ancient Israel thornbushes provided fuel, especially in places where trees were scarce. Shown here is the plant referred to in Ecclesiastes, which is known as spiny or thorny burnet.

people cannot determine what is good in any ultimate sense.

Do not be quickly provoked. A distinguishing mark of wisdom is patience and deliberation, in contrast to a fool's rash and passion-driven responses. Wise people seek to understand the bigger picture and set experiences into that broader context. They suspend judgment until they have a sufficient basis for responding and remain aware of their own limits—both of which provide protection against rash judgments.

7:10 *Why were the old days better than these?* People tend to isolate the good things from the past and celebrate "the good old days," while forgetting the bad things. Qoheleth's commitment to reality includes a commitment to the way the past really was. He also understands the importance of living in the present and discourages focusing on the past in ways that debilitate people and prevent them from doing useful work in the present. He commends a balanced view that values the past and learns from it while being rooted solidly in the present.

7:11–12 *Wisdom is a shelter . . . the advantage of knowledge.* Ecclesiastes recognizes the advantages of wisdom and wealth but also their limits. The word for "shelter" means "shade" and is often used as a metaphor for protection or for that which is short lived. The ambiguity suggests that the protection of wisdom and wealth is an "advantage," but a short-lived one that does not extend beyond death. Neither wealth nor wisdom provides the kind of ultimate advantage for which Qoheleth is searching.

7:14 *God has made the one as well as the other.* Life in the world will involve good and bad times, but Qoheleth assures us that both happen within the framework of God's providential oversight. Qoheleth encourages us to take advantage of opportunities to enjoy in the present rather than waiting for a future about which no one can be certain.

Theological Insights

Qoheleth asserts in 6:12 that no one knows what is good for a person and then cites proverbs exploring what is good in 7:1–12. This creates the tension that is typical of Ecclesiastes. Qoheleth's observations demonstrate the complex nature of the world and emphasize the limited nature of human perspective. Some experiences turn out, in hindsight, to be very different from how they initially appeared, and unpleasant things, like funerals or rebukes, often contribute to positive outcomes in a person's life. God's pervasive work of providence makes it unlikely that we can identify the pieces of a puzzle that may span generations and involve events that seem independent and unrelated. Consequently, people should be careful about passing judgment on the experiences of life or on God's work and character on the basis of their experiences.

Qoheleth's conclusions come largely from human observation and the experiences of life. This section makes it clear that this kind of empirical approach is unable to discern what is good for people, and the section provides a clue to the basic problem with empiricism. It enables the sage to see that the world is bent and broken but cannot take him any further, because he is confined to examining a fallen world that often appears chaotic, senseless, and enigmatic. Qoheleth's approach gives him no way to see the world from a perspective

Qoheleth asserts that "no one can discover anything about the future" but must instead trust in God's sovereignty. The Israelites were forbidden to engage in practices like divination that were used in the ancient world to obtain information about the future. In this Assyrian relief from the palace at Nimrud, a priest, wearing the flat hat, stands over a slaughtered animal. Its entrails would be studied and the omen literature consulted to receive answers to yes or no questions (865–860 BC).

that includes re-creation and redemption.[6] It is only special revelation that discloses such categories to us and makes it clear that God's ultimate purposes are moving not just toward our personal salvation but toward the restoration of all things and a world where evil does not exist and everything functions according to Yahweh's order. God's people today live in the same world that Qoheleth did and experience the world in much the same ways that he did. The confusing, enigmatic, and unjust elements that perplexed this sage still characterize life in the world, and Christians feel pain and frustration in the same ways. The revelation of the new covenant gives us a larger perspective on God's plan and purposes, but the experiential realities remain essentially the same.

Teaching the Text

Qoheleth calls us to recognize that God is the sovereign Creator of the universe and human beings are finite creatures. It is essential to understand our human limits: we can rarely know what is good in any ultimate sense, we are mortal, and we cannot figure out what will happen in the future. Qoheleth also notes the importance of balance as we focus appropriately on the past and the future but recognize that

the present is the only context we have for choosing and acting. He makes it clear that what is good cannot be determined by what brings us immediate pleasure. We should recognize the pleasure and security that wealth and wisdom can provide but also hold such things loosely because we understand they are fleeting and do not give ultimate meaning to life. Qoheleth affirms the importance of a good reputation; the need for living with humility, openness to instruction, and correction; and the importance of patience and the avoidance of anger and rash responses.

Qoheleth makes it clear that people cannot succeed in a dispute against God and should accept their creaturely limits and live in submission to the Creator. Disputes against God can take the form of rash and angry responses directed to God, but they can also take the form of alternative visions of what reality ought to be like. People are often deluded into thinking that the world is (or should be) different from what it is; they are also indoctrinated into thinking about humans in ways that do not appropriately reflect their potential and limits. Hope must be based on the way things really are rather than on the way someone (even someone with impressive academic or theological credentials) says they are or should be.

Illustrating the Text

To dispute with God about his purposes in the world is absurd.

Poetry: "Invictus," by William Ernest Henley. Isaiah likens disputing with God to the absurdity of the clay arguing with the potter (Isa. 29:16), describing well the generation to whom Isaiah and other prophets were called. Despite the fact that the discipline of God left no spot on their bodies unbloodied and unbruised, these people recklessly pursued their godless course, a defiance affirmed in a poem by Victorian poet Henley (1849–1903).

> Out of the night that covers me,
> Black as the Pit from pole to pole,
> I thank whatever gods may be
> For my unconquerable soul.
> In the fell clutch of circumstance
> I have not winced nor cried aloud.
> Under the bludgeonings of chance
> My head is bloody, but unbowed.
> Beyond this place of wrath and tears
> Looms but the Horror of the shade,
> And yet the menace of the years
> Finds, and shall find, me unafraid.
> It matters not how strait the gate,
> How charged with punishments the
>   scroll.
> I am the master of my fate:
> I am the captain of my soul.[7]

God's goodness surrounds us, even in a fallen world.

Personal Testimony: A friend of mine (Edward's) diagnosed with bone cancer was told that she probably had no more than five years to live. Defying the odds, she amazed the doctors by living another seventeen years, enjoying life to a remarkable degree. She had a profound impact on many people and demonstrated deep trust in God. Shortly before she died, she said that those years had been the best of her life. In the midst of pain, she grew more than she thought possible in her relationship with God and with her family. She came to see dimensions of Psalm 33:5 ("The earth is full of [God's] unfailing love") that she had never imagined. Her life testified to the truth that God's good providence can accomplish beautiful and significant things.

Church Missions: The familiar account of the killing of five young missionaries in the 1950s as they tried to bring the gospel to the Auca Indians in Ecuador illustrates the principle of God's goodness. Many Aucas came to faith in the aftermath of those deaths. Many young people volunteered for missions after hearing about the story. The martyrs' families had ongoing ministries. Under the metanarrative of God's providence, anything can happen. Who knows, finally, what is good? Jim Elliot's wife, Elisabeth, noted that Jim's credo was captured in the words that he had written in his Bible: "He is no fool who gives what he cannot keep to gain what he cannot lose."[8]

Ecclesiastes 6:10–7:14

Teaching the Tensions of Life

Most readers of Ecclesiastes are struck by the tensions in the book. Qoheleth points out that injustice is a frustrating reality in the world (3:16; 5:8; 7:15; 8:14), but also expresses confidence that justice will prevail (3:17; 8:12–13). The author affirms the value of wisdom over folly (2:12–14), but recognizes that both the wise and the foolish die and questions the value of being extremely wise (3:15). Some of his statements sound very pessimistic and skeptical (e.g., 3:19; 4:2–3; 9:2), while others are the epitome of piety and orthodoxy (such as 12:13). Such tensions are perplexing for most students of this book. Miller and others[1] have suggested that a key to understanding this characteristic of Ecclesiastes lies in Qoheleth's teaching methods.

Miller argues that Qoheleth's rhetorical strategy involves connecting with his audience by first presenting an idea with which they agree on the basis of tradition or experience (a strategy that Miller calls "ethos"). Qoheleth then presents another idea that stands in tension with the first (a strategy that Miller calls "destabilization"). Miller says, "Tensions at this level of the book do not represent an incoherence in the author's mind nor a failure in his attempts to express himself. Rather they represent the problematic circumstances to which the book is addressed."[2] Qoheleth's goal in this is to bring his audience to a new understanding of the world and its place in that world (a strategy that Miller calls "restabilization"). Miller says,

> He has identified the problems, contradictions, and frustrations of his audience's world, and has an alternative to offer. He will not present this alternative by denying the realities which he has identified. The chaos and injustice are still there. He wants his audience to accept the things that they cannot control, but to change their own way of being and doing over which they do have some control.[3]

An example of this is seen in the tension generated by injustice in the world. Ogden suggests that Qoheleth's inclusion of the proverb about death in 7:2 may be connected with 3:17, where he says that "God will bring into judgment both the righteous and the wicked." Ogden says,

> [Qoheleth's] problem is to find some way of coming to terms with death, especially when it comes to the oppressed and poor who so frequently die without witnessing justice (4:1–3), or when it strikes the wealthy who have never found enjoyment in their material accomplishments (6:1–6). If there are so many in society who are unable to "enjoy" life as God provides it, then the sage is confronting a problem of monumental proportions—God's very justice is at stake.[4]

Qoheleth's reflections on death and injustice involve an issue that has perplexed many other biblical authors. Vawter's comments about the author of Psalm 49 are appropriate for Qoheleth as well: "We have the situation of a man grappling with a problem to which there was no traditional answer, or rather, to which there was a traditional answer [the doctrine of retribution] which now seemed inadequate."[5] It is impossible to know what was in Qoheleth's mind, especially given his unique teaching methods (12:11). It is interesting to note that these are the questions that played a significant role in the understanding of the afterlife that developed between the Old and the New Testament eras and that the New Testament, in the light of the resurrection of Jesus, came to understand as definitive and authoritative.

Qoheleth also understood that many tensions cannot be rationally resolved but must remain as faith intersects with the experiences of life. Ecclesiastes affirms the sovereignty of God and his ongoing providence and recognizes realities of human experience that call into question God's goodness and concern for his people. Both Ecclesiastes 5:18–6:2 and 7:13–14 set this tension in clear relief. Qoheleth's use of these proverbs should warn us against a rush to judgment about God's governance of the universe. Wisdom dictates that we exhibit patience before pontificating about what is good. The same caution that is appropriate in interpersonal relations is also vital in our efforts to understand the meaning of life and the work of God and can go a long way toward delivering us from situations where we have to say with Job, "Surely I spoke of things I did not understand, things too wonderful for me to know" (Job 42:3).

As Qoheleth observes that "death is the destiny of everyone" (7:2), he also tries to resolve how God's justice operates and concludes that there will be a future time when God will judge every deed (3:17). Revelation 20 describes the last judgment, the time when justice is finally served. Many artists have tried to illustrate that scene. This mosaic from the Baptistery of San Giovanni in Florence (1300 AD), shows Christ Pantocrator and the Last Judgment.

Finally, some maintain that Qoheleth here and in chapter 8 is arguing against traditional wisdom and seeking to correct its naïve claims on the basis of his own observations and experiences, but it seems far more likely that he is just doing what sages do. Fox says,

> Wisdom books always incorporated earlier wisdom, reshaped it, and went beyond it. . . .
>
> Different sages had different ideas, and dialectic was unending, because Wisdom was a living, growing literature. . . . [Qoheleth] never sets himself against traditional (which is to say, earlier) wisdom, but simply folds traditional wisdom into his own teachings and moves in a direction of his own.[6]

Sages understood that proverbs were general truths, and they were not so naïve as to think that wisdom provided guarantees against trouble. They understood that wise people can reduce risk by skillfully applying wisdom to life, but they also recognized that in a complex world no amount of human wisdom can guarantee outcomes.

Affirming Human Limits and Fearing God

Big Idea *Human wisdom and righteousness are limited, and fearing God should be first priority.*

Understanding the Text

The Text in Context

Ecclesiastes 7:13–14 functions both as a conclusion to the previous section and as an introduction to the verses that follow. Verses 15–29 assert that humans cannot alter the work of God or know what will happen in the future and emphasize the futility of attempting to subvert these realities. The rest of this section affirms the importance of living in the fear of God and argues that this produces the balance that reflects God's order. Qoheleth recognizes the importance of living with full awareness of human limits, including the pervasive reality of human depravity. He points out in this section how human sinfulness negates attempts to achieve wisdom and righteousness in any comprehensive or ultimate sense.

Historical and Cultural Background

People outside Israel experienced the world in the same way as Qoheleth did. The idea of retribution (that good people should be blessed and wicked people punished) was recognized in Mesopotamia and Egypt, and people struggled to explain the enigmatic experiences of life. Their different theological perspectives produced solutions very different from those in Israel, but there are parallels between their struggles. Lambert notes, "As soon as human reason tries to impose a man-made purpose on the

Israelites were not the only ones who struggled with the observation that righteousness did not guarantee prosperity. Egyptian and Mesopotamian cultures struggled with these ideas as well. The seventh-century BC Mesopotamian text (shown here) known as *Ludlul Bel Nemeqi* ("I Will Praise the Lord of Wisdom") features a man who praises his god while enduring suffering and calamity in spite of a pious lifestyle.

universe, intellectual problems arise. The big problem in Babylonian thought was that of justice [why retribution does not seem to work in practice]. . . . The universal incidence of death seemed another injustice."[1]

Ludlul Bel Nemeqi and the Babylonian Theodicy struggle with whether piety is a guarantee of prosperity, and the author of *Ludlul* expresses frustration that humans cannot distinguish between good and bad or understand the ways of the gods. Mesopotamian literature sometimes reflects a negative understanding of human nature. According to Kramer this was "so pervasive that one Sumerian pessimist could say, 'Never has a sinless child been born to his mother.'"[2] While the conclusions are, on the surface, similar to Ecclesiastes 7:20 and 29, the conclusions flow out of profoundly different theological assumptions.

Interpretive Insights

7:15 *the righteous perishing . . . the wicked living long.* Wisdom emphasizes the doctrine of retribution, but Qoheleth's observations make it clear that there is more to reality than this. There are many reasons why people experience what they do in life, including the sovereign activity of God. Estes says, "The observable patterns of life that are taught in traditional wisdom must be supplemented by a recognition that the sovereign God cannot be confined to formulas that finite humans have developed."[3]

7:16–17 *Do not be overrighteous . . . overwicked.* Qoheleth encourages living with balance and avoiding extremes. What being wicked involves seems generally clear, but there is little consensus about the meaning of being overly righteous. Some think it is a warning against pretense or hypocrisy,

- Human wisdom, while valuable, is limited and elusive.
- Human righteousness is limited.
- Human depravity is a fundamental reality in the world.

while others suggest that Ecclesiastes is warning against becoming a fanatic in trying to achieve perfection. In this context, Qoheleth may have in mind the attempt to gain a secure future by careful religious observance. Seow says that Qoheleth is rejecting "overconfidence in righteousness and wisdom. He has in mind specifically the notion that it is possible for one to be so righteous that one could always avert destruction and extend life."[4] Wisdom and righteousness do not guarantee protection from difficult and tragic experiences. At the same time, Qoheleth affirms the traditional wisdom view that the pursuit of folly often leads to a person's early demise and thus should be avoided.

7:18 *to grasp the one and not let go of the other.* The antecedents of "one" and "the other" are not clear. Some suggest that Qoheleth is commending a balance that includes some righteousness and some evil.[5] Ecclesiastes 12:13 connects the fear of God with keeping his commandments, while Job associates it with turning from evil (Job 1:1; 2:3; 28:28). This seems to preclude the possibility that Qoheleth is commending a balance that includes some righteousness and some evil.

Whoever fears God will avoid all extremes. Fearing God elsewhere in the Old Testament means that a person recognizes who he or she is (a creature) and who God is (the Creator) and then lives in the light of those realities.[6] This involves living in willing submission to God and his purposes and keeping his

Qoheleth and Traditional Wisdom

Some commentators contend that Qoheleth is taking issue with traditional wisdom, but, more likely, he wants to correct misunderstanding that can result when a person loses sight of the nature of wisdom sayings. Garrett notes that the wisdom found in Proverbs typically

> emphasizes the general truth over some specific cases and, being a work of instruction, frames its teachings in short, pithy statements without excessive qualification. It is not that the wisdom writers did not know that life was complex and full of exceptions, but dwelling on those cases would have distracted attention from their didactic purposes. It is general truth that those who fear God and live with diligence and integrity will have lives that are prosperous and peaceful but that those who are lazy and untrustworthy ultimately destroy themselves. And general truths are the stock in trade of Proverbs.[a]

These wisdom teachings were not all-encompassing statements about reality but generalizations. Qoheleth wants to correct the idea that wisdom sayings are comprehensive and invariable laws; he wants to bring his readers to a more balanced and realistic understanding of the complexities of life in a fallen world.

[a] Garrett, *Proverbs, Ecclesiastes, Song of Songs*, 57.

commandments. The NIV's translation "avoid all extremes" is an interpretive paraphrase of the Hebrew, which says, "comes out with both of them." The person who "fears God" will have a deep awareness of the destructive potential of folly and avoid it to the degree possible. That person will also be characterized by righteousness, but not the kind that supposes that people can control what happens to them by righteous living. Such a person will faithfully embrace God's instruction and live that out before God and others. The result will be a life characterized by qualities like compassion and justice—things in which God delights.

7:19 *Wisdom makes one wise person more powerful than ten rulers.* Qoheleth affirms both the value of wisdom and its limits. Wisdom cannot give ultimate meaning to life, eradicate the difficulties of life, or eliminate death. It does, though, have immense value and can sometimes enable one to succeed against much larger and stronger forces (see Eccles. 9:13–16; Prov. 21:22; 24:5). Wise strategy often allows people to secure victory in situations where all the odds are against their winning. Obviously power and wisdom are not antithetical, and hopefully a leader will have both.

7:20 *no one . . . righteous, . . . who does what is right and never sins.* The human potential for wisdom is limited, and so is the potential for righteousness. The quest for perfection is futile in a fallen world, and even the most energetic and valiant efforts to achieve righteousness will be mixed with evil. Legalism often produces an obsession with righteousness. From the people who bring an entitlement mentality into their relationship with God because they believe they have earned enough "righteousness points" to deserve protection from all trouble, to those who make lists of every possible offense they may have committed that day, an obsession with righteousness takes many forms.

7:21–22 *Do not pay attention to . . . your servant cursing you.* An awareness of human limits should impact the way we deal with others and their faults. A master has power over a servant and can inflict punishment for the offense, but Qoheleth exhorts the master to give the servant the benefit of the doubt. Our limited ability to know the motives of others or the circumstances that have prompted their offense should generate patience and kindness toward them, as should the awareness that we sometimes do similar things. Garrett says, "The teaching of the whole text is that the reader must accept that all are sinners and learn to deal with people as they are."[7] Qoheleth will warn us in 10:20 that we cannot count on the same response if we offend those with power over us.

7:23–25 *to search out wisdom and the scheme of things.* Wisdom, while of great value, is inadequate to explain the anomalies and enigmas that Qoheleth points out. Much practical wisdom for living according to God's order can be discerned, but "the scheme of things" eludes people completely. The term translated "the scheme of things" is related to a verb that means "to think, plan, or count," and Seow says, "The image conjured up for us is that of a merchant or an accountant poring over the documents, trying to give an account of every item, perhaps to assign everything to one side or the other of the ledger and then to tally it all up in order to arrive at the balance."[8] Despite great effort, Qoheleth could not find the wisdom needed to "understand the universe and control life."[9] Even with God's special revelation, God's people still lack the wisdom to grasp the scheme of things.

7:26 *the woman who is a snare, whose heart is a trap.* Qoheleth likely has in mind not women in general but Madam Folly as personified in Proverbs 1–9. She is the antithesis of Lady Wisdom; she is an immoral woman who seduces young men away from wisdom and leads them into disaster. (See the "Additional Insights" section after this unit.)

7:28 *upright man . . . upright woman.* This is an interpretive rendering of the Hebrew, which does not include the word "upright." The Hebrew is quite ambiguous and says, "One man among a thousand I found, but a woman among all these I have not found" (ESV). (See the "Additional Insights" section after this unit.)

7:29 *God created mankind upright, but they have gone in search of many schemes.* Qoheleth recognizes that much of the dysfunction he observes in the world is the result of human failure to live according to God's order. Estes says,

> The rarity of wisdom . . . is attributable to the choices that humans have made. Alluding to the creation narrative in Genesis 1–2, in which God made humans in his image and proclaimed all of his creation good, Qohelet says that God made them morally upright. After the fall into sin, however, humans are unable to live in conformity with God's upright standard, and instead

As Qoheleth tried to understand wickedness and folly, he observed how the seductive woman easily ensnared young men who were not walking the path of wisdom. These young men became trapped much like the deer in this Assyrian relief (palace at Nineveh, 645–635 BC).

they have chosen many forms of moral corruption.[10]

Qoheleth makes his point through a play on the words "scheme of things" (vv. 25 and 27) and "schemes" (v. 29). Both terms have similar sounds and likely come from the same Hebrew root. The first word involves the kind of explanation that would give the seeker a full understanding of the way things are and the way God works in the world. Qoheleth is unable to discover such wisdom. What he has found instead is that human beings who were created morally upright (a common meaning of the word "upright") by God have sought out a variety of "schemes" that take them away from God's order and purposes.

Theological Insights

The central focus of this text is on human limits in a world maintained by the sovereign God. Despite the sage's effort to fully understand reality, the scheme of things eludes him. Enigmas remain that Qoheleth cannot explain. What he does recognize is that, at the very core of every human being, there is a preference for folly rather than wisdom. Despite God's creating people upright, they seek out alternatives and schemes rather than living in the fear of God as God designed them to do. Just as some people seek wisdom as a means of exerting control over their own destiny, some also suppose they

can exercise control over God and the future by pious living. Qoheleth makes it clear that such schemes do not work; they reflect the refusal of the creature to live in submission to the Creator. The one who lives in the fear of God avoids being ensnared by folly and instead is characterized by the kind of righteousness that pleases God.

Teaching the Text

This section affirms the value of wisdom and its contingent and limited nature. Provan says, "[Wisdom] is a good and useful thing that allows us to arrive at important conclusions about the world. . . . Nevertheless, possessing wisdom is far from enabling complete mastery over experience, and it certainly does not solve the problem of death."[11] Often the desire for knowledge/ wisdom and even the motivation for human righteousness seem to be prompted by the desire to find "a key that can be used in independence of the Creator to unlock the secrets of the universe, to shape existence after mortal desires, and to control life."[12] Among the things that are important to emphasize in this section are the following:

1. Wisdom, or any other human accomplishment, including righteousness, "is not magic. God is not an object to be manipulated, nor does God's world belong to human beings."[13]

2. Wisdom and folly do not respect gender. Both wise men and women exist, though they may be few and far between. It is important to recognize that our personal failure to find a wise man or a

Wisdom was valued in all the cultures of the ancient Near East. Thoth, shown here in his baboon form (1450–1280 BC), was the Egyptian god of wisdom. The Book of Thoth is featured in an Egyptian myth where it is highly desired because it contains all the wisdom of the world.

wise woman reflects both their rarity and the limited nature of our observation and experience. The distribution of wisdom across genders and cultures is one of God's gracious gifts to us. It enriches us by allowing us to gain wisdom from others whose perspectives and experiences are different from ours.

3. A life of trusting dependence on God (fearing God) disabuses us of the idea that we can earn divine favor and control the future by human effort. A life that flows out of a right relationship with God produces the righteousness that God desires from his creatures.

Illustrating the Text

To deny that human depravity exists in ourselves and others is a profound mistake.

Literature: "The Man Who Corrupted Hadleyburg," by Mark Twain. In this story (1899), almost a sermon, by Twain (1835–1910), Hadleyburg has the reputation everywhere of being an "incorruptible" town. Its people are thought to be responsible and honest and carefully schooled in how to reject temptation. The town motto is "Lead us not into temptation," and the people rest smugly in their flattering labels. One day, however, they offend a stranger passing through, who pledges to get revenge by corrupting the town. He later drops off a sack of gold at Mr. and Mrs. Richards' house, requesting they present it to the person in town who, in the past, gave the stranger invaluable advice and twenty dollars for his needs.

A note with the sack further instructs that anyone claiming to know that advice should write it down and give it to the Reverend Burgess, who will open the sack at a town meeting and find the answer. The news of the sack of gold filters through the town, greed begins to work on the spirits of almost everyone, and they begin guessing what the advice might be, even though not one of them recalls having helped a stranger. To further cause trouble, the stranger sends a note to every household, telling them what the advice is. Corrupted by greed, all nineteen of the town's couples submit their "answers" to Burgess and begin planning how to spend the money. Clearly, no town is incorruptible.

Human wisdom will always be flawed.

Anecdote: An old joke tells of a man who got too near the edge of a cliff. When the ground gave way, he slipped over the edge. As he fell, he managed to grab a small tree growing on the side of the cliff. He had never been a religious person, but as he saw the soil beginning to crumble around the roots of the tree, he decided to pray. He called out, "God, if you are up there, please help me!" After a brief pause, he heard a voice saying, "This is God. I heard you, and I will help you. I want you to let go of the tree." The man thought for a minute and said, "Is there anybody else up there?"

Poetry: "Wisdom," by Langston Hughes. Hughes (1902–67) appears to have had the right perspective on human wisdom, as illustrated in his simple poem titled "Wisdom." In this poem, Hughes declares that he is humbled by the knowledge that humanity's wisdom is very limited; if it were not, people would do things very differently.

Wisdom and Gender | The Scheme of Things

Ecclesiastes 7:26–28 contains perhaps the most difficult verses in this book, and a key issue has to do with the identity of the "woman" that Qoheleth found / did not find (vv. 26 and 28). Many argue that Qoheleth was a deeply entrenched misogynist, but several considerations make it unlikely that these verses have any relevance for the question of misogyny. Verses 23–25 make it clear that Qoheleth has been unable to find sufficient wisdom to fully understand life and the work of God in the world. He has, though, found one thing in his quest: a "woman" who entraps those who come near her. Qoheleth's language is similar to that used in the early chapters of Proverbs, where young men are warned about the dangers of the adulteress and the immoral woman. There are also close parallels between the sage's words and passages in Proverbs where wisdom and folly are personified as women. Passages like Proverbs 9:13–18 describe Madam Folly in much the same way as the woman is described in Ecclesiastes 7:26, and this is likely what Qoheleth has in mind. It is difficult to imagine a reader familiar with wisdom's depiction of folly not relating Qoheleth's words to such passages. Qoheleth has not found the wisdom he is seeking, but he has found plenty of folly in the world.

While Qoheleth uses the Hebrew word *'adam* ("man, humankind") in the generic sense of "humankind" throughout the book, he seems to make a distinction between male and female in Ecclesiastes 7:28, though the focus of the distinction remains ambiguous. Was he searching for a person of great wisdom or great righteousness, or was it the ability to consistently resist the seductions of folly? Or was it something less tied to the context, like a person he could relate to at a deep and intimate level or someone he could genuinely understand? If he was seeking a person with great wisdom or righteousness, Qoheleth's conclusion illustrates the limited nature of human experience and the problem with trying to construct a model of reality from one's own limited experiences of life. Wise women are identified elsewhere in the Old Testament (2 Sam. 14:2; 20:6), and the woman in Proverbs 31:10–31 is described in terms of virtues that are regularly associated with wisdom (diligence, kindness, careful planning for the future, skill in business, and providing for the needs of her family). According to Proverbs 31:26 her words reflect wisdom, and she is characterized by the fear of the Lord, which is the essence of wisdom.

Ecclesiastes 7:29 makes it clear that the problem of folly, lack of righteousness, or the propensity to lead others astray is not gender specific but is innate to humanity. Some have argued that the distinction made in verse 28b is a sexist quote that Qoheleth is rejecting[1] (i.e., "some people say, 'I have found one man out of a thousand, but not a single woman,' but what I have found is that people [male and female] have sought out schemes"). Others have argued that the verse has to do with human relationships and that Qoheleth has shifted his focus from "the scheme of things" (v. 27) to a single aspect of life that he cannot understand completely: people and human relationships, especially male-female relationships.

Ecclesiastes 7:23–28 describes Qoheleth's search for the wisdom that will enable him to understand all that happens in the world ("the scheme of things"). Despite his diligent ("adding one thing to another," v. 27) and persistent search, he is unable to find the wisdom he is seeking. What he finds instead is folly, and verse 29 suggests that the pervasive folly in the world is a consequence of human refusal to embrace God's order. Instead of submitting to God's wisdom, people pursue their own alternative schemes that lead to the dysfunction and disorder that Qoheleth observes in the world. Thus not only is life in the world complicated by human limits that make it impossible for any person to find wisdom in a full and comprehensive sense, but it is also negatively impacted by the chaos that results from the human propensity to reject God's order in favor of independence and autonomy.

As Qoheleth searched for wisdom the folly of the world was revealed instead, often personified as Madam Folly, who would ensnare those who were not seeking to please God. The painting on this small Greek amphora (425–400 BC) illustrates the enticement away from wisdom toward disaster.

The Power of Wisdom and Folly

Big Idea *We should recognize the realities of life in the world, acknowledge human limits, fear God, live wisely, and enjoy life.*

Understanding the Text

The Text in Context

Qoheleth continues highlighting the benefits of wisdom and exploring the questions that began in Ecclesiastes 6:11–12. The section begins with two questions in 8:1 that set the context for the rest of the unit. Qoheleth concludes that truly wise individuals are very difficult to find but affirms wisdom's great value and its essential role in enabling people to succeed in difficult situations. Dealing with a king, whose power cannot be resisted, requires great wisdom, skill, and patience, but a truly wise person can sometimes bring about significant changes in policy and direction through careful interaction with the monarch. Qoheleth's example also demonstrates the limits of wisdom, because it exposes the servant's inability to predict or control the king's responses. Qoheleth continues to point out the inequities and injustices that exist in the world, along with the realities of human depravity and inability to understand the work of God. He also insists that living in trusting dependence on God is the wise way to respond to injustice. He highlights the tension that exists between faith assertions and experience as he expresses the confidence that, despite what he sees and experiences, things will go well for those who fear God but will not go well for the wicked.

Historical and Cultural Background

Compositions from Egypt include advice for dealing with a rich and powerful person. The Instruction of Ani warns the young man not to talk back to a superior but rather let him have his way. The young man is told to speak nicely to his superior and is reminded that when the superior's anger has subsided, he may well return to praise the servant.[1] Perhaps the closest parallel is in the proverbs of Ahiqar, advisor to Assyrian kings Sennacherib and Essarhaddon. Ahiqar says to be very careful around the king and to listen carefully to what the king says. He compares the king's words to fire and recommends

In 8:2 Qoheleth provides wise counsel for interacting with a powerful king. Similar advice was recorded in the papyrus of Ahiqar, in which Ahiqar says, "When a royal command is given you, it is a burning fire. Execute it at once, lest it flare up against you and singe your hands. But rather let the king's command be your heart's delight" (Coogan, *Reader*, 207). The papyrus page shown here was found in Elephantine, Egypt, and dates from 524 to 504 BC.

obeying the king's commands quickly, since otherwise they may consume you. He also warns that inappropriate words directed to the king can be fatal.[2]

Interpretive Insights

8:1 *Who is like the wise?* Qoheleth makes it clear that truly wise people are rare, even as he affirms both wisdom's limits and its value in dealing with difficult and potentially dangerous situations in life.

A person's wisdom brightens their face. This proverb probably describes the effect that struggling with a difficult problem or resolving a complex issue can have on a person's appearance. Just as it is often possible to see in a person's face that he or she is perplexed, so one can often tell when the problem has been resolved.

8:2–6 Qoheleth gives practical advice about how to deal wisely with the king (or other powerful individual). When the king is determined to pursue a policy that appears to be wrong or harmful, it is important to avoid responding in ways that

Key Themes of Ecclesiastes 8:1–17

- Wisdom helps people avoid detrimental consequences.
- Wisdom helps people successfully work through complex situations in life.
- The potential harm that can be done by people with power over others should not be underestimated.
- Despite appearances, justice will finally prevail.
- Despite enigma, injustice, and things beyond our control, we should fear God and enjoy life.

reflect a lack of loyalty to the king. It is tempting to react with anger or revulsion or to join in a rebellion against the ruler. Qoheleth's advice is to be patient, obey the king, and look for opportunities to turn the king away from the ill-conceived course. In such situations it is essential to keep the power and authority of the king clearly in view—he has ultimate authority on the human level, is answerable to no other human being, and does whatever he chooses. Wise people can often identify the right time and the right way to bring about significant changes for good. The dangers inherent in such situations are obvious because of many factors that not even the most skilled sage can predict or control.

8:2 *Obey the king's command.* Doing what the king commands demonstrates loyalty to him, and it is rare for a king or leader to be open to criticism from someone whose behavior or attitude marks him or her out as disloyal. However, many texts like Daniel 3:13–18 or Acts 4:13–21 make it clear that when a king commands something immoral or contrary to God's truth, God's people must do what is right, despite the consequences.

because you took an oath before God. It is uncertain whether "God's oath" (ESV) refers to God's promise giving David's descendants authority to rule or to a subject's oath of loyalty to the king. The NIV's translation, "because you took an oath before God," is an interpretive rendering of the Hebrew.

8:3 *a bad cause.* This could involve anything from harsh, angry, and demeaning words directed to the king to participation in outright rebellion.

8:5–6 *the proper time and procedure.* Dealing with powerful people exposes our limited ability to determine the right time and correct way.

8:8 *power over the wind.* The word translated "wind" can mean "wind," "the human spirit," or "life/breath," and the verse probably plays on all these meanings. Human limits are evident in the inability of humans to know the future, to capture the wind, or to prevent death. No one can extend these limits, not the wisest sage or the king who often seems to think he is in complete control of his world.

no one is discharged in time of war. War is illustrative of many things over which people have little control. War is sometimes forced on people by enemies whose attacks leave no option except to resist, and generally citizens are given little choice about serving, irrespective of the reasons why the war was declared.

wickedness will not release those who practice it.

While evil often appears to contribute to people's success, wisdom claims that evil ultimately recoils on itself and leads to their shame (e.g., see Pss. 7:14–16; 34; 73).

8:9 *when a man lords it over others to his own hurt.* The pronoun "his" can refer to either the one victimized by the abuse of power or to the abuser himself, and the ambiguity is probably intentional. When people pursue a course at odds with God's order, they often end up enslaved to the evil they have practiced and become so habituated to evil that they lose both the desire and the ability to change.

8:12–13 *it will go better with those who fear God.* Despite evidence to the contrary, Qoheleth affirms that justice will finally occur. Provan says, "How is justice to be done? Qohelet never explains himself. He simply expresses his confidence in the moral nature of the universe while noting various data that bring this into apparent question. Unable finally to resolve the puzzle himself, he then characteristically advocates that the reader get on with life

Qoheleth observes that wickedness continues "when the sentence for a crime is not quickly carried out" (8:11). Law codes were developed to administer justice, and many include punishments for specific crimes. The Code of Hammurabi (shown here) is perhaps the most well known, recorded by Hammurabi, ruler of Babylon, 1795–1750 BC.

and not worry too much about the details, which lie with God."[3]

For Qoheleth the key to getting on with life is to "fear God." He does not explain how that resolves the tension; he simply affirms that living in the fear of God is the solution. This means trusting God in terms of when and how justice takes place, and it leaves open the possibility that justice sometimes prevails in ways that are not evident to us.

8:15 *I commend the enjoyment of life.* Qoheleth again commends "enjoyment of life" in the face of circumstances that people can neither change nor understand. This does not reflect nihilism or the abandonment of moral responsibility in the pursuit of pleasure. Rather, it is the enjoyment of the gifts God gives when he provides the opportunity.

8:17 *all that God has done.* Humans must live in the world aware that God is at work but with little sense of what it means or where it is going. This is a fundamental reality of life under the sun, and Qoheleth's advice is to fear God and enjoy life as there is opportunity.

Theological Insights

Qoheleth affirms the value of wisdom but also reveals its limits by highlighting perhaps the most difficult aspect of living wisely—the application of wisdom to the complex issues of life. His example confronts us with the difficulty of dealing with people who have significant power over us, and such situations demonstrate our limited ability to know the proper time or the right way to respond. Qoheleth again emphasizes that no one can fully understand life and the work of God. Despite

what he observes about the realities of life, Qoheleth also makes important faith assertions in 8:12–13 when he expresses his confidence that despite what he sees in the world, God will judge the righteous and the wicked, though he does not indicate when or how this will occur. He again contends that fearing God constitutes the right way to live in a fallen world. Moving beyond the hopeless realities defined by human experience and discovery will only be possible through a life that is centered in God and that draws from his special revelation. This hope comes not from finding answers about why things happen but from trusting God and his purposes. Even as Qoheleth affirms these things, he again calls us to eat, drink, and enjoy.

Teaching the Text

Three things stand out as important teaching points in this chapter. The first is the value of wisdom for living in the world. People must contend with the reality of human depravity and with the necessity of living under the authority of those who possess great power in society and who sometimes use that power in tyrannical ways. The prudent and timely application of wisdom can often allow a person to avoid danger and to succeed in such situations. On the other hand, an angry response to someone who has authority over us can result in the loss of a job, significant career damage, or serious legal problems. Inappropriate responses can cause irreparable damage in relationships and thwart success in many arenas. In some cases, foolish responses can even cost people their lives. The acquisition of wisdom requires deliberate

Ecclesiastes 8:1–17

For the fourth time Qoheleth "commends the enjoyment of life," saying "there is nothing better for a person under the sun than to eat and drink and be glad" (8:15). This drinking cup is made of both gold and silver and was produced in Syria, probably during the fifth century BC.

and focused effort and persistent practice, and it is a process that must continue over one's lifetime.

A second point has to do with the limits of wisdom and the temptation of depending on wisdom or skill to the neglect of trusting God. Given the things that can be accomplished through wisdom skillfully employed, it is a short step to supposing that a person can control life and its outcomes through wisdom. As Goldingay points out, "The occupational hazard of the wise man is to walk by calculation rather than by faith."[4] Qoheleth's examples make it clear that things like human finitude and our inability to predict the future seriously impair our acquisition of wisdom. And then there is the matter of our inability to understand the work of God, or what is going on in the hearts and minds of other people so as to predict their moods and responses. Situations like the one Qoheleth describes expose our inadequacies in terms of sufficient wisdom and reveal our need to trust God. Qoheleth calls us to live in the fear of God as we experience circumstances that we can neither understand nor control.

The third important emphasis relates to the dissonance that the realities of life often create for the life of faith; such circumstances sometimes call into question God's own revelation about who he is and how he works. There are many abuses of human power, and ordinary individuals are often unable to resist or alter the course of oppressive and unjust uses of power. The

wicked receive honor and popular reverence, often even after they die. Such realities raise questions about God's moral governance of the world. Despite what Qoheleth sees around him, he concludes that "it will be well with those who fear God, because they fear before him. But it will not be well with the wicked" (8:12b–13a ESV), and he calls us to live by faith in the presence of such realities. Qoheleth does not explain the basis for his confidence or describe how or when this will occur. Further explication will have to come from some source other than Ecclesiastes, though finite human beings will never fully understand the work of God in the world. In the midst of the tension and the mystery that surrounds it, Qoheleth's counsel is clear: fear God, enjoy life in the world, and leave the moral governance of the universe in God's hands. (See also the "Additional Insights" section following the unit on Eccles. 9:1–18.)

Illustrating the Text

Wisdom is an invaluable help in working through the complexities of life.

Anecdote: A doctor encountered a disturbing situation at a hospital where he worked. Instead of angrily confronting those in charge of hospital policy, contacting the newspapers, or going over the head of hospital leadership and appealing to the board, he waited for a propitious time to challenge the policy appropriately and winsomely. He was successful in getting the policy changed. A different approach could have had very different results; he could have lost his standing among his colleagues or, worse yet, his job. And his loyalty could have been questioned by his bosses. Godly wisdom was effective in accomplishing what needed to be done.

Human wisdom has limitations; we must still walk by faith.

Quote: *Crowded to Christ*, by L. E. Maxwell. Maxwell was the founder and principal of the Prairie Bible Institute of Three Hills, Alberta, Canada. In his autobiography, he writes,

> Many Christians . . . reduced to great straits . . . cry in unbelief, "I am shut up, and I cannot come forth." In their grief

and bondage they pray for an increase of faith, convinced that if they could only believe in the *greatness* of God, then they could trust Him to handle their difficulties. . . . They therefore struggle for greater faith, but this does not bring them into God's presence. . . . When we believe that God is *good*, we can believe that God is *great*.[5]

We are to fear God in circumstances that we cannot comprehend or control.

History: Sometimes situations like the one described in 8:2 and following involve moral issues that allow no compromise and where obedience to the king would result in overt participation in the evil. Often people do not have the option of resigning from situations where evil is pervasive, and they must remain in bondage to the circumstances. One example is Helmuth von Moltke, who was assigned a position in counterintelligence for the Nazis, even though his Christian faith made him deeply opposed to what they were doing. He believed it would be wrong to engage in violence against the government, but he was able to use his position to save the lives of many people. Moltke was finally convicted of treason and sentenced to die when he made it clear that his ultimate loyalty was to God. That decision cost him his life.[6] Many are confronted with similar choices as they stand before wicked leaders who demand that they participate in actions that are fundamentally contrary to God's order. There are times when wisdom and a commitment to God's truth require uncompromising loyalty to God's truth, whatever the cost.

Live with Trouble and Uncertainty—Then You Die

Big Idea *Life offers ambiguous support for God's moral governance—good and bad things happen to both righteous and wicked people, and each dies with little observable difference between them.*

Understanding the Text

The Text in Context

"No one can comprehend what goes on under the sun" (8:17), and certainly people cannot understand God's work, which encompasses all creation and eternity (3:11). Qoheleth maintains that the experiences of life are too ambiguous to serve as a clear indicator of God's favor toward a person, and he sees no obvious difference between the righteous and the wicked in the manner and circumstances of their deaths. He asserts that life offers opportunities that do not continue past the grave and encourages his readers to live aware that death is coming. He obviously believes that the way a person lives makes a difference, but he does not explain what the difference is. Again the sage calls his readers to enjoy life and to find delight in the things around them. Finally, he reminds them that "time and chance happen to them all" (9:11) and insists that we do not control outcomes and destinies as we live in the world. He encourages people to engage in life with all their might, while reminding them that wisdom, valuable as it is, is often not appreciated by others, a point he will expand in chapter 10.

Historical and Cultural Background

Questions relating to human mortality, the meaning of life, and so on are common to all times and cultures, and it is not surprising that similar explanations are found in widely separated cultures. Parallels have been seen between Ecclesiastes and such diverse material as ancient Greek literature and even the writings of Albert Camus and other modern existentialist philosophers. Two ancient parallels with this section of Ecclesiastes stand out. One comes from a group of Egyptian tomb inscriptions known as The Harper's Songs, which, according to Lichtheim, "lamented the passing of life and urged enjoyment of life while it lasts!"[1] The second is a passage in The Epic of Gilgamesh that calls for the enjoyment of life as Gilgamesh reflects on the death of his friend and diligently searches for immortality. The list of things to enjoy includes items similar to those in Ecclesiastes 9:7–9, and follows the same order.[2] The broad popularity of Gilgamesh throughout the ancient Near East likely accounts for the similarity rather than direct literary dependence.

Interpretive Insights

9:1 *all this.* The author likely refers to the conclusions reached in 8:16–17.

the righteous and the wise . . . are in God's hands. While many today would conclude from the sage's evidence that it is a random universe and that there is no God, Qoheleth never doubts God's existence or his sovereign oversight of life.

no one knows whether love or hate awaits them. Good and bad things happen to all people, and it is impossible to differentiate between good and bad people on the basis of their external circumstances. Nor can people predict what the future holds for them; things may get better, or they may get worse, and it seems to matter little whether a person is righteous or unrighteous. Kidner says,

We have only to use our eyes without prejudice, according to Psalm 19 and Romans

Key Themes of Ecclesiastes 9:1–18

- Life is lived under the sovereign oversight of God.
- People have limited understanding of life as it comes from God.
- What happens to people often depends more on things outside their control than on their wisdom and diligence.
- What the future holds for a person (righteous or wicked) cannot be predicted.

1:19ff., to see that there is a powerful and glorious Creator. But it takes more than observation to discover how He is disposed towards us. . . . We shall have . . . only an uncertain answer about the Creator's character from the world we live in, with its mixture of delight and terror, beauty and repulsiveness.[3]

9:2 *All share a common destiny.* The "common destiny" is death, and the lack of any observable distinction in death between those who are righteous and those who are not creates a theological tension. Kidner says, "The things that are supposed to matter most to [God] turn out to make no difference—or none that anyone can see—to the way we are disposed of in the end."[4]

9:4–6 *Anyone who is among the living has hope.* Biblical hope normally involves the confident expectation that God will do what he has promised. The Hebrew word for "hope" used here occurs only three times in the Old Testament, and its exact meaning is uncertain. It does not describe glorious possibilities to be anticipated after death but refers to what a person can expect or

The Harper's Songs from ancient Egypt offer advice similar to that of Qoheleth. This relief from the tomb chapel of Paatenemheb (1333–1307 BC) features a blind harpist and a portion of the Harper's Song of Intef. This song encourages the listeners to follow their desires and enjoy life because death will come.

be confident about while she or he is alive. Qoheleth recognizes that there are certain advantages to being alive and sees these advantages and opportunities as terminated when a person dies. The Old Testament recognizes that personal existence continues after death but understands that existence to be a shadowy or shady one in comparison to life in the world (e.g., Job 3:13–22; 10:21–22; 14:10–14; Isa. 14:9–15). Job desires death because it will provide relief from the pain and turmoil he is experiencing. At the same time, death affords no opportunity to do the things one can do in life, and according to Ecclesiastes 9:5–6 the dead know nothing, have no more reward, do not experience the same emotions as the living, and have no more share in what is done under the sun. Life, with all its problems, is a known commodity, while what happens after death is largely unknown and includes some undesirable features. In that sense life is to be preferred over death.

a live dog is better off than a dead lion! Dogs were scavengers and were viewed with contempt, while lions were regal animals and seen as noble creatures. It is better to be a living, contemptible dog than a highly admired, but dead, lion.

9:7 *God has already approved what you do.* This time Qoheleth's exhortation to enjoy consists of imperatives, and he indicates that "God has already approved" of the enjoyment. This does not mean that God gives unlimited approval for people's actions, irrespective of what they are. Rather, it suggests that God has given us gifts, and it is his intention that they provide pleasure and enjoyment.

9:10 *do it with all your might.* Qoheleth's observations could lead one to resignation and despair, but he urges his readers to greater diligence, because he sees a basis for confidence and hope in fearing God and trusting in his providence. This does not guarantee a life that is materially prosperous and trouble free, but it does enable people to face an unknown future confidently, because they know God's purposes cannot be thwarted by the enigmatic experiences that are part of life.

9:11 *time and chance happen to them all.* "Chance" does not reflect the modern idea of chance or luck but rather describes that which happens apart from the intention or awareness of those involved in a matter. Outcomes, according to Qoheleth,

"Anyone who is among the living has hope—even a live dog is better off than a dead lion!" (9:4). Staged lion hunts were enjoyed by the kings of Assyria. This relief from the north palace at Nineveh shows King Ashurbanipal hunting lions from his chariot. He aims his spear at an attacking lion while a previous kill lies under his horses' hooves. By the end of the hunt, all the lions that had been released into the hunting area would have met their demise (645–635 BC).

are often determined by factors outside a person's understanding or control. While modern thinking often attempts to be more precise in establishing categories of causation, the biblical authors were too pragmatic to concern themselves with such things, and while they realized that both human and divine elements contribute to outcomes, they recognized that the complexities of life make it impossible to accurately distinguish between them. For the biblical authors the key question was whether anything in the realm of "time and chance" takes place apart from God's awareness and control, and the answer was a resounding no. If a person can be assured of God's favor—and one can infer that Qoheleth sees this as a result of fearing God—and recognizes that God is both sovereign and beneficent, that individual can live with confidence and hope in the midst of uncertainty and difficulties. Such trust in God does not change the harsh realities in the world, but it does show that there is more to reality than the enigmatic experiences of life. The awareness that God is at work and is accomplishing his purposes—even if we have only a minimal understanding of what those purposes are—provides a basis for hope and confidence.

9:15 *a man poor but wise . . . saved the city . . . nobody remembered.* Wisdom is often not appreciated, even by those who benefit (or could potentially benefit) from it. Wise people (especially poor ones) are often ignored and their wisdom dismissed. This is the case in society, and even in the church. Provan says, "The implication of vv. 15–17 is that wealth and social class are far more impressive to people, generally speaking, than wisdom and that people will listen more readily to people of great wealth and high social class than to a poor but wise man." Despite wisdom's value, Provan says, "In practice wisdom and its purveyors are undervalued, so that remedies are not found when needed."[5]

9:16–18 *one sinner destroys much good.* Despite wisdom's great value, a small amount of folly can completely undermine a wisely crafted plan. While examples are legion, perhaps the most striking ones are those where fools are put into positions of authority and power.

Theological Insights

The experiences of life do not unequivocally support the idea that God always rewards the righteous and punishes the wicked, and Job argues that there is much evidence that calls retribution into question (e.g., Job 21). Estes says,

> The categories of traditional wisdom, with its theology of retribution, are simply insufficient to account for how God works in his world. Even though observation can suggest a general correspondence between acts and consequences, the enigmas in life that have been cataloged by Qohelet demonstrate that it is illegitimate to extrapolate a rigid, comprehensive law of cause and effect by which God governs his world.[6]

Qoheleth's points also raise significant theological issues. Ogden says, "The idea that death should come to all without regard to one's character, religious commitment, or behavior in general, does raise a moral question: is God truly just?"[7] Qoheleth affirms that everyone—whether wise, foolish, righteous, or wicked—is in God's hands and insists that the experiences of life provide little basis for determining God's disposition toward a person, since good things and bad things happen to everyone.

Qoheleth contrasts wisdom and folly, saying that "wisdom is better than weapons of war" (9:18). This relief shows the walls of Lachish being assaulted by a siege machine as it moves up the siege ramp. Archers on the wall and below the wall shoot arrows at each other as the battle rages. Torches are thrown from the wall in an attempt to stop the siege machine. In the end, the city was defeated (palace at Nineveh, 700–692 BC).

Teaching the Text

Farmer says, "Human beings must live out their lives without being able to find out precisely what God has in mind to do. Mortals must run the risk of choosing to act without knowing what the ultimate results of their actions will be."[8] Qoheleth makes it clear that a person's circumstances in life provide no certain basis for determining God's favor or lack thereof. He affirms the importance of embracing life and diligently pursuing such things as work, knowledge, and wisdom before we go to the grave. He does not explain why this matters but implies that the way we live makes a difference.

Again we find Qoheleth's regular emphasis on fearing God and keeping his commandments, and even in the midst of uncertainty and enigmatic circumstances we can be certain that a life characterized by trusting dependence on God is worth pursuing. The sage's statement that we are to enjoy because "God has already approved what you do" (9:7) must be understood in the light of his instruction to fear God, which makes it clear that enjoyment is to be done in ways that are consistent with God's instruction and values. Qoheleth's exhortation here suggests that it is God's intention for us to enjoy the things he provides us in the world. Farmer says, "Enjoy what you have to eat, to drink, and to wear. Enjoy married life and throw yourself energetically . . . into whatever work needs to be done. . . . Qoheleth asserts that this (enjoying the everyday aspects of life) is what God wants us to do."[9]

What happens often depends more on factors outside our control than on our wisdom, diligence, and skill. This awareness can produce frustration and fear, but the knowledge that God's providence is active in the world has the potential to relieve some of that frustration if we can be assured of his favor. Since the experiences of life present ambiguous testimony regarding God's favor, the answer to such questions as God's favor toward us or the nature of his providence will have to come from some source other than what happens to us in the world. The world does not always appreciate a person's wisdom, and life lived according to God's order will often have to be its own reward, since it will not always generate public acknowledgment and respect. It only takes a little folly to ruin a well-conceived and effective plan, and it is important to emphasize the need to avoid folly as we live in the world.

Illustrating the Text

The indirect relationship between earthly behavior and reward is simultaneously a proof of God's sovereignty and a test of our faith.

Science: Explain about the phenomenon of conditioning. This is a process whereby a creature learns a connection between a behavior and a result (as when a lab monkey hits a button to get food). The way scientists measure the strength of conditioning is through a process called "extinction trials." These break the correlation between behavior and reward and measure how long the creature will repeat it before losing hope and giving up.

The easiest conditioning to extinguish is a 1:1 correlation; as soon as the reward stops, the behavior is easily extinguished. A more sparse correlation (like 3:1 or 10:1) is stronger and harder to extinguish. The hardest conditioning to extinguish is a random payback schedule, as when the behavior is sometimes rewarded after being done once, sometimes after ten times, and sometimes after thirty or one hundred times.

Invite your listeners to replace the lab monkey's button pushing with our faith in God and food pellets with earthly blessings. If God wanted to be our favorite vending machine, he would just adopt a 1:1 payback schedule (one good deed = one blessing) or perhaps a more strenuous works-based ratio (ten prayers = one answer, or one year of tithing = one promotion at work). If his interest were simply in good behavior, this would work, as long as he never broke the correlation between works and rewards.

Instead, this passage assures us that the correlation between godly behavior and earthly rewards is truly random. This tells us that God is sovereign and is lovingly conditioning us toward inextinguishable dependence and trust that endure regardless of reward. His interest is not mere good behavior, but humble acceptance of his sovereignty and enduring trust in his goodness despite circumstances.

A little folly does a lot of harm; avoiding foolish behavior is a reward in and of itself.

Props/Visual Aid: Set up some large prop dominoes up front. Alternatively, you could use regular dominoes and have a camera enlarging the view for your listeners or use a video clip of a domino toppling stunt. (You could also use another type of chain reaction, like the game *Mousetrap*, or any type of "Rube Goldberg" machine.) Ask listeners what will happen if you topple the first domino (or otherwise start the machine). The answer will be obvious: a small act will set off a complex and unstoppable reaction with results that are often hard to predict. In the same way, a little bit of folly can set off a chain reaction that harms others and causes regrettable results.

Personal Stories: Tell about a time when you made a seemingly small choice that set off a chain reaction of unintended consequences. The story can be humorous, grave, or cautionary. Invite listeners to consider how a seemingly small act of folly can have ripple effects that are hard to take back. Share the regret you have and explain how you would appreciate a "do-over." Assert that avoiding the choice in the first place would have been a reward in and of itself when considered in hindsight.

Justice in Life and in Life after Death

Many commentators conclude that Qoheleth's tensions reflect a reaction against traditional wisdom and his rejection of the faith claims of Israel's religious tradition. We have suggested that his observations are, in part at least, designed to confront his readers with the existential tensions that regularly occur between life and the claims of faith. He wants his readers to forge out a worldview that takes full account of reality in the world, and this must include what can be known through both general revelation and special revelation. This section, in many ways, brings Qoheleth's tensions to a climax, and many see 9:1–10 as perhaps the most pessimistic section in the book. It is impossible to get into Qoheleth's mind to fully explicate his own personal conclusions. He has, though, pointed out certain pieces of the puzzle that have the potential for resolving a bit of the tension. He has emphasized that humans cannot understand the work of God, in part because God's work is not limited by time; human knowledge, limited by time and space, cannot comprehend what God may be doing outside those boundaries that confine us. Qoheleth tells us that the end of a matter may be better than its beginning (7:8), and he makes it clear that we cannot always know what is good (6:12). What he points out leaves open the possibility that God may be providentially working toward some good purpose despite our failure to see and appreciate what that purpose may

be, and the stories of Joseph, Ruth, and Esther clearly illustrate such possibilities.

At the same time, Qoheleth's claim that justice will prevail, or that it will go well with the person who fears God in contrast to the person who does not, seems to be contradicted by even one example of a righteous victim or a wicked oppressor dying before justice occurs. This is clearly the case if Qoheleth's observation that death brings personal existence to a full and final end represents his settled conclusion on the matter. It seems likely that the sage is at least "probing the possibility that there may be some meaningful existence beyond the grave."[1] Farmer suggests that "Qoheleth is still weighing the evidence of his senses over against traditions which have been handed down for generations in his community of faith."[2] It is likely that Qoheleth's intention is not to communicate his own personal conclusions on these issues but to make clear to his readers where any approach limited only to what people can observe and experience will lead. Through his teaching he goads his readers toward reaching their own conclusions in the light of the evidence he is presenting. It is clear that questions such as what happens after death cannot be answered on the basis of human observation, since human discovery cannot penetrate beyond the grave.

This understanding of Qoheleth's words seems more consistent with his advice about how a person should live in the light of these realities than with the view that Qoheleth has reached a settled conclusion rejecting the possibility of any sort of afterlife. Qoheleth's observations have made it clear that injustice, oppression, and folly are not always resolved under the sun, and his advice to be diligent and wise and to live in the fear of God and with an awareness that we will die makes little sense if life under the sun is all there is. At the same time, Qoheleth recognizes that a search for wisdom, limited to what we can see and experience in the world, can do little besides speculate about such cosmic issues as the work and purposes of God or what lies beyond the grave. As Longman recognizes, "The answer to Qohelet's frustration is divine revelation,"[3] and the fuller revelation that provides definitive answers to these questions would come only with the death and resurrection of the Word become flesh. In the meantime, Qoheleth's pragmatic exhortation to fear God and keep his commandments is advice that remains the essence of God's desire for his people in every age.

In 9:5 Qoheleth makes some observations about death. He says, "For the living know that they will die, but the dead know nothing; they have no further reward, and even their name is forgotten." Some Egyptian pharaohs tried to erase the memory of their predecessors. For example, when Thutmosis III came to the throne he had the image of Hatshepsut removed from this relief at the temple of Hatshepsut at Karnak. The chisel marks show the place where the figure of Hatshepsut used to stand.

Embrace Wisdom as You Face Life's Folly and Uncertainty

Big Idea *Wisdom, despite its limits, is essential to counter the folly and uncertainty that characterize life in the world.*

Understanding the Text

The Text in Context

Ecclesiastes 10 presents a number of traditional sayings and examples illustrating both wisdom's value and things that can thwart wisdom's effectiveness. While Qoheleth uses a variety of wisdom forms in the chapter, he regularly makes his point by citing proverbs, each of which contributes a single point of truth to the sage's overall message.

Historical and Cultural Background

Proverbs were commonly used by sages throughout the ancient Near East, and proverbs similar to those in Ecclesiastes can be found among Israel's neighbors. Ecclesiastes 10:5–7 describes a world of societal upheaval, and comparable descriptions can be found in Egypt. According to Seow, The Prophecies of Neferti describes "a land in turmoil. . . . It is a world that has been turned upside down."[1] This is also the case with The Admonitions of Ipuwer, which,

according to Shupak, "concludes by pinning the blame for the decline into evil days on an unnamed regnant king."[2] This resembles Qoheleth's description of the damage that can be done by corrupt or incompetent people in government positions.

Interpretive Insights

10:1 *dead flies . . . a little folly.* Tiny amounts of contamination can ruin valuable goods; dead flies can ruin a container of expensive oil or perfume. A foolish mistake can cause a carefully designed project to fail. Qoheleth emphasizes the great damage that even a little folly can do in order to motivate his readers to avoid folly assiduously.

10:2 *right . . . left.* These terms do not have the political connotations often associated with them today and likely indicate nothing more than that the two people are going in opposite directions. In the biblical view the heart, while corresponding closely to the mind, is the central core that makes a person what he or she is. It is analogous to a computer that controls a system, and the way the heart controls an individual reflects the way that person is programmed. The wise person and the fool are committed to different worldviews; they are programmed with fundamentally different values, and their words and behavior will reflect that difference.

10:4 *anger rises against you, do not leave your post.* Qoheleth's advice here is similar to 8:2–3 and 9:17. Wisdom regularly touts the benefits of calm, rational responses to angry individuals, especially those who have authority over us. Rash, defensive responses typically increase the other person's anger and reduce the likelihood of rational solutions. In such situations, the most positive results are generally obtained through quiet and soothing words delivered in the right way and at the appropriate time.

10:5–6 *the sort of error that arises from a ruler.* The "ruler" could be any person in authority, and "error" usually involves something done by accident or inadvertently. According to verses 6 and 7, the ruler's error was putting the wrong people in important positions, and the damage resulting from inept people in responsible positions can be immense. His contrast between rich and poor does not reflect the modern rhetoric of class warfare; his concerns likely focus on a person's competence for the task. Qoheleth wants important positions in government to be filled by capable and competent people, irrespective of considerations such as social status or wealth. His complaint has to do with competent people being moved aside in favor of inept and inexperienced people

Key Themes of Ecclesiastes 10:1–20
- Pursue and practice wisdom—it reduces the friction in life and helps a person succeed.
- Avoid folly—it regularly leads to difficulty and disaster.
- A little folly can contaminate valuable goods and undermine important projects.
- Do not let risk paralyze you into inaction.

who happen to have the right political or family connections.

10:7 *slaves on horseback.* Qoheleth describes a society that has been turned upside down. Normally, only the wealthy would have owned horses, and slaves would have had to travel on foot. Here the normal expectations have been reversed, with chaos the likely result.

10:8–9 *Whoever digs a pit may fall into it.* These proverbs emphasize the risk attached to many everyday activities. Accidents happen and unexpected things occur as people engage in ordinary activities of life, and wisdom cannot totally prevent such things from occurring. It does, though, compel a person to carefully evaluate risks and potential benefits before undertaking a task and also equips people to engage in activities wisely and carefully. Wisdom, while reducing the likelihood of accidents, does not totally eliminate the risks of living in the world.

10:10 *ax is dull . . . more strength is needed.* The context suggests that the NIV conveys the probable meaning

A proverb from Ecclesiastes 10:10 says, "If the ax is dull and its edge unsharpened, more strength is needed, but skill will bring success." Shown here are three ancient ax heads.

of this difficult verse. Wisdom (better than NIV's "skill") enables a person to work more intelligently and produce more in less time and with less effort. Before cutting wood, a wise person will give appropriate time and attention to sharpening an ax—and then to keeping it sharp.

10:11 *If a snake bites before it is charmed, the charmer receives no fee.* "Fee" more likely means "advantage" or "benefit" here. Snake charming is a mysterious skill, but even possessing such an esoteric ability provides neither the snake charmer nor the one who hires the charmer any benefit unless the ability is applied in a timely and appropriate way. The consequences of missed opportunities can be painful and expensive, and as Fox says, "No one, *not even*

the skilled man, can undo damage after the fact."[3] This proverb affirms the value of wisdom even as it identifies an aspect of folly that can thwart its potential benefits.

10:12–15 *fools . . . do not know the way to town.* Wise words bring favor to both the speaker and those to whom the words are directed, while foolish words regularly create havoc. The last part of verse 15 says that the fool does not "know the way to town"; the expression may be similar to our saying that a person does not have the sense to come in out of the rain. Given the pervasive presence of fools and the propensity of so many for folly, wisdom is essential for minimizing folly's destructive impact.

10:16–17 *Woe to the land whose king was a servant.* The word translated "servant" can refer to a youth[4] or to an administrator who has seized the throne by force. The sage's point is that this king lacks the maturity and training for the position he holds—and, in the light of verse 17, perhaps also lacks the character for the job. Incompetent and corrupt politicians/officials can destroy much good, and even the wisest citizen can often do little to prevent the harm that results. The king of noble birth is one who has the training, experience, and wisdom to lead his people effectively. He chooses leaders committed to the people's well-being, and the leaders eat and drink at the right times and in the appropriate

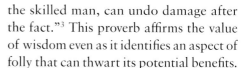

"Through laziness, the rafters sag; because of idle hands, the house leaks" (10:18). The typical house roof in ancient Israel was flat and required continual maintenance in order to stay watertight. Although no archaeological remains of roofs exist, this roof, seen from the interior of the reconstructed four-room house at Tel Qasile, Israel, shows typical crossbeam construction over which poles were placed. Reeds may also have been used. This layer was then covered with mud, after which a final layer of plaster was applied.

ways. The result is a nation that is genuinely fortunate or blessed.

10:18 *rafters sag . . . house leaks.* This verse may continue the description of the corrupt leaders of verses 16–17 since "house" can also refer to a political dynasty. More likely it is simply a statement about buildings and necessary maintenance. In ancient Israel, "flat roofs . . . were covered with lime, which eventually cracked and allowed rain to seep in . . . , since no run-off was provided."[5] Failure to do required maintenance or to attend to necessary tasks can cause significant damage to an important project, a well-built structure, or a political dynasty.

10:19 *money is the answer for everything.* Many understand this notoriously difficult clause to be affirming the importance of money in acquiring things like food, drink, and clothing that enable a person to enjoy life. Others suggest that the verb means "to be busy or occupied with" and describes the preoccupation with money that characterizes many people—certainly the corrupt leaders of verses 16–17. With all the ambiguity surrounding this clause, this is not a verse on which to build a significant theological structure.

10:20 *Do not revile the king even in your thoughts.* In 7:21–22 Qoheleth advised patience when people overhear negative and unbecoming things about themselves from someone over whom they have authority. Here he recognizes that people over us will not always show the same courtesy and may exact harsh punishment. Things said in the most private and secure places often get back to the person about whom they were said—sometimes in most unusual ways—and this can create unpleasant consequences. The folly of a single rash comment can destroy much good, and the only way to be sure the words will not get back to someone is not to say the things at all.

Theological Insights

Qoheleth's examples illustrate both the value of wisdom and its vulnerability to folly, and they are designed to motivate readers to avoid folly and to embrace wisdom as they live in the world. Destructive consequences can result from one's own bad choices, but they can also come from the folly that is pervasive in the world. Damage resulting from one person's failure to relay essential information to someone who needs it or from someone giving incorrect instructions about a crucial part of a project can harm an entire community.

Qoheleth insists that folly is self-evident to everyone except fools and their close associates, but people still reject wisdom in favor of folly. Such behavior demonstrates the flaw in human nature that Qoheleth observes in 7:29. Human depravity and folly combined with power can bring immense suffering to people, and it is rarely the case that the wisdom of a few wise people can counteract the damage from foolish policies imposed on people by bad leaders or inept, powerful bureaucrats.

Risks and uncertainties in the world are not always related to folly; some are inherent in life. Risks are a part of necessary activities like building or working in the field, and while wisdom can significantly reduce these risks, wise people cannot always avoid unfortunate consequences. Human depravity with its propensity for folly, and the uncertainties that come from human inability to know the future, seem to leave little basis for hope and confidence apart from God's providence and the knowledge that the righteous and the wise and their deeds are in the hands of God (9:1).

Teaching the Text

This chapter affirms the value of wisdom for living in the world but also recognizes that folly is a pervasive presence that can, even in small doses, undermine the best-constructed plans of wise people. The principles emphasized by Qoheleth in this chapter can be readily supplemented by similar teachings in Proverbs and could provide a basis for extended teaching. Qoheleth emphasizes the responsibility of leaders to appoint the right people to the right positions, whether in government, the workplace, or the church. Appointments made on the basis of things like nepotism, political loyalty, or wealth often have negative outcomes. Competence, good character, and demonstrated wisdom are much better criteria for leadership, and few things are more destructive than folly amplified by power. Qoheleth also points out that wisdom does not secure guarantees against unpleasant consequences in life but can reduce their likelihood. Risk is an innate part of many necessary endeavors, and while it cannot be eliminated entirely, it can be reduced by careful choices about what to do and when to do it. Often the greater folly is to be so paralyzed by risk that nothing is done and opportunity is missed because of bad timing.

Qoheleth does not see these realities as a reason for despair or disengagement from life; rather, he concludes that they make

wisdom even more essential and should motivate us to pursue wisdom and practice it diligently. Wisdom has been described as "lubrication for life"; it reduces the friction people experience as they live life. Examining aspects of wisdom emphasized in the chapter—the wise use of words, patience, taking appropriate risks, diligence—and exploring ways to develop and apply these skills to life constitute important teaching points for this chapter.

Illustrating the Text

Folly must be confronted, since it leads to difficulty.

Literature: *The Wind in the Willows*, by Kenneth Grahame. This famous children's book (1908) by Scottish writer Grahame (1859–1932) portrays a great fool, Toad, whose friends (Badger, Rat, and Mole) try to rescue him from his follies. Toad tires easily of good activities and is lazy and prone to wanderlust and self-aggrandizement. He easily loses "all fear of obvious consequences" and gives "animals a bad name . . . by [his] furious driving and [his] smashes and [his] rows with the police." The wise Badger tells him, "Independence is all very well, but we animals never allow our friends to make fools of themselves beyond a certain limit; and that limit you've reached."[6] This is how we need to think about and handle fools.

The reality is that fools are put in power.

Literature: "The Emperor's New Clothes," by Hans Christian Andersen. Anderson's classic fairy tale is about a fool in charge, revealing the author's "tongue-in-the-cheek attitude towards the pompous incompetents

of the world." The emperor is so "excessively fond of new clothes that he spent all his money on them."[7]

When two swindlers come to town pretending to be weavers of the "most beautiful stuffs imaginable" with a "peculiar quality of becoming invisible" to everyone not fit for his or her position, the emperor is sure these must be "splendid. . . . By wearing them I should be able to discover which men in my kingdom are unfitted for their posts . . . [to] distinguish the wise men from fools." Before ordering the clothes, he sends two faithful ministers to observe the weaving. Both see nothing, yet are quiet for fear of being thought unfit.

The emperor finally visits "the crafty imposters." Seeing nothing, he thinks to himself, "Am I a fool? Am I not fit to be Emperor? Why, nothing worse could happen to me!" Then he says, "Oh it is beautiful." The emperor then marches in a great procession wearing his new "clothes" until a child exclaims, "But he has got nothing on." While the emperor sees the truth, he thinks, "the procession must go on now"

as the chamberlains hold up his invisible train. This is a true portrait of a fool.

History: Many who went through the Russian Revolution of 1917 and were able to leave the country describe situations where people totally lacking the requisite experience and skills were put in charge of estates or appointed to important government jobs. The appointments were made largely on the basis of party loyalty, and in most cases, the result was harmful to those they were supposed to serve.[8]

A little folly can lead to great damage.

Sports: Late in the deciding game of the World Series, a shortstop takes his eye off what should be a routine ground ball. The ball rolls past him into the outfield, and the other team scores the winning run. His team is denied the season's ultimate prize, and a single mistake ruins an otherwise well-executed season. A defensive back commits an unnecessary infraction late in the Super Bowl, his team incurs a penalty that keeps the opponent's winning drive alive, and the championship is lost. Examples of the ruin that a little folly can cause abound: in politics, corrupt or shortsighted decisions operate to the detriment of the people served; in business, an improperly transcribed number can cause great harm to a company; in industry, a carelessly monitored process can result in the production of a harmful drug—not to mention many such examples in everyday household life.

Take Risks Wisely, Remember God, and Enjoy Life While You Still Can

Big Idea *Life offers few guarantees. Work diligently and wisely, and remember God as you engage life.*

Understanding the Text

The Text in Context

Six times Qoheleth has affirmed the importance of enjoying life, and he returns to that point in Ecclesiastes 11:7–9. He has reminded readers that they should live with the awareness that they will die, and he repeats the point in 12:1–7. In 12:7 he returns to the question he has raised in 3:21. Qoheleth has affirmed God's judgment in 3:17 and 5:6 and again addresses this in 11:9. He begins the book with a poem on the recurring cycles of nature and the fleeting character of human life, and he ends it with a poetic description of the deterioration and dissolution of life. Finally, the book ends in 12:8 as it begins in 1:2 with the declaration that all is *hebel*.

Literary features also tie the subunits of this section together. Ecclesiastes 11:2–6 identifies four things that human beings do not know (what disaster may come, the

path of the wind/spirit, the work of God, and the best time for planting), while 11:10 points out what people should know (God will judge everyone). In 11:8 Qoheleth calls the reader to enjoy/rejoice and remember, and in 11:9–10 he repeats the call, this time using imperatives to emphasize the importance of enjoyment. Finally, 12:1–7 expands on the theme of remembering.

Historical and Cultural Background

People in other ancient Near Eastern cultures experienced the world in the same way the Israelites did, and their descriptions of human experience parallel Ecclesiastes at many points. Descriptions of the difficulties of old age occur in Egypt in The Instruction of Ptahhotep and The Tale of Sinuhe, and they occur in Sumerian poems as well.[1] Another parallel is found in The Harper's Song from the Tomb of King Intef, which, according to Lichtheim, "lamented the passing of life and urged enjoyment of life while it lasts!"[2] Both this text and Ecclesiastes connect the exhortation to enjoy with the fact that death awaits everyone, but the Egyptian text reflects resignation, and Ecclesiastes hope.

Interpretive Insights

11:1 *Ship your grain across the sea.* The Hebrew says literally, "Send your bread upon the face of the waters for in many days you will [or 'may'] find it." The metaphor is most likely a reference to trade and commerce, though some have argued that it refers to charity. The principle can be applied to many areas of life. People are sometimes confronted with decisions about participating in activities such as trade, which appear risky, or charity, which seem to offer little chance for a return on one's investment. Qoheleth affirms the importance and wisdom of engaging in such endeavors. Guarantees rarely exist in life, but Qoheleth sees greater folly in doing nothing than in prudently living life with its risks and uncertainties.

- Take risks but distribute them to minimize adverse outcomes.
- Do not let the inability to predict the future paralyze you into inaction.
- The work of God pervades all of life, but people cannot fully understand it.
- Enjoy life, but remember: judgment, old age, and death are coming.
- Live a God-centered life while you are still young.

11:3 *clouds . . . pour rain . . . a tree falls.* When conditions are right (clouds full of water), it is inevitable that rain will fall. When a tree falls, it stays in the place where it has fallen. These things happen according to certain principles, which we do not fully understand and generally remain beyond our control. The farmer knows it will rain at some point but cannot predict whether it will come at the right time and in the right amounts to produce a bumper crop or do damage. Such things are largely unpredictable, and people remain at the mercy of such occurrences. Accidents happen, and outcomes often depend on factors that cannot be predicted, but people must act despite the uncertainty.

11:4 *Whoever watches the wind will not plant.* People can focus on things that might go wrong in ways that lead to "the paralysis of analysis." One must proceed on the basis of reason and common sense, but in the absence of guarantees.

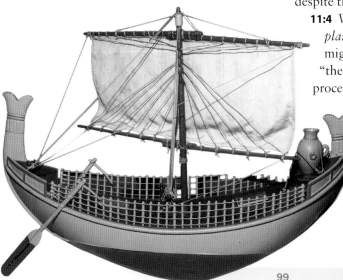

Qoheleth's advice in 11:1 is to "ship your grain across the sea; after many days you may receive a return." This model represents a fourteenth-century BC Canaanite merchant vessel similar in design to those later used by King Solomon.

11:5 *work of God.* Qoheleth likely has in mind God's providence, which brings blessing and benefits but also allows misfortune. While we do not fully understand providence, we know it is operating and determining outcomes.

11:6 *do not know which will succeed.* Because many things are unpredictable, it is imperative to work both hard and intelligently. Guarantees are rarely possible, but wisdom can maximize chances for success. Diversified efforts may not guarantee success, but inaction and folly will likely lead to failure.

11:8 *enjoy them all . . . remember the days of darkness.* Qoheleth structures his advice around the themes of enjoying and remembering. He calls his readers to a balanced perspective that recognizes the good and the bad as well as the pleasant and the unpleasant. While darkness is often a metaphor for death in Ecclesiastes, "days of darkness" probably represents difficult and painful times in life, and the sage affirms the importance of remembering those times. As 12:1–2 makes clear, advancing age that precedes death is a central focus of the days of darkness.

Everything to come. This likely refers to what happens in this life. Seow says, "For Qohelet . . . everything is *hebel*—not just what comes after death; all the experiences of life, and life itself, are *hebel*; they are all ephemeral and beyond human ability to control. It is unlikely that the author is talking about what comes after death, about which he insists no one knows anything (3:21; 10:14)."[3]

11:9 *God will bring you into judgment.* Qoheleth encourages young people to enjoy life rather than to delay pleasure until they have more opportunity and greater resources, but their enjoyment must be constrained by the fact that "God will bring every deed into judgment" (12:14)—another of Qoheleth's faith assertions. (See the "Additional Insights" sections following the units on Eccles. 6:10–7:14 and 9:1–18.) While pleasure and the enjoyment of life are gifts of God to be fully embraced, they must be pursued according to Yahweh's order. Provan says, "Qohelet's advice is to start early on this pathway of joyful existence before God . . . in the sure knowledge that life will only ever become more challenging as time passes and as we move inexorably toward the darkness of death."[4]

11:10 *banish anxiety . . . cast off troubles.* A person's focus should be realistic and balanced; obsessively focusing on the negative can be toxic and blind that individual to good and pleasant things. When possible, wisdom dictates that people remove themselves from anxiety-producing situations. This can take many forms, including avoiding folly and the painful outcomes it regularly produces.

youth and vigor are meaningless. Youth lasts only a short time (the likely meaning of *hebel* here). Before people know it, they will be facing the difficulties of old age and impending death.

12:1–7 For further comments on the poem on old age and dying, see the "Additional Insights" after this unit.

12:1 *Remember your Creator.* In addition to the exhortation to remember the days of darkness, Qoheleth now tells his readers, "Remember your Creator," thus adding a significant dimension to the message of the book. This involves recognizing the Creator as the sovereign Lord.

According to Walton, one important aspect of creation was to give function to things and to bring order to the world.[5] Remembering God includes remembering God's control over life and death, his control over peoples' fortunes and well-being, and the fact that he will judge each individual and has made everything beautiful/appropriate in its time. This makes it possible to find enjoyment in a world characterized by difficult things.

in the days of your youth. Waiting until a person is old to remember God will result in missed opportunities for wise living and the pleasure it brings. That person will also be poorly equipped to deal with the challenges of old age, since the habits developed over one's lifetime are difficult to break.

12:8 *Meaningless!* The book ends with the same words with which it began. The claim that everything is *hebel* focuses not so much on whether life has meaning but on human mortality and the nature of life in the world. Life is filled with mystery, and people live in a world where the benefits that result from living wisely are sometimes thwarted by factors outside their understanding and control. Qoheleth's examples raise questions about whether life has meaning and whether there is a way to live so that one's life really matters. At the same time, his references to God's providence, his exhortation to accept one's lot and enjoy life in the world, and his advice to live wisely and fear God provide a basis for hope as we live our brief lives under the sun.

Theological Insights

Qoheleth brings together many of the points he has emphasized throughout the book, and his references to God provide coherence and establish the tone of his message. He describes God as Creator and Judge. His assertion in 9:1 that "the righteous and the wise and what they do are in God's hands" acknowledges God's providence as he works out his purposes in the world. While much about the work of God remains incomprehensible to humans, enough can be understood to know that there is a plan, and this can provide a basis for hope and confidence.

Life is filled with enigmatic experiences and things that do not operate the way we know they should. Our inability to control life and secure the outcomes we desire is evident at every turn. We see, if only in hindsight, evidence of God's providence, but we lack the ability to identify it as it happens and can rarely determine where it is going. A coherent understanding of God's providence comes, not from the experiences of life, but from God's revelation to us. Qoheleth's appeal to God's providence comes as one of his "faith assertions," and its inclusion is critical in terms of the book's message.

If a person can be certain of God's goodness and favor, God's providence allows that individual to live with confidence and hope despite the difficulties of life. This knowledge allows us to set the difficulties and inequities of life in a context where, as Ogden puts it, we can "recognize the enigmas and frustrations of the human experience, but at the same time . . . grasp life as a divine gift and enjoy it in all its mystery."[6]

Teaching the Text

Qoheleth affirms the importance of remembering God and enjoying the blessings he provides. When a person (hopefully while young) embraces human limits, fears God, and lives aware of the difficulties of life and the finality of death, that individual can enjoy life and live it to its full potential. Qoheleth's principles apply broadly in life—to work, to financial matters, to charity, and to ministry. We must avoid rash commitments and diligently use wisdom in all we do, but we cannot wait until we have guarantees of success before

acting. Qoheleth has made clear the futility of trying to lay up treasures on earth. We must be generous and show compassion in the face of the need that exists around us. We should invest our time and energy in planting seed in rich, fertile soil, but when our only option involves planting on rocky soil, we should do that with diligence, trusting God to accomplish what he desires. God's providence oversees our circumstances and the outcomes of our efforts, and one never knows what he may do through our efforts, even in unlikely places.

Qoheleth's exhortation to remember the Creator is a call to a life that is centered in God and lived under his authority and instruction. The remembering to which Qoheleth calls us flows out of a realistic understanding of life and involves recognizing that despite the realities of life in the world, God is still sovereign. It involves rejoicing in beautiful and delightful things around us and recognizing that they come from God and attest to his goodness and to the goodness of his creation. Seow says, "Human beings are supposed to enjoy life . . . because that is their divinely assigned portion, and God calls one into account for failure to

"However many years anyone may live, let them enjoy them all" (11:8). This Greek statuette of an elderly nurse holding a young child brings to mind the contrast between youth and old age and Qoheleth's teaching to live life following God's teaching and rejoice in the blessings he provides (300 BC).

enjoy. Or, as a passage in the Talmud has it: 'Everyone must give an account before God of all good things one saw in life *and did not enjoy.*'[7] For Qoheleth, enjoyment is clearly God's intention for humanity.

Illustrating the Text

Prudent actions that get thwarted by adversity are not shameful; becoming paralyzed by uncertainty is.

Bible: James 4:13–17 offers good reinforcement for this point. James points out the same ephemeral nature of life and asserts that if you know the good you can do today but fail to do so, that is sin in and of itself. Also, Matthew 25:14–30 relates Jesus's way of reinforcing this truth. In the parable of the talents, he explains how the man who hid his one talent was paralyzed by a false understanding of the master and was liable to judgment for his refusal to take even the most minimal risks in managing the talent given him.

Sports/Fitness: Talk briefly about batting averages. Explain that if a player entered the batter's box once, got a base hit, and then never stepped up to the plate again, he would have a perfect batting average but would be a worthless and forgotten player in the history of baseball. Then, compare this scenario to Babe Ruth's career. In his era, the average player struck out only 8.1% of the time. By contrast, Ruth struck out nearly twice as often as his peers, or 15.8% of the time (1,330 times over 8,399 official at bats). In fact, he led the league in strike outs five times in his career, averaging 61 strikeouts per season over his 22-year career. On the other hand, Babe is still ranked third in the all-time list of home-run hitters. In other words, stepping up to the plate and swinging repeatedly involves both risk and opportunity; if your goal is to seem perfect by avoiding risk, you may look good on paper but you will never make a mark on history, either.

We are not just accountable to avoid folly, we are also accountable to enjoy and appreciate God's gifts and his presence.

Creeds and Confessions: Many are familiar with the Westminster Shorter Catechism and its answer to the question, "What is the chief end of man?" The reply is that we are intended "to glorify God and to enjoy him forever." This confessional statement condenses the truth taught in Ecclesiastes and other passages into one overarching theme. We are not primarily made to be good, to be wise, or to save ourselves through works. Instead, we are primarily made to glorify a sovereign Lord who is most glorified and pleased when his creatures are utterly dependent on, and finding unceasing delight in, him.

Quote: Charles H. Spurgeon. Spurgeon, the great nineteenth-century preacher, once said, "It is not how much we have, but how much we enjoy that makes happiness." This resonates in sympathy with this passage in Ecclesiastes, emphasizing the difference between benefitting from God's favor and providence on the one hand, and truly enjoying it on the other. We are plagued, it would seem, not by a lack of God's goodness to us but rather by our own failure to recognize and enjoy those manifold kindnesses. This passage teaches that we will be held accountable for stewarding our awareness and joy in the face of God's providence.

A Poem about Death

As noted in the "Text in Context" section on 11:1–12:8, the poem in 12:1–7 is well integrated into both the larger unit in which it is set and the book itself by virtue of its emphasis on remembering and its expanded discussion of death. It also could easily stand as an independent poem describing the difficulties and challenges of growing old, and according to Fox the poem is "the most difficult passage in a difficult book."[1] It seems appropriate to provide some additional discussion of the poem. The poet describes old age and the end of life in terms of a storm and a dilapidated house. Estes says that the poem "is not precisely allegorical, but rather is a more impressionistic collage."[2] Poetry is normally designed more to affect the reader than to inform, and thus the author's purpose is less to describe the details of growing old than to produce in the reader a feeling and attitude about the end of life.

Verse 2 compares the troubles of old age to a storm. The sky becomes dark and clouds obscure the normal sources of light; then after the rain falls, the storm clouds often return again.

In 12:3–7 the poet describes aging and death in terms of the deterioration of a house and the cessation of activity on the part of those who have lived and worked there. The picture of aging in verses 3–5 gives way to a description of death in verses 6–7. Many suggest specific allusions in these descriptions (e.g., the keepers of the house are a person's arms, the strong men are his legs, the grinders are his teeth, the grasshopper dragging itself along the ground represents the difficulty many old people have getting around), but these suggestions quickly become speculative and uncertain. The context makes the general

Ecclesiastes 12:1–7 poetically describes the aging process. Descriptions of the difficulties of old age have also been found in a piece of literature from Egypt known as the Instruction of Ptahhotep (2465–2325 BC). Battiscombe G. Gunn's translation reads, "The end of life is at hand; old age descendeth [upon me]; feebleness cometh, and childishness is renewed. He [that is old] lieth down in misery every day. The eyes are small; the ears are deaf. Energy is diminished, the heart hath no rest. The mouth is silent, and he speaketh no word; the heart stoppeth, and he remembereth not yesterday. The bones are painful throughout the body; good turneth unto evil. All taste departeth. These things doeth old age for mankind, being evil in all things. The nose is stopped, and he breatheth not for weakness (?), whether standing or sitting" (Gunn, Instruction). Shown here is a painting of Ptahhotep from his tomb at Saqqara.

meaning of the poem clear, and uncertainty about details does not lessen its impact. Farmer even suggests that "the ambiguity of the imagery contributes to rather than detracts from the effectiveness of the passage. Rather than spelling out the specifics of the process of aging, the metaphors evoke an atmosphere of decline and decay,"[3] and this makes the poem more broadly applicable to a variety of individual experiences.

The expression "go to their eternal home" in verse 5 does not have to mean more than dying or going to the grave. It is, though, sufficiently ambiguous to allow the possibility of more, and it seems likely that Qoheleth intends to leave open that possibility.

The silver cord that is severed and the golden bowl that is broken in verse 6 are obviously valuable items. Most suppose that the verse describes a lamp that consisted of a golden bowl that held oil to provide light for the house; the bowl was then attached to a support by a silver chain (though nothing like this has ever been found in ancient Israel). Another possibility is that the golden bowl of the lamp sat on a silver lamp stand, though there is little evidence for such items made of gold and silver in private homes. The point of the metaphor is that something that was beautiful, functional, and of significant value now lies destroyed and useless—a most appropriate figure for death. Pieces of a shattered pitcher lying by a spring and the wheel once used to draw water now broken beside the well (v. 6) serve as poignant images of death. Only broken artifacts remain where there was once life and vigorous activity. One thinks of abandoned towns where remains of broken dishes, toys, and other items disclose tiny fragments of the story of those who once lived there.

In 12:7 ("dust returns to the ground . . . spirit returns to God who gave it") Qoheleth answers the question he has asked in 3:20–21. He alludes to Genesis 2:7 and 3:19 and describes death as the separation of body and spirit—the reversal of what God did in creating human beings. Most argue that there is no suggestion of an afterlife here and that Qoheleth sees death as the ultimate end for the human. We would argue that this is not necessarily the case. Certainly there is no developed view of the afterlife in Ecclesiastes, but it seems likely that Qoheleth leaves open the possibility. As Bartholomew points out, "To see death . . . as the end makes nonsense of Qohelet's insistence that finally judgment comes before God. For this judgment to be a reality, there must be life beyond death, and although Qohelet lived prior to the revelation of the New Testament, he envisions, albeit without elaboration, that life which is a gift of God returning to God, its eternal home."[4]

Just as Qoheleth begins with a poem describing the fleeting nature of human life under the sun, so the book ends with a poem reminding its readers of the reality of death and its inevitability. Perhaps the poem's graphic description of the deterioration of life and the debilitating effects of old age is intended as both a warning and a motivator for each student to begin immediately to live in trusting dependence on God; it would be folly to wait until it is too late.

The Conclusion of the Matter:

Fear God and Keep His Commandments

Big Idea *Fear God and keep his commandments.*

Understanding the Text

The Text in Context

This epilogue, probably written as an addendum, identifies Qoheleth as a sage who did his work carefully and communicated his ideas accurately to his students; it also assures us that his words are true. This section captures the essence of the book's teaching as it asserts that fearing God and keeping his commandments are the central responsibilities of every person. Qoheleth has presented his ideas in ways that raise many questions and provide few answers, and this likely reflects his desire to engage his readers in the struggle to find their own answers to his open-ended questions.

Our understanding of life and the work of God is quite limited; life is filled with things over which we have limited control; and there are many basic questions about life and death that cannot be answered on the basis of human experiences, which are often shrouded in mystery. The tensions created by these realities must be resolved by faith in a beneficent and sovereign God, or they cannot be resolved at all. Qoheleth's claim is that living a life centered in God will enable a person to live in the most meaningful and advantageous way, and in a way that pleases God.

Historical and Cultural Background

Literature from antiquity deals with questions similar to those in Ecclesiastes. Several Egyptian texts advise people how to live in a world full of anomalies and uncertainties, and there are texts that deal

In 12:9 Qoheleth is identified as a sage, imparting "knowledge to the people." In Mesopotamia there were primeval sages, known as the *apkallu*, who brought wisdom to humankind. They are represented on this cultic water basin by the figures wearing fish-type garments (704–681 BC).

with issues like old age and the reality that death comes to everyone. This epilogue is similar to the colophon found at the end of literary compositions in Egypt and Mesopotamia that provides information about the author or the scribe who copied the text. Seow points out that the epilogue of The Instruction to Kagemni from Egypt also ends with a warning not to go beyond what is written in that piece,[1] perhaps similar to the warning in 12:12. He also points out other parallels in both Kagemni and The Instruction to Ani. While similarities abound between Ecclesiastes and other compositions from the ancient Near East, Qoheleth's answers and the advice he gives are fully consistent with Israelite theology.

Interpretive Insights

12:9 *Not only was the Teacher wise.* The statement that the Teacher was wise is likely an assessment of his competence and insight. It is a claim that what he has presented in Ecclesiastes reflects wisdom rather than folly.

pondered and searched out and set in order. Qoheleth worked in a meticulous and deliberate way. He thought carefully about the material, chose the exact words to communicate his ideas accurately and effectively, and arranged his composition in just the right way to accomplish his intended goals. While this verse describes the human aspect of his work, the inclusion of this book in the biblical canon attests to the superintending work of God in inspiring Ecclesiastes—a point perhaps implied in verse 11.

12:10 *what he wrote was upright and true.* Some argue that while Qoheleth tried hard to write what is "true," he did not

Key Themes of Ecclesiastes 12:9–14

- The Teacher was wise and wrote what was true and upright.
- The words of the wise are like goads and nails.
- God will bring every deed into judgment, including every hidden thing.

succeed, but the NIV's translation likely reflects the correct interpretation. An inspired assessment of the material by the biblical author is helpful when dealing with a difficult book like Ecclesiastes, because it affirms that Qoheleth's teaching does not come from a cynic whose teaching was unorthodox and heretical.

12:11 *The words of the wise are like goads.* A goad is a pointed stick used to guide and prod animals in the direction the herder wants them to go. A wise teacher sometimes uses sharp and painful words to guide students as they think through difficult issues. Estes says, "The images of the goad and the nail at least refer to the ability of the wise sayings to provoke people to good conduct [and I would add to good thinking as well], and the nail may also suggest the stability that wise teaching provides to those who receive it."[2]

given by one shepherd. "Shepherd" may be a generic way of referring to wisdom teachers in general and may point to the way the sage guides people in their thinking and behavior. Many, though, conclude that the shepherd is God (see the NIV footnote) and affirm that wisdom originates with God and comes to us with his authority (cf. Prov. 2:6; Job 28:23, 28). It likely confirms the inspired character of this sage's teaching.

12:12 *Be warned . . . of anything in addition to them.* This is not a warning against intellectual pursuits, nor does it contrast canonical and noncanonical material; rather, the author is affirming the adequacy and authoritative nature of the material in this book. It perhaps warns as well about people who are "always learning but never able to come to a knowledge of the truth" (2 Tim. 3:7). One can examine complex intellectual issues from an almost infinite number of perspectives and end up with nothing but questions and novel theories. Many of Qoheleth's questions can be pursued indefinitely and will likely remain unanswerable. He does give some clear answers, and it is essential to embrace those and apply them as we live in the world.

12:13 *Fear God and keep his commandments.* Qoheleth has not previously connected fear of God with obedience to God's commandments, but that connection is regularly found throughout the Old Testament. Keeping God's commandments is an essential response to understanding who God is and who we are.

12:14 *God will bring every deed into judgment.* Ecclesiastes does not explain how or when God's judgment will occur, and our inability to understand the work of God means that we will not always know when justice has been meted out. At the same time, Qoheleth gives examples of people who have persisted in evil (4:1; 7:15) with no overt indications that justice has been done. Job describes similar situations and seems to describe wicked people who die without any indications that justice has been meted out (Job 21:7–26). It is likely that Ecclesiastes at least leaves open the possibility that judgment may occur after death.

Theological Insights

As Ecclesiastes reaches its conclusion in these verses, several essential points are clear. The first is that while tradition is important, it cannot be allowed to obscure reality and the truth of what life in a fallen world is like. Qoheleth's observations make it clear that reality is often more complex than our traditions would lead us to believe. He believes that the life of faith must look reality square in the eye and engage in the struggle to integrate experience with faith. He sees little value in gaining worldview coherence by denying the realities of human experience in the world.

Qoheleth also recognizes the sovereignty of God and his ongoing providence. This provides the potential for resolving many of the tensions between faith and experience, but only if there is a solid basis for knowing that God is good and gracious—the very thing that the painful and enigmatic experiences of life call into question. Qoheleth's emphasis on enjoying life and finding pleasure in what we do offers one important way to learn to appreciate God's goodness.

Garrett says that this final exhortation to "fear God and keep his commandments" (12:13)

> binds together all the separate strands of the Teacher's thought. . . .
>
> For us the "meaninglessness" of life which the Teacher so ruthlessly exposes would seem to lead to despair or nihilism; for him it is an incitement to true piety. The insignificance of all that is done under the sun leaves him awestruck and silent before God. His inability to control or predict the future provokes him to dependence on God. The futility of attempting to secure his future through

The final instructions of Ecclesiastes are to "fear God and keep his commandments" (12:13). For Israel, God's commandments were contained in the law given to Moses. The importance of God's law was also recognized by early Christians. Scenes of Moses receiving God's commandments were often included in their funerary reliefs, like the one shown here from the sarcophagus of the physician Ioannes (Constantinople, fifth century AD).

wisdom or acts of religion . . . leads him not to impiety but to an understanding of the true nature of obedient trust.

Seen in this light, to "keep his commandments" is not to behave with the self-satisfied arrogance of religious presumption. . . . Rather, it is the deepest expression of humble acceptance of what it means to be a human before God.[3]

Teaching the Text

This final section of the book identifies the central core of the Teacher's instruction as living in trusting dependence on God, in obedience to his commandments, and with awareness that he will judge all our actions. Qoheleth insists that life in the world is *hebel*; it is short and filled with things that we can neither understand nor control. Experience regularly confronts us with reminders of life's painful and fragile nature and of our own human limits. The experiences of life provide little basis for discovering whether life has meaning or how to live so that our lives really matter— and then there is the matter of injustice and oppression. There appears to be no way to live so as to guarantee the outcomes we desire or to predict what will happen in the future—except that we will die. We are left with the question of how a person should live in the light of such realities.

The epilogue makes it clear that "all is *hebel*" is not the final word, for it affirms the central importance of a life centered in God. Qoheleth has made clear that what is gained in the world will be lost at death, thus underscoring the futility of trying to find meaning and lasting value in what is accomplished in the world. The experiences of life will take us only so far in understanding reality, and they leave us unable to answer many important questions about life, faith, and God. Moving beyond the limited perspective of human observation and experience is possible only when God reveals the answers to his people. They must, of course, embrace those answers by faith—another essential characteristic of a life centered in God.

The world is filled with disruptive and painful elements. At the same time, much remains that God has created and declared to be very good, and one of God's purposes for humanity is to enjoy the blessings that come from him. A beautiful sunset, food, and relationships with family or special friends can remind us of God's goodness. Regularly reflecting on such things is important to keep a balanced perspective in a world filled with evil and pain. Qoheleth calls us to remember the difficult times of life, the fact that we will finally die, and that God will judge every deed. At the same time, we are to remember our Creator and his providence. It is life lived in the fear of God and obedience to his commandments that serves us well both in this life and in whatever comes after death. This balanced perspective enables us to live with hope and confidence.

The fuller revelation of the New Testament has advanced our understanding far beyond what Qoheleth knew. We have a much clearer understanding of human depravity and the impact of sin and human rebellion on both individuals and culture. We know much about the afterlife and God's coming judgment that the author of Ecclesiastes did not know, and yet life is still shrouded in mystery and uncertainty for the Christian. We do not know what will happen tomorrow; we cannot interpret the things that happen to us or identify the many variables that contribute to outcomes in our own lives. We still struggle with evil and the same realities of life as did Qoheleth. We experience life the same way Ecclesiastes describes it, and we find the providence of God as elusive and uncertain as did this Old Testament sage. We have the same struggles understanding the work of God and knowing how he is working out his purposes in our lives. We face the tension between the assertions of faith and the experiences of life in the world in ways that are little different from how Qoheleth

encountered them, and the advice he gives is as relevant for us as it was for his original readers. These are points that should be emphasized in teaching this section.

Fear God and keep his commandments. Rejoice and find delight in the things that come from God's hand. Understand the way things really are in a fallen world and also remember your Creator. It is only in living the way Ecclesiastes commends that we understand the meaning of humanness and discover the true meaning of life. Living in the fear of God is the antithesis of self-fulfillment. Instead, we faithfully live according to God's instructions and leave the outcomes with him. We gratefully receive the gifts that come from his hand and find delight in God himself, and as the New Testament makes clear, those who live in trusting dependence on God are the ones in whom God delights and whom God uses to accomplish his purposes.

Illustrating the Text

The words of the wise are like goads and nails.

Definition: Goad.

The goad itself was a long stick, usually five to seven feet long, but sometimes as much as nine feet long, with a sharp point fixed to one end. The farmer would use it to prick the cattle forward when they grew weary. When oxen were yoked and harnessed to the plow, the farmer would take the plow in one hand and a goad in the other and spur the oxen to drag the plow through the ground. . . . The image of prodding the reluctant or lazy creature made this a useful metaphor for sharp urging, such as the prick of conscience, the nagging of a mate, or the "words of the wise," which are "firmly embedded nails" in human minds (Eccles. 12:11).[4]

A wise teacher guides students as they think through difficult issues.

Anecdote: Qoheleth's teaching methods are like those reflected in a rabbinic story told by Perry. Several students asked their teacher questions, and his answers did not correspond with what he had taught them before. When they pointed this out, he commended them for their astuteness. "The case was not that he didn't know but rather he wanted to stimulate his students." The students then referred to Rabbi Joshuah, who used to say, "Whoever learns but does not labor at it is like a man who sows but does not reap."[5] Probably such skills as those Qoheleth desires in his students can only develop as they struggle with the issues of life, forging out their own answers.

If we fear God, we can take prudent risks, undeterred by the lack of guarantees.

Church Missions: Wilbur and Evelyn Aulie were among the first translators to go to Chiapas, Mexico, under the auspices of Wycliffe Bible Translators, where they served for many years. There was immense risk in pursuing such a course, and Wilbur was the victim of beatings and harsh treatment from people who did not want them there. Furthermore, Wilbur had had polio as a child, making the necessary walking through the mountains difficult. Nevertheless, the Aulies learned the language, translated the Bible into Chol, and ministered to the people with love and kindness. Evelyn also provided medical help as a nurse. Later they retired, but upon their return to the States, they concluded that their hearts were in Mexico and went back.

When Wilbur died, his body was taken to Chiapas to be buried. His son, Bruce, describes what happened.

> For one who never sought the limelight, I think he would have been embarrassed by the huge turnout for his funeral. Services were held in three different communities en route to the burial site. Hundreds of Chol Indians streamed out of villages and joined the funeral procession. Some came on foot from five and six hours away. The burial plot was on a ridge where Wilbur and Chol colleagues would stop to pray for the Chol people. . . . A handful of very old Chol men insisted on digging the grave with picks and shovels. . . . People recounted how the villages used to be—alcoholism, machete fights in which people would lose their arms and heads—now transformed by the gospel of grace.[6]

A similar outpouring of gratitude took place when Evelyn died. The impetus for living with risk is often enhanced by a strong sense of God's calling to a task.

"The words of the wise are like goads" (12:11). This Egyptian model of an agricultural scene shows the farmer holding a goad in one hand to direct the oxen as he manages the plow with the other.

Ecclesiastes 12:9–14

Introduction to Song of Songs

The Greatest Song: A Song about Love

Centuries of discussion have produced little consensus about Song of Songs, and significant disagreements remain about almost every aspect of the book. Many things contribute to the uncertainty, including its erotic language and themes, the fact that God is not mentioned in the book,[1] the absence of anything relating to salvation history, and the fact that despite the erotic language there is no explicitly moral teaching in the book. Many have struggled with what is obviously love poetry in the canon of Scripture, and the appearance of such material in the canon also raises questions about how the material should be understood—is the primary purpose of the poetry to describe love between a man and a woman (in marriage?), or is the human relationship really intended as a metaphor for God's love for his people (Israel, the church, or the individual believer)? The book contains many words that are not known outside this book, though most are names of spices, plants, and the like, thus impacting only our understanding of details rather than the major flow of ideas. The point of many of the book's metaphors is difficult to understand because of the great gulf between the original culture and the world of today's readers. Comparing the girl's hair to "a flock of goats descending from the hills of Gilead" (4:1) and her nose to a tower, while obviously compliments, fail to come across that way to most modern readers. Solomon's relationship to the book and the events it describes is problematic as well, since the statement of 1 Kings 11:1–8 regarding his seven hundred wives and princesses and three hundred concubines seems to preclude the possibility of his being a role model for an ideal relationship between a man and woman.

While some have suggested that the book is an allegory, the purpose of which is to describe God's relationship with his people, others have argued that the author is relating historical events but still see the book's primary purpose as describing

God's relationship with his people. Both of these approaches agree that the plain sense of the text is not its primary meaning and reflect the idea that human love, including its physical and sensual aspects, is not a topic worthy of inclusion in divinely inspired Scripture. While the popularity of this approach has diminished, this method was dominant throughout most of the history of the church, and many who departed from it found themselves excommunicated. Few would argue that the Song was written as an allegory, since it lacks the clues that an author normally provides to alert readers to such intentions in the piece.[2] Often the allegorical interpretation was preferred to make it easier to deal with the erotic language and subject matter, and it may well reflect an interpretive method brought to the text rather than representing the original author's intention. As John Walton has pointed out,[3] the authority of the text must reside with the author's intention rather than in its allegorical interpretation. Many biblical scholars and leaders have interpreted the book allegorically, and believers through the centuries have been helped practically

Love poetry was a part of the literature in many cultures in the ancient Near East. Perhaps the oldest-known love poem is the one found on this Sumerian tablet (2037–2029 BC). A section of the poem shows the passion and desire of the bride: "Bridegroom, let me caress you, / My precious caress is more savory than honey, / In the bedchamber, honey-filled, / Let me enjoy your goodly beauty" ("The Oldest Love Poem," www.istanbularkeoloji .gov.tr).

and devotionally. An important distinction must be made between what may be devotionally helpful and what is exegetically derived. Often the points affirmed by interpreters of the Song are biblically correct principles that can be supported from other passages of Scripture; what is doubtful, however, is that these points can be exegetically determined from the text of the Song of Songs.

The general consensus today is that the Song describes the love between a man and a woman, but this conclusion has not produced agreement about the purpose of the book or the story it tells. The book consists of a number of different poems, but these are not connected by a narrative framework that clearly tells the story of the lovers. Some conclude that there is no story; rather, it is an anthology of poems celebrating the beauty and virtue of human love, written by various authors at different times. Some think these poems were used during wedding celebrations in ancient Israel, while others have proposed that the material had its ultimate origins in the fertility cults, which flourished in the ancient world and existed in Israel despite the condemnation of such practices in the Law and the Prophets.

Certain expressions and themes (e.g., daughters of Jerusalem) recur throughout the book and suggest its unity and the probability of a connected story. At the same time, it is not clear what that story is, and some have appropriately described the book as an impressionistic collage rather than a descriptive narrative. Ambiguity about who is speaking in the various dialogues adds uncertainty, and some have compared the book to a play that lacks stage directions. As a result of this vagueness, a number of assumptions must be made to construct a unified story from the poetry. Many proposals for reconstructing the story of the lovers have been made, some of which can be rejected on textual or theological grounds, while others can be dismissed as unlikely. Perhaps to a greater degree than with any other book of the Bible it is impossible to present a particular view of the book as *the* correct interpretation. It is possible to say of several proposals for reading the Song that "this particular reading of the Song is offered as one among several that are plausible and defensible from the text itself without unduly 'straining' the meaning of the text or 'reading into' the text what is not there."[4]

Conclusions about the kind of literature, the nature of the language and metaphors, the major points taught by the book, the story recounted in the book, and so on, must, of course, result from a careful study of the text itself; but in the case of the Song of Songs, these decisions cannot be made entirely on that basis, since even the most careful study will leave us with several possibilities, which *may* be, rather than with one conclusion, which *must* be. At the same time, decisions about these matters will be applied to the text and will determine the interpretation of various details throughout the book. A thorough study of these issues is beyond the scope of this volume, but it is important to identify some of these issues and encourage careful consideration of these preliminary questions.

Date and Authorship

The Song of Songs begins with a statement that many believe identifies Solomon as the author ("Solomon's Song of Songs," 1:1). The Hebrew preposition used here is a common way of indicating authorship, but the preposition could also mean "the Song of Songs about Solomon" or "for Solomon" or "commissioned by Solomon." Thus a decision about authorship will have to be made on some basis other than this statement. The references in 1:5 and 8:11–12 do not necessarily connect Solomon with the poems, but those in 3:7, 9, and 11 do. The mention of Solomon in 1:1 also ties him in some way to the book, even if it does not identify him as the author.

Many conclude that the story involves Solomon's relationship with a woman whom he truly loved, in contrast to wives he married for political expediency, and it is also possible that Solomon is describing what might have been had he lived according to the great wisdom and insight for which he was famous. Others have suggested that Solomon is not the hero of the book and that there are three major characters rather than two (a view sometimes called the "shepherd hypothesis"). According to this view, a young girl, who was in love with a shepherd from her home town, has been taken to Jerusalem by Solomon to become a part of his harem. Despite the splendor of the court and the benefits she would enjoy as Solomon's wife, the girl rejects his advances and is finally allowed to return to the shepherd, whom she truly loves.

Prior to the nineteenth century, the references to Solomon were understood as affirming Solomonic authorship, and many who deny that Solomon wrote the book still acknowledge that the statement in 1:1 is likely a claim about authorship. Solomonic authorship would require a date near the mid-tenth century BC and would be consistent with what is known about his literary pursuits and interest in wisdom and the natural realm.[5] Many today question the traditional date, largely because some linguistic evidence suggests a later date. The book contains some grammatical features more characteristic of Hebrew from a later period than from the time of Solomon (though some of these may reflect dialectical differences in the Hebrew used during the time of Solomon). There are also words that may have been borrowed from Persian or Greek. At the same time, there are grammatical features characteristic of an early date, so the linguistic evidence is at best ambiguous.[6]

Too much ambiguity exists to conclude with certainty that Solomon wrote the book, and we are left with little basis for

Song of Songs describes the love relationship between a woman and her beloved. A beautiful illustration of this expression of love from the ancient world is this painted relief from Amarna (ca. 1335 BC). It shows a royal couple in their garden. The queen holds lotus blossoms in her left hand and waves fragrant mandrake fruits under her husband's nose, indicating her desire for his love.

determining the date or the authorship of this problematic book. The book describes love and romance from a woman's perspective, and some have suggested that it may have been composed, at least in part, by a woman. The Song of Deborah (Judg. 5), the prayer of Hannah (1 Sam. 2:1–10), and the prayer of Mary (Luke 1:46–55) were likely composed by women, and given the lack of definitive indicators as to the author and date of the Song, this suggestion cannot be rejected out of hand. Fortunately, our understanding of the message of the book does not depend on an exact knowledge of authorship or date. It is even possible that the ambiguity regarding these matters is a deliberate part of the book's design. As Richard Hess says, "The environment of the Song can be situated in a variety of possible times and places. This itself may betray the intention of the Song to speak more widely of love than a defined historical circumstance would allow."[7]

Solomon and the Structure of the Book

Solomon's role in the book is intertwined with issues of authorship, the date of the book, its unity, and the story told in the book. Those who view the book as an anthology of poems generally conclude that there is no story and that the separate poems were written by many different people over a long period of time. Those who conclude that the book consists of a unified story will be greatly influenced in their understanding of the story by their conclusions about Solomon's role in the book. Solomon's bad example as the husband of many wives is a major problem for Solomonic authorship. He was much better at originating and collecting wisdom than he was at applying it to his own life, though perhaps his Spirit-illuminated wisdom allowed him to describe an ideal relationship that he never experienced. It is also possible that the book was not intended to tell a story about Solomon and that he functions more as a literary device than as a character in the story.

The approach in this commentary will divide the book based largely on thought units and will suggest that the book describes a relationship between one man and one woman rather than the three-character view. I also maintain that the book is about an ideal relationship rather than an actual one and that the characters are generic ones representative of all lovers. It is possible that the poem describes their relationship from courtship to marriage and beyond, but the poetry is not sufficiently precise to allow us to know where in their relationship a particular episode fits. This makes it difficult to argue that material prior to the marriage scene in 3:6–11 describes their courtship while the material after that deals with the period after their marriage. As Tom Gledhill says, "In the Song all the complex emotions of courtship are jumbled up together in a somewhat bewildering cycle of movements."[8] The poems are about love and romance and move back and forth with little concern for the chronology of the relationship. Daniel Estes says, "The Song uses a collage or kaleidoscope of scenes that suggests a story . . . in a fashion analogous to the impressionistic paintings of Monet and the impressionistic music of Debussy."[9]

Song of Songs and Sexual Morality

A striking feature of the book is the absence of clear moral teaching (perhaps with the exception of 2:7; 3:5; and 8:4), and this likely is related to the purpose of the book and the pedagogy of wisdom. The book describes and celebrates love and romance between a man and a woman, and didactic discussions of morality would take away from the basic point the Song is making. In proverbial

Introduction to Song of Songs

instruction an individual proverb generally captures a tiny cross section of truth rather than providing a comprehensive treatment of a topic, and this is true even when moral and ethical considerations are obviously relevant. People are expected to bring the appropriate moral and ethical principles to bear as they apply the principle to life. The only context in which we have Song of Songs is the context of the canon, and it likely presupposes that moral values must be brought from that broader tradition. Gledhill says, "If we look at the wider biblical context, we see with the utmost clarity that the ancient Hebrews possessed a very rigid moral code; premarital sexual relationships were prohibited. . . . Adultery was considered a more serious sin. . . . So the Song gives us no license to flout the moral codes of God's covenant people."[10]

It is also important to respect the poetic form of Song of Songs. According to Leland Ryken, poetry "is the interpretive presentation of human experience in an artistic form. It [is] . . . a more concentrated form of discourse. . . . Concentration is achieved through the use of images, symbols, allusions, metaphors, similes, emotive vocabulary, and multiple meanings."[11] The abundance of such literary devices contributes to notorious difficulties in interpreting love poetry, and there is a wide range of opinions about the way and extent to which the Song describes the sexual activity of the couple. Cheryl Exum points out that the romantic encounters in the Song are described through "the indirection of language, through innuendo, double entendre, and metaphor," and she adds, "What form intimacy takes here and elsewhere, though it may be strongly suggested, is never literally described. Moreover, an imaginative reader can find sexual innuendo and double entendre everywhere. Like beauty, double entendre is in the eye of the beholder."[12] This gives the text an important quality: it can be read either very explicitly or as subtly erotic.

Those who see the book's language as explicitly sexual find human anatomy and sexual encounters in almost every scene. Such interpretations make it difficult to

The lily is a prominent image in the figurative language in the Song of Songs and is used to describe the woman and the romantic encounters of the lovers. Lilies probably refer to lotus flowers, very common in Egyptian art. Shown here is a painted ivory carving of a royal princess gathering lotus blossoms and picking grapes (Amarna Period, fourteenth century BC).

recognize the broader aspects of relationships and often see little relevance in the moral teaching of the rest of the Old Testament for interpreting the Song. The book, almost certainly, is about love rather than sex, and the descriptions of intimacy involve far more than physical sexual activity. As Gledhill says,

> That the Song is about sexual love is not disputed. But that must be seen in its widest context, for love between the sexes is more than physical expression; the lovers in the Song interact in many other ways, praising each other, going out in the country together, just quietly being in each other's presence. Their mutual commitment is not just for the purposes of physical pleasure.[13]

Recognizing the nature of poetic language and the subtle and reserved ways in which the episodes are depicted in the Song (e.g., the way the couple's sexual experience is described in 4:12–5:1) allows a reader to appreciate the fact that love can express itself in many different ways besides the physical.

Song of Songs in the Broader Biblical Context

In the early chapters of Genesis, God creates Adam and makes the woman as an appropriate helper for him. The account makes it clear that human beings were not made to function independently and autonomously but were made for relationships. The companion that God designs for the man is not an inferior partner but a helper who brings strengths to match the man's weaknesses. This interdependent relationship is a fundamental part of God's design and suggests that the one-flesh relationship includes far more than the physical and sexual. The fall and God's judgment on humanity have brought significant dysfunction to male-female relationships, and what is often observed and experienced in male-female relationships reflects something quite different from God's design. The question of how the relationship between a man and a woman is supposed to work is rarely addressed in the Hebrew Bible. We often catch glimpses of dysfunctional relationships (Isaac and Rebecca, Jacob and his family, David and Bathsheba, Amnon's rape of his half sister Tamar, Solomon and his wives), but it is far more unusual to see a relationship that works according to God's order. Proverbs often contrasts the positive and the negative potential of marriage relationships, but we are still left wondering what this one-flesh relationship, functioning according to God's design, looks like in practice. It seems likely that Song of Songs is a picture of this kind of relationship between a man and a woman. The relationship that we see in the Song is characterized by love, mutual respect, and praise for and delight in each other, and as Exum points out, we learn by observing the relationship and hearing what the characters say to each other.[14] The power of the Song lies in its ability to draw us into the experience of the couple to participate vicariously in that relationship. In the process we learn significant things about how the one-flesh relationship that God designed is supposed to work.

Introduction to Song of Songs

Passion, Praise, and Delight

Big Idea *The love of a man and a woman brings passion and delight.*

Understanding the Text

The Text in Context

Solomon's connection with Song of Songs sets it in the context of Old Testament wisdom, with its focus on discovering the basic principles that operate in the world. This also anchors the book in a context that affirms the moral teaching of Old Testament wisdom literature. As is common with other wisdom literature, Song of Songs teaches by allowing the reader to observe the couple and listen to their conversations. The book starts in the middle of the lovers' story, which is never brought to an end. We observe their relationship at various points in its development. The poetry engages our emotions and draws us into the lovers' experience as we learn about love and romance through that vicarious experience.

Historical and Cultural Background

While parallels exist between the literature of Israel's neighbors and Song of Songs, similar examples extend more broadly across cultures, reflecting the universality of love and romance. Sumerian poetry sometimes describes sexual encounters between deities—often represented by the king or a priest/priestess. The purpose and use of these poems is debated, though they were likely used in the cult to enhance fertility and prosperity.[1] There is no evidence that the Song was ever used in this way, and the Mesopotamian material seems to have limited relevance. A group of Egyptian love poems reflects the same excitement and delight as Song of Songs and describes similar obstacles to the couple's coming together to express their love. The couple's determination to overcome difficulties and pursue their relationship is also a common theme, and similar metaphors are used in both the Song and the Egyptian love poems. The parallels do not suggest literary dependence but reflect each culture's treatment of issues that are innate to male-female relationships. The parallels do make it clear that the biblical poetry did not develop in a vacuum but drew from a common tradition of language and experience.

Interpretive Insights

1:1 *Song of Songs.* This type of construction is often used to indicate a superlative idea (e.g., "king of kings" or "holy of holies"). If Solomon was the author, perhaps this was his greatest composition; if not, the poem may be so designated because of its artistry or theme.

1:2 *Let him kiss me . . . your love is more delightful than wine.* This woman is not passive, waiting for the man to act; she participates fully in their romantic activity, often initiating it. The jussives (e.g., "let him . . .") and imperatives in subsequent verses convey the energy and urgency of her desire. "Love" often refers to lovemaking, and she finds the euphoric and intoxicating effect of his love to be even greater than that of wine. The poetry leaves the exact nature of the love/lovemaking ambiguous; such ambiguity characterizes the Song and is typical of love poetry.

1:3 *your name is like perfume poured out.* To pour out perfume would more broadly disperse the fragrance. Perhaps hearing her lover's name produces this effect. A person's character was often associated with his or her name, and perhaps the woman's reflection on his noble qualities triggers the delight described here.

1:4 *Let the king bring me into his chambers.* "The king" may refer to Solomon (either a literary figure or the historical individual) or may reflect the way the woman sees her lover (he is her king). The Hebrew would normally be translated "the king brought me" (cf. ASV, ESV, and most commentaries) and may indicate that the perspective has

- The lovers delight in each other.
- The lovers praise each other.
- Praise has the power to change people.

changed from anticipation to description. "Chambers" can refer to different kinds of rooms, including bedrooms, and ambiguity remains regarding the couple's intention. They are in love and want to spend time together in private.

We rejoice and delight in you . . . your love. The speakers are probably the daughters of Jerusalem. The object of the verbs "rejoice" and "delight" is ambiguous, though it is likely the man. The Hebrew suffix on "your love" refers to the man.

1:5–6 *I am darkened by the sun.* The woman's words are probably directed to women whose skin reflects the benefits of never having worked outside. She indicates that her skin is dark because she has had to work in the vineyards. This suggests that she is from a poor family. Her sun-darkened skin would be seen by some as "a sign of

In 1:5–6 the woman declares that she is dark skinned. Whether this indicates she is from hardworking peasant stock or emphasizes her exotic, otherworldly beauty is debated. The contrast in skin tones was captured in this painting found in the grave chamber of Nefferronpet (Luxor, Egypt, thirteenth century BC).

Song of Songs 1:1–2:7

lower social status"[2] and therefore as incompatible with beauty.

my own vineyard. Sometimes in the Song "vineyard" or garden refers to a literal one, and at other times it refers to the woman's body. Both meanings are evident here.

1:7 *where you rest your sheep.* The man is described as a shepherd, as is the woman in verse 8. The shepherd motif is common in love poetry, though it is also a metaphor for the king in the ancient Near East. She wants to know where he will be so that she can be with him during the day.

Why should I be like a veiled woman . . . ? The meaning of "veiled woman" is uncertain. Hess, based on reliefs from Lachish, suggests that the term may refer to the type of cloak worn by a woman tending sheep.[3] Thus, she would be saying, "I do not want to tend my sheep with the other shepherds; I want to be where you are."

As the woman's beauty is praised by her beloved, he remarks that "her cheeks are beautiful with earrings" (1:10). These gold earrings are from Phoenicia (seventh to sixth century BC).

1:8 *most beautiful of women.* This is likely the man's response to his lover's question in verse 7. He has feelings for her like those she has for him and thinks she is the "most beautiful of women." He is interested only in her—no matter how much others may love him—and he will obviously welcome her visit.

1:9 *my darling.* The man regularly calls the woman "my darling" in the Song, and the term occurs only here in the Hebrew Bible. The masculine form of the word means "friend, companion." It is a term of endearment, and as Exum indicates, "It can have an intimate sense as well as a more general one."[4]

a mare among Pharaoh's chariot horses. Horses were used primarily for war, and seeing these animals pulling war chariots would have been impressive, suggesting qualities like nobility, beauty, and strength. Stallions normally pulled war chariots in Egypt, and Pope notes an instance when the prince of Qadesh sent a mare into the Egyptian army to distract the stallions and make them ineffective in a battle.[5] Bergant says about this same incident, "The tantalizing presence of the mare was able to throw those otherwise well-disciplined horses into total confusion and disarray. . . . The metaphor implies that her charms are able to unsettle even the most disciplined of men. Her mere presence can cause them to lose control of themselves."[6] The woman here has that effect on her lover.

1:11 *We will make you earrings of gold.* The women's desire to make earrings for the girl apparently reflects a change from their criticism of her implied in verse 6.

1:12–14 *a sachet of myrrh . . . a cluster of henna blossoms.* The scent of the woman's perfume[7] causes her to think of her lover as "a sachet of myrrh" between her breasts. Myrrh, a reddish gum resin from South Arabia, was used in making incense for the temple, as well as for cosmetics. She also thinks of him as "a cluster of henna blossoms from . . . En Gedi," a beautiful and fertile oasis in the barren desert. He stands apart from other men in as dramatic a way as En Gedi contrasts with the surrounding desert.

1:15 *How beautiful you are.* The man describes his lover by using words that she will echo back to him in verse 16 and reinforces his compliment by repeating the word "beautiful."

1:16 *How handsome you are, my beloved!* The woman uses masculine forms of the adjectives that her lover used to describe her.

our bed is verdant. The forest and the beauty of nature remind her of the special delight she finds in her lover. "Bed" suggests the possibility of a sexual encounter, though one cannot determine from such an intentionally provocative text whether these words reflect imaginative anticipation or describe present or past experience.

1:17 *The beams of our house are cedars . . . firs.* Nature, with its lush greenery and breathtaking beauty, is a fitting context for the couple as they find delight in each other.

2:1 *I am a rose of Sharon, a lily of the valleys.* The "rose" may be a crocus or meadow saffron, and the woman may be comparing herself to a beautiful wildflower or saying that she is only a common wildflower. Keel argues that the "lily" is actually a lotus and notes the importance of this as a symbol of life and regeneration in ancient Egyptian iconography. Scarabs and paintings from Palestine show that it was viewed in similar ways there.[8] In this case she would be making a very positive statement about herself.

2:2 *Like a lily among thorns.* The man turns the woman's words into a compliment by telling her that she stands out from the other women like a beautiful flower in a field of thornbushes. Keel says, "He contrasts the life and refreshment he receives from his partner with the troubles and deadly boredom associated with other women."[9]

2:4 *banner.* This probably refers to a flag identifying tribal or military units. Carpenter and Grisanti suggest that her beloved's "love protectively hovers over his lover . . . or is displayed for all to see."[10] Based on a similar Akkadian word, it is possible that the phrase should be translated, "His intention toward me is love."[11]

2:5 *raisins . . . apples . . . faint with love.* The woman's desire for her beloved has made her lovesick, and she asks for raisins and apples. Gordis says, "She is calling for concrete food, to be sure, but *at the same time*, by her choice of fruits that are symbolic of love, she is indicating that only the satisfaction of her desires will bring her healing."[12] In an Egyptian poem a young man says about the woman he loves, "She will make the doctors unnecessary because she knows my sickness."[13]

2:6 *left arm is under my head . . . right arm embraces me.* Her words describe an intimate embrace.

2:7 *Do not arouse or awaken love.* This refrain occurs again in 3:5 and 8:4, and according to Longman it is the woman's warning "to other women who may look on the relationship and want to experience something similar; she is, in essence, telling them not to force it. Wait for love to blossom; don't hurry it."[14] As Hubbard points out, the experience of love "is too powerful, too all-consuming to be lightly aroused, unless the couple have the commitment, the desire, and the right opportunity to enjoy it."[15] The refrain probably also warns about the physical expression of love prior to a commitment in marriage, which in the Bible establishes the proper context for full physical intimacy.[16]

Theological Insights

The one-flesh relationship between a man and a woman was designed by God and is one of his good gifts to humanity. Despite the damage resulting from humanity's rebellion against God, good and mutually beneficial elements are still evident in many relationships between men and women. At the same time, male-female relationships are often characterized by abuse and turmoil rather than delight. Song of Songs shows us a man and a woman relating in ways that likely reflect God's order, even in a fallen world. Setting this relationship in nature and describing it in terms of its beauty suggests that love between a man and a woman, including its physical and sexual expression, is as fundamental to God's order as are these other elements of creation.

Teaching the Text

The lovers' praise for each other characterizes the entire book. They find appropriate metaphors for expressing their passion and delight in things around them that evoke pleasure and awe. The beauty of nature; delightful aromas of perfumes, spices, and trees; tastes; and the intoxicating effect of wine create experiences that enable them to describe the exhilaration they find in their

When the woman compares herself to a "lily of the valleys," her lover praises her as a "lily among thorns" (2:1–2). The lily may be referring to a lotus flower, like the one this woman holds in this ancient Egyptian painting (1200–1100 BC).

love for each other. The praise that dominates their conversations reflects mutual adoration and delight, and the expression of their feelings is mutual as well. Their praise flows out of a profound respect for the other and a deep awareness of the other's worth. Such praise is essential in relationships. The praise of the woman's lover has the power to reduce her insecurities and assure her of her worth in his eyes. Such affirmations can change people's self-understanding and motivate them to greater diligence in meeting their partner's needs and desires. Her lover's praise reassures her and encourages her in the face of criticism and elevates her reputation in the eyes of those who have disparaged her. Focusing on what we value and things that bring us delight in the one we love contributes to a growing appreciation of his or her worth and is important as relationships grow. Love is stimulating and intoxicating; it transforms ordinary things into extraordinary ones; it is exhilarating and overwhelming. Praise, mutual respect, and love play major roles in keeping passion and delight alive and in moving a relationship toward maturity.

Illustrating the Text

Lovers delight in each other.

Quote: *Addresses on the Song of Solomon*, by H. A. Ironside. "We delight to speak with those whom we love. One of the wonderful things about love is that when someone has really filled the vision of your soul, you do not feel that any time that is taken up communing with him is wasted."[17]

Poetry: The metaphors used in praise of the beloved in the Song of Songs, such as "mare among Pharaoh's chariot horses" (1:9) and "a cluster of henna blossoms" (1:14), reflect the Song's cultural setting. Love poetry, both ancient and modern, is replete with examples of this rich use of metaphor. "Oh, thou art fairer than the evening air clad in the beauty of a thousand stars," wrote Christopher Marlowe (*Dr. Faustus*, act 5, scene 1); "She walks in beauty like the night of cloudless climes and starry skies; and all that's best of dark and bright meet in her aspect and her eyes," wrote Romantic poet Lord Byron ("She Walks in Beauty"). More recent is Oscar Hammerstein II's song "All the Things You Are."

Elizabeth Barrett Browning

Because the love story between Elizabeth Barrett Browning (1806–61) and her husband Robert Browning is so powerful and provides such a striking example of the transforming power of love and praise, a number of Elizabeth's famous *Sonnets from the Portuguese* (1850) will be used as illustrations throughout this part of the book. Elizabeth's father controlled her life, and she suffered from ill health. Because of an injury, she believed she would never walk or marry. Her relationship with poet Robert Browning changed all that, and their courtship generated a rich body of poetry.

Praise has the power to change people's lives.

Poetry: *Sonnets from the Portuguese*, by Elizabeth Barrett Browning. In "Sonnet I," Browning (see the sidebar) describes the transforming power of love as the difference between life and death. Some of the lines follow:

> I saw, in gradual vision through my
>   tears,
> The sweet, sad years, the melancholy
>   years,
> Those of my own life, who by turns
>   had flung
> A shadow across me. Straightway I was
>   'ware,
> So weeping, how a mystic Shape did
>   move
> Behind me, and drew me backward by
>   the hair;
> And a voice said in mastery, while I
>   strove,—
> "Guess now who holds thee?"—
>   "Death," I said, But, there,
> The silver answer rang,—"Not Death,
>   but Love."[18]

Song of Songs 1:1–2:7

My Beloved Is Mine, and I Am His

Big Idea *Mutual commitment is the key to a relationship that works according to God's order.*

Understanding the Text

The Text in Context

This long speech by the woman consists of Song of Songs 2:8–17 and 3:1–5. The first part captures the woman's excitement as she eagerly anticipates the arrival of her lover. She describes him as a gazelle or young stag and pictures him leaping and bounding over the mountains as he comes to her. His excitement is also evident as he waits outside her house, peering inside, hoping to catch a glimpse of her. He invites her to enjoy the beauty of springtime as they see, hear, touch, and smell the exciting things that come with springtime renewal. He wants to be with her, to see her and hear her voice. Both of these poems begin with the two apart, and they come together in the course of the poem. In the second poem, the woman, fearful because of his absence, diligently seeks her lover but cannot find him. Finally, she finds him and refuses to let him go until she has brought him safely to her mother's house. The section ends with the same adjuration to the daughters of Jerusalem found in 2:7.

Historical and Cultural Background

Several Egyptian poems are written only in the female voice, as is this section of the Song. Common themes in both are the frustration and fear of separation and the deep yearning to be together in a private place. There are also comparisons with flowers, fragrances, and lush foliage, and in one Egyptian poem the girl compares the arrival of her lover to a gazelle,[1] though her point is different from that in Song of Songs 2:9 and 17. Themes of excitement and passion, separation and coming together, seeking and finding are also common in Egypt. Such common themes reflect universal human experience rather than literary or cultural borrowing.[2]

Interpretive Insights

2:8–9 *My beloved!* The woman regularly calls her lover "my beloved." The term can also mean "brother" or "cousin" and in the plural can mean "love" or "lovemaking." Its use in the book makes it clear that this is a term of great intimacy and endearment.

Look! Here he comes, leaping . . . bounding. The Hebrew particle *hinneh* that begins this line, and occurs again in verse 9, indicates something present and immediate. The energy and immediacy are amplified by the participles (translated as "comes," "leaping," "bounding," "stands," "gazing," "peering") that dominate verses 8–9. The girl is excited and filled with anticipation.

like a gazelle or a young stag. The image of gazelles or stags bounding over the hills generates feelings of excitement and delight. A homonym for "gazelle" means "beautiful" and is likely part of what the metaphor is meant to communicate. (See also the commentary on Song 4:5.)

2:14 *dove in the clefts of the rock.* When the man is outside the woman's house and separated from her by walls and windows, he describes her as a dove in a place inaccessible to him. The softness and color of the dove convey the idea of gentleness, and the sound the bird makes is soothing. The dove is a symbol of peace and love in many cultures, and as Bergant notes, "It was also used as a representative of the goddess of love in several ancient cultures."[3]

face . . . voice. He wants to see her and to hear her sweet voice. The word translated "face" by the NIV actually means "form"; he wants to experience the delight of looking at her and hearing the sound of her voice.

2:15 *little foxes that ruin the vineyards.* The woman probably cites a popular proverb or song. Some argue that the foxes may be

Key Themes of Song of Songs 2:8–3:5

- Being together produces excitement, anticipation, and delight.
- Separation produces frustration and fear.
- Love must develop naturally and without coercion, and full physical intimacy must wait for the right time, the right place, and the right person.

"womanizers" who could derail the relationship through their immoral intentions toward the girl, and certainly the relationship could be adversely affected if her lover were involved in such behavior. Others suggest that "little foxes" destroy grapevines by digging for insects near the roots, damaging the plants and preventing the vine's full growth. In this case, the woman would be expressing her desire that they deal with every obstacle that might prevent their relationship from progressing.

2:16 *My beloved is mine and I am his.* At the center of this relationship is the mutual commitment of the couple to each other, and this constitutes the foundation that makes growth toward maturity possible. While details are sparse, it is likely that such commitments were publically

The endearment "my beloved" is used throughout Song of Songs. This limestone statue from an Egyptian tomb represents Ptahkenuwy with his spouse. One of the inscriptions on the base refers to her as "his beloved wife" (Tomb G 2004, Giza, 2465–2323 BC).

formalized through covenants of betrothal and marriage.

he browses among the lilies. In 1:7 the woman asks her lover to tell her where he shepherds or grazes, and while "graze" has no object in Hebrew, the context suggests that the object is "your flock." In 2:16 she uses the same verb (NIV: "browses") but now with an object, "lilies," or more likely lotus flowers. In 2:1 she describes herself as a "lily" or lotus, and he repeats this description in 2:2. As Bergant notes, "The sexual nuances here are obvious. Pasturing is a metaphor for love making. The man finds his nourishment and pleasure in making love with the woman."[4] She recognizes that he finds delight, satisfaction, and nourishment in her charms, and clearly this is mutual.

2:17 *turn . . . like a gazelle or like a young stag.* The woman envisions her lover as "a gazelle or young stag" in 2:9, and she uses similar words at the end of the section. It is unclear whether her exhortation to "turn" expresses her wish for him to return home or is an invitation for him to spend the night. If the context for this episode is prior to marriage, the exhortation may reflect the fact that, despite her passion and desire, this is not the time or place for the full physical expression of their love, so she reluctantly sends her lover away as they await the future.

rugged hills. While "rugged hills" (Heb. *beter*) could refer to hilly terrain characterized by numerous ravines, it could also refer to her breasts and express her desire or invitation for sexual intimacy. The Hebrew term might also be the name of a town near Jerusalem (see the NIV footnote).[5]

3:1 *I looked . . . did not find him.* Verses 1–4 may describe a dream or something the woman imagines as she longs for her absent lover at night. Despite her desire and fervent search, she could not find him. This likely describes the common fear of losing someone precious, which seems even more ominous at night, as imagination runs wild.

3:4 *mother's house . . . one who conceived me.* The mention of conception raises the possibility that the woman's goal was a sexual encounter with her lover and perhaps reflects what she imagined as she fantasized about the full physical expression of their

The woman compares her beloved to a gazelle. His excitement as he comes to her is like the leaping and bounding of these agile creatures as they travel the mountains. Shown here are three gazelles on a hillside in the Judean wilderness.

love in marriage. Campbell, though, has suggested that "in some circle of custom, hinted at by the Song of Songs passages; Genesis 24:28; and Ruth 1:8, the 'mother's house' was the locus for matters pertinent to marriage, especially for discussion and planning for marriage."[6]

3:5 *Do not arouse or awaken love until it so desires.* This is likely a warning to the young women watching this couple to wait for such a relationship to develop rather than trying to force it. It is also a warning about the physical expression of love apart from the appropriate context. See the commentary on Song of Songs 2:7.

Theological Insights

It is difficult to derive theological insights from poetry; it is not unlike trying to diagnose Job's malady from the poetry in that book. In Song of Songs the task is complicated by the nature of love poetry, with its propensity for ambiguity and for double meanings that both reveal and hide, and by the complex nature of love and romance and its inexplicable effects on those caught up in it. Gaining theological insights in this book is made even more difficult by the book's failure to mention God or morality. The context for the book, as we possess it, is the canon of Scripture and the Old Testament wisdom literature, and this allows us to affirm that the relationship between a man and woman, in its sexual, emotional, psychological, and spiritual dimensions, is a part of God's "very good" design (Gen. 1:31). Among the things in Proverbs 30:18–19 that are too wonderful for the sage and beyond his understanding is "the way of a man with a young woman," but verse 20 makes it clear that male-female

relationships can also go terribly wrong as it affirms that the adulteress eats and drinks and wipes her mouth and says, "I've done nothing wrong." Developing a useful understanding of relationships, how they work, and where they can go wrong cannot be limited to narrowly focused texts like this section. That task requires bringing together knowledge available from general revelation[7] and integrating it with moral and theological understanding that comes to us in special revelation. (See also the "Additional Insights" section after this unit.)

Teaching the Text

Passion, excitement, and desire characterize the woman's speech as she describes her lover and their relationship in terms of beautiful and delightful things in the world around them. This section affirms the importance of making praise an intentional part of a relationship. Focused reflection on the good attributes of the person we love and regularly communicating our praise contribute to a growing appreciation for the beauty and worth of our beloved. Regularly expressing appreciation to that person fuels the flames of the relationship and helps keep passion and excitement alive and growing.

In 2:16 the woman describes their mutual commitment, and this is a fundamental characteristic of a relationship that functions according to Yahweh's order. Appearance, charm, a delightful personality, and other pleasing qualities may be nice, but a successful relationship between a man and a woman begins with a fundamental and irrevocable commitment to each other. Most marriages in the ancient world were

The Delight of Anticipation

arranged, and the couple's respect for parents and the values of the clan and culture led to a commitment rarely based on love but which would hopefully blossom into love. Such commitment creates an environment where the trust, respect, and valuing of the other that we see in the Song can develop. Commitment provides a solid basis for love and romance, while romance and passion without commitment regularly lead to pain and futility.

The Song acknowledges the excitement and passion between this man and woman and the physical desires that love engenders. When the Song is set in its canonical context, the implication is that sexuality and its related desires are a good and beautiful part of God's design and order, though they must be enjoyed in the right ways and at the appropriate times. Both wisdom literature and the rest of the Old Testament see the commitment of marriage as the one appropriate context for the full physical expression of love. Many find it unimaginable that the woman, after expressing such intense desire and longing, could conclude that this was not the time or place for their sexual intimacy to begin. Hess says,

This picture of delayed gratification challenges all who would see this book either as a biblical license for free sex or as a manual for a successful marriage. It is neither. . . . It is erotic love poetry that makes no apology for appealing to all of the senses that God has created. Yet it also affirms that there is an order to this wonderful gift of sex. Its potency and wildness does not mean that there is no restraint.[8]

The idea that the couple was not married and that they anticipated and desired the full physical expression of their love but did not engage in it prior to a commitment in marriage sounds strange in today's culture, but it does seem more true to life than many secular and post–sexual revolution interpretations. Anticipation has always been an important part of love and romance.

Illustrating the Text

Sexuality and desire are designed by God as good and beautiful gifts.

Poetry: "A White Rose," by John Boyle O'Reilly. In this poem, O'Reilly (1844–90), using the colors of roses metaphorically, contends that love that contains desire is a superior love.

> The red rose whispers of passion,
> And the white rose breathes of love;
> O, the red rose is a falcon,
> And the white rose is a dove.

But I send you a cream-white rosebud
With a flush on its petal tips;
For the love that is purest and sweetest
Has a kiss of desire on the lips.[9]

In God's design, sexuality is best enjoyed in the right ways and at the right times.

Personal Testimony: My (Edward's) wife once taught in a high school program designed to help girls who were pregnant or already had babies to finish high school. As she heard many of the girls' stories, a common pattern emerged. Many of them had never experienced true love from anyone, though they deeply desired love. Over and over they reported how they had become sexually involved with someone because they thought such intimacy would bring the commitment and love they so desperately wanted. What they consistently discovered, however, was that love really cannot be forced or manipulated by physical intimacy. Instead, their "intimate encounters" brought them only pain and difficulty—something they did not anticipate.

Quote: *Sex for Christians*, **by Lewis Smedes.** "We cannot depersonalize our sex acts without dehumanizing ourselves in some measure. Our sexuality defines our personhood too fully."[10]

The desire of the woman for her beloved is illustrated by her search for him through the dark city streets and squares. This aerial view of ancient Beersheba shows what a city layout would have looked like. The path through the gate entrance in the foreground wall approaches the plaza through an inner gate with chambers where watchmen would have rested between rounds. The open plaza and the streets that led to public buildings and private residences are clearly visible.

Boundaries as Part of God's Order

While the Song of Songs and the rest of Scripture provide important details about relationships that function according to God's order, this must be supplemented with the wisdom that comes through human observation, tradition, and trial and error. Because the Song blurs past, present, and future as well as anticipation and experience, it is impossible to be certain about chronology and the flow of the story. One can, however, read the story in a way that sees this section (2:8–3:5) as describing the couple before they were married and suppose that the couple's behavior before marriage was consistent with biblical moral values and what we know of Israel's cultural expectations. Reading the story in this way also illustrates important principles about relationships and how they develop. The ambiguity of the Song's language captures something of the complicated character of relationships and the multifaceted nature of human responses. Bergant says that the

Song of Songs recognizes the power of passion but cautions, "Do not arouse or awaken love until it so desires" (3:5). This plaque shows a man and woman with their arms entwined. In the ancient world, this display of affection would only have been appropriate for married couples (Ur, 2000–1750 BC).

logical tensions that we see in the Song may capture some of this: "What could appear to be contradictory descriptions are really metaphorical attempts to portray various features of these complex individuals and the passionate emotional attachment that they have for each other."[1] Of course, the emotions of romance are often overpowering and pull people in very different directions. Moral values and cultural expectations regularly define appropriate responses, though intense romantic passions often lead people to act in disregard of such conventions. Certainly one of the important teachings of the book is to alert people to the power of love and passion and warn them that such powerful forces must be constrained by God's order so as to bring the delight and mutual help that God intended rather than pain and misery.

Relationships involve the whole person, and healthy relationships must develop in a balanced way. The Song describes the physical urges that are innate to human sexuality. While these urges are a part of God's design and are good, when isolated from the emotional and psychological aspects of relationships they can reduce this good gift of God to lust, with its profoundly devastating consequences. This section of the Song likely illustrates the role of thought and imagination in developing relationships. Gledhill says,

> Our imaginations often run far ahead of our physical reactions and they in turn run far ahead of what our actual relationship may be able to bear at that particular moment. When the physical outstrips the fully personal, emotional and psychological integration of the two lovers, the danger signals should start flashing. Adulterous thoughts, thoughts of fornication are all too easy to entertain in the abstract, divorced from a relationship that is developing healthily at its own pace. It seems that the girl in the song recognizes that here. She wants their love to be consummated, but she is in great tension, because she knows that the time is not yet ripe. . . . For the Christian, the appropriate time is always within marriage, never outside it.[2]

Physical intimacy can easily result from a desire for immediate personal gratification and pleasure. When it is separated from a context of commitment and profound respect for another person made in God's image, God's gift is distorted and often leads to pain and chaos. The sexual revolution has made it difficult for modern readers to read a section like this without supposing that the couple's interactions led to intercourse. While it goes beyond what the text actually teaches, it is worth pointing out that the biblical morality, while appearing naïve and antiquated to many moderns, does deliver those who practice it from many common problems, such as guilt that adversely impacts future relationships, sexually transmitted diseases, unwanted pregnancies, destroyed marriages with the consequent damage to both children and parents, and other detrimental effects of sex without commitment. In addition, sexual intercourse appears to play an important role in psychological and physiological bonding between a man and a woman, and it seems likely that the inevitable (but often unwanted) bonding that takes place in casual sex has the potential for causing people significant problems in future relationships. Abandoning God's order in this area appears to lead not to the freedom that many people imagine but to enormous negative consequences and even bondage. Perhaps these ancient sages and those who practiced their teaching were on to something when it comes to how a relationship between a man and a woman is supposed to work. It is difficult to imagine that the broader biblical values are not presupposed by the author of this book.

You Are Beautiful, My Love:
Delight and Consummation

Big Idea *The lover praises his beloved.*

Understanding the Text

The Text in Context

Song of Songs 3:6–11 describes a royal wedding. Nothing explicitly connects it to the marriage of the man and the woman in the Song, but the best way to integrate the section with the rest of the book seems to be to understand it as describing their wedding, which through their eyes is a royal one. The poem suggests that in the eyes of each lover the other is royalty. The luxury, extravagance, and excitement described in the passage suggest the value they place on committed love.

Song of Songs 4:1–7 is defined by the words, "How beautiful you are, my darling" (4:1), and the unit ends with similar wording. In 4:9–15 the man praises the woman's beauty and describes its effect on him. His praise gives way, in 4:16, to the woman's invitation for him to make love to her, an invitation that leads to the consummation of their relationship in 5:1.

Historical and Cultural Background

Descriptions of lovers as "brother/sister" and of a woman's sexuality as a verdant garden are found in Mesopotamian and Egyptian love poetry and reflect a common stock of metaphors from which poets drew. Terms like "you have stolen my heart" (4:9) are also found in Mesopotamia and Egypt. The poem of descriptive praise in 4:1–5 is the first of four examples in the Song of poems describing a woman's beauty.

Similar poems, called *wasfs*, are known from Arabic literature. The descriptions typically begin with her head and move to her feet. These similarities demonstrate that the biblical literature did not originate in a cultural vacuum but reflects the language, shared experiences, and literary techniques of the Near Eastern cultures in which Israel was situated.

Interpretive Insights

3:6 *Who is this coming . . . ?* The author captures the excitement and anticipation of observers as they strain to see an approaching procession. They cannot make out the particulars, and it is only as the entourage comes closer that they begin to discern specific details. The "smoke" rising in the distance heightens the mystery and raises the excitement as they watch the procession approach. "Myrrh," "incense," and "spices" create an aura of luxury and extravagance and add a sensory dimension to the experience.

3:9–10 *King Solomon made for himself the carriage.* The word translated "carriage" is used in later Hebrew for the enclosed platform on which a bride was carried in a wedding procession. The splendid and extravagant nature of this piece of furniture is reflected in the costly and exotic material used to make it.

Garden imagery is used in love poetry throughout the ancient Near East. In Song of Songs, going to the garden and enjoying the delights of the garden may figuratively describe the sexuality of the woman, the physical attraction between the lovers, or the lovemaking itself. In this beautiful painted ivory plaque, Queen Ankhesenamun and King Tutankhamen stand in the royal garden as she offers him lotus flowers she has picked. Her outfit suggests that she is ready to respond to his passion (from the lid of a coffer from King Tutankhamen's tomb, Eighteenth Dynasty, ca. 1370–1352 BC).

Key Themes of Song of Songs 3:6–5:1

- The lover praises his beloved's remarkable beauty.
- Through the eyes of love he sees no defect in her.
- His delight in her magnifies his passion and desire for her.
- He respects her and waits for her willing participation in their lovemaking.

Historical Record or Poetic Ideal?

As Estes points out, "If the song were written as an imaginative poetic lyric rather than as a realistic autobiographical narrative, then the characters . . . could be regarded as idealizations of love. It could well be . . . that the Song of Songs is intended to be read as an extended proverb . . . of ideal intimacy instead of as the historical record of the relationship between two specific individuals."[a]

[a] Estes, "Song of Songs," 274–75.

3:11 *the crown . . . on the day of his wedding.* The crown was probably a headpiece worn by a groom rather than a royal crown. Isaiah 61:10 also mentions the headdress of a groom on his wedding day.

4:1 *Your eyes behind your veil.* The veil may support the idea that a wedding is being described. Van der Toorn says that "the principal ceremony in which the veil played a role is the wedding"[1] and adds, "It is indeed likely that the Israelite bride wore the veil as an ornament and as a symbol of chastity to be lifted at the consummation of the marriage."[2] The veil was removed in the privacy of the bridal chamber, and the guests saw her face only after she came out of the chamber. This practice often remains a part of the modern Jewish wedding ritual. As the man here looks at his beloved through the veil, which is obviously intended to conceal, his words may relate

Song of Songs 3:6–5:1

to earlier descriptions of her as a dove in inaccessible places in the rocks (2:14). Bergant says that this seems to be "the kind of concealment that beguiles rather than hides." Such a veil "accentuates the mysteriousness of the woman's eyes and makes them even more alluring."[3]

Your hair is like a flock of goats. The metaphor of goats descending down a hillside suggests dark, wavy hair gently flowing over her shoulders and down her back and perhaps recalls similar scenes the two have enjoyed in the country.

4:2 *Your teeth are like a flock of sheep.* The man praises both the whiteness and the evenness of the woman's teeth—something that would have been unusual in antiquity, where modern dental practices did not exist.

4:3 *halves of a pomegranate.* This may reflect the pattern or colors he sees as he observes her through the veil. The pomegranate was known for its sweetness and is frequently found in ancient Near Eastern literature and imagery as a symbol of love, fertility, and fruitfulness; sexual and erotic nuances are probably also reflected in his description. Keel suggests that the word for "temple" actually indicates the mouth or palate. The word for "halves" often means "slit" or "slice," and Keel suggests that the metaphor describes her open mouth, seen through her veil.[4]

4:4 *tower of David, built with courses of stone.* This ornamented tower was likely part of the defensive

structures of some city and was impressive, beautiful, and strong. Keel suggests that the metaphor refers to rows of necklaces, such as those depicted in many images from the ancient Near East.[5]

4:5 *twin fawns of a gazelle.* The man describes her breasts using the same metaphor that she has used to describe him in 2:16–17. Twin fawns grazing in a flower-filled meadow stir up feelings of softness, tranquility, and delight. Keel notes the numerous images of gazelles that have been found in Palestine—often depicted with lotus flowers[6]—and argues that gazelles, lotus flowers, and breasts are regularly symbols of life and renewal.[7] He adds that gazelles are sometimes depicted with love goddesses and in connection with the tree of life and says that they are "representatives of a joyful lust for life."[8]

4:6 *mountain of myrrh . . . hill of incense.* "Mountain" and "hill" are metaphors for her breasts, while perfumes and spices capture the pleasure and delight he anticipates as they make love. (See also the commentary on Song 1:12–14.)

4:8 *crest of Amana . . . top of Senir . . . summit of Hermon.* Amana, Senir, and Hermon, mountains in the Lebanon or Anti-Lebanon range to the

The woman's neck is described by her beloved as a tower built with stones on which shields hang. This may be a metaphor for the style of necklace depicted on this statue of a goddess found at the ancient city of Mari (Tell Hariri, Syria, 1850–1760 BC).

north of Israel, are impressive but some-what inaccessible. They are noted for their awe-inspiring beauty but are full of danger because of the terrain and animals such as lions and leopards. The metaphor reflects the woman's fears that make her, despite her passionate desire for her lover, reluctant to give herself fully to him. He sees her awesome beauty but recognizes that she remains inaccessible.

4:9 *my sister, my bride.* The "brother/sister" language is a term of endearment indicating the closeness of the lovers' relationship.

with one glance . . . one jewel. Her beloved is overwhelmed by the sight of her and by her presence. A single glance or the sight of a single stone from her jewelry is enough to sweep him off his feet.

4:10 *more pleasing is your love than wine.* The man repeats her praise for him in 1:2–3 and expands on her words. Her love/lovemaking and the exhilarating fragrance of her perfume are intoxicating and better than fragrant spices.

4:12 *a garden locked up . . . a spring enclosed, a sealed fountain.* Kings in the ancient Near East took great pride in their gardens,[9] which were places of relaxation and pleasure and produced an abundance of delightful sights, tastes, and smells. Love poetry often uses garden as a metaphor for female sexuality, as is the case here. Abundant water is necessary for a garden to flourish, and the lover describes his beloved as a garden, a spring, and a fountain. She is, though, a "garden locked" and a "sealed fountain" and remains inaccessible to him. Despite his passion for her, he wants her as a willing partner in their lovemaking and awaits her invitation before

enjoying the full delights of her love. Given the context, it is likely that Munro is correct when she suggests that the woman's reticence is related to "her independence and, in particular, her virginity. Neither is to be wrested from her."[10]

4:13–14 *orchard . . . choice fruits . . . every kind of incense . . . all the finest spices.* According to Exum this "cluster of metaphors . . . create[s] an overall picture of the woman as a fragrant . . . garden, where a bountiful meal of erotic delights awaits him."[11]

4:16 *my garden . . . his garden.* The man's praise is interrupted by her invitation to come into her garden—which she now describes as *his* garden—to enjoy its delights. Genuine love is characterized by a profound respect for the other; it must be freely and graciously given and received as a gift.

5:1 *I have come into my garden.* This verse is the midpoint of the book in terms of verses, and many see it as the high point of the book. The lover accepts his beloved's invitation, enters the previously locked garden, and enjoys its delicacies to the full. His acceptance of her gift of commitment to him is clear from his frequent repetition of the possessive suffix "my" in the sixteen words he speaks. Their sexual encounter is described in a way that elevates the experience above the coarse and purely sensual. As Bloch and Bloch say, "In our day it is the innocence of the Song, its delicacy, that has the power to surprise."[12]

Eat, friends, and drink. The invitation to eat and drink is likely directed both to the couple and to readers of the book; it stands as an invitation to learn about God's order from what they see and hear as they observe the lovers. They are to put into practice the attitudes and actions that are displayed here.

Theological Insights

Perhaps the central theological insight has to do with the good gift of relationship between a man and a woman that is part of the order God established at creation. This section describes the passion and delight of the man as he reflects on the beauty of this woman whom he loves and shows us that the sexual relationship between a man and a woman is a part of God's design, as is the mystery and delight of being in love with another person. The physical and sexual expression of love is celebrated in this passage and is seen as a gift from God to be enjoyed. The respect that the man has for the woman and the giving of one to the other that is central to love are clearly depicted and likely reflect a fundamental aspect of how this relationship is supposed to function.

Teaching the Text

The Song begins in the middle of an established relationship, presumably, because the principles emphasized in the Song are not contingent on how a relationship begins. It seems likely that God's order for relationships includes things like commitment, respect, love, and appreciation. Most marriages in Israel were arranged, and many would have begun with the two people having few feelings for each other beyond a sense of commitment to each other and the relationship—perhaps because cultural and family expectations gave them few other options. It is likely that the Song describes essential principles about how a relationship between a man and a woman should work, and these principles contribute to an environment that allows the relationship to grow and flourish.

This section shows us the mutual excitement, passion, and delight that can be experienced between a man and a woman. It demonstrates that love, including its sexual expression, is not manipulative or coercive but must be freely given and gratefully received. We see a relationship where both of them respect each other and value the other's needs and desires as much as their own. While the couple's mutual delight and desire for each other are evident throughout the Song, this passage focuses primarily on the man's passion as he praises his beloved's beauty.

Neither this section nor the book itself addresses the question of morality, but it seems unwise to teach the section without addressing these issues, especially in a culture that increasingly seeks to divorce sexual expression from morality. It seems appropriate to connect this to Genesis 2 and

The groom praises the beauty of his bride, remarking on many of the features that can also be seen in this tomb painting of an Egyptian woman. Notice her flowing hair, earrings, tiered necklace, and the perfumed cone on her head (tomb of Menna, fifteenth century BC).

affirm that, while a sexual relationship is an obvious part of the one-flesh relationship, it is only one part. The suitable helper that God made for Adam was not an inferior partner but one designed with strengths to complement the man's weaknesses. It seems obvious that the man is designed to help the woman at her points of weakness as well. The mutual help strengthens their relationship and facilitates their growth toward maturity—relational, emotional, intellectual, and spiritual. Its primary purpose is not personal sexual pleasure but to enable men and women to function as God designed them to.

Illustrating the Text

The lover's praise for the beloved demonstrates the value of committed love.

Psychology: John Gottman (b. 1942) is a psychologist and prominent researcher in marriage and parenting at the University of Washington. Gottman stresses the importance of praise between individuals. Based on over thirty years of research on relationships, he points out that in good and long-lasting relationships positive comments and behaviors between the parties outweigh negative ones by about twenty to one. In contrast, in relationships where the positive and negative comments and behaviors are equal, Gottman concludes, it is virtually certain the relationship will not last very long. He has also identified what he calls the Four Horsemen, which are behaviors that, if left unchecked, will quickly doom a relationship. These behaviors are criticism, contempt, defensiveness, and stonewalling. In contrast, among the things that he has found to be keys to lasting relationships are respect, acceptance, and friendship. Further, he notes the importance of mutuality in good relationships. Both partners need to feel that they have influence over the other and that the other seriously considers their opinions and responses. Many of these factors are also reflected in the Song of Songs.[13]

Poetry: *Sonnets from the Portuguese*, by Elizabeth Barrett Browning. In "Sonnet XXI," Browning shows the delight of hearing repeated affirmations of affection.

> Say over again, and yet once over again,
> That thou dost love me. Though the
>   word repeated
> Should seem "a cuckoo-song," as thou
>   dost treat it.
> Remember, never to the hill or plain,
> Valley and wood, without her
>   cuckoo-strain
> Comes the fresh Spring in all her green
>   completed.
> Belovèd, I, amid the darkness greeted
> By a doubtful spirit-voice, in that
>   doubt's pain
> Cry, "Speak once more—thou lovest!"
>   Who can fear
> Too many stars, though each in heaven
>   shall roll,
> Too many flowers, though each shall
>   crown the year?
> Say thou dost love me, love me, love
>   me—toll
> The silver iterance!—only minding,
>   Dear,
> To love me also in silence with thy
>   soul.[14]

A Wedding Described | Beyond Physical Beauty

While the suggestion must be understood as tentative, several things suggest that the description of a wedding may extend beyond Song of Songs 3:6–11. Posner says, "It appears that processions for both the bride and groom were a central part of the celebrations."[1] This was still the case in New Testament times and is confirmed by various rabbinic sources. Posner further notes that "until the destruction of the Temple both the bride and groom wore distinctive headdresses, sometimes of gold."[2] Munro points out that "the image of the veil may belong specifically to wedding imagery, as does the term of address, *kallâ*, 'bride' (4.9, 11, 12; 5.1), for although the Song is not concerned with marriage as such, it is

possible that elements are drawn from the marriage ceremony in order to celebrate love."[3] Van der Toorn makes it clear that the mention of the veil here does not prove that a wedding is being described, but he also affirms that the veil played an important role in the wedding ceremony—something that he asserts "is generally acknowledged."[4] Many understand "bride" to be a term of endearment in the Song and argue that it has nothing to do with the marital status of the lovers. The term is used six times in the Song, all in 4:8–5:1, and it normally means "bride" or "daughter-in-law." When it does not mean "daughter-in-law," it refers to a woman who is either married or a bride at the wedding ceremony. Garrett says, "There is no reason to assert that 'bride' does not have its normal meaning here. In the quasi-story that stands behind the Song, the man and woman are newly married. . . . It would be peculiar to use

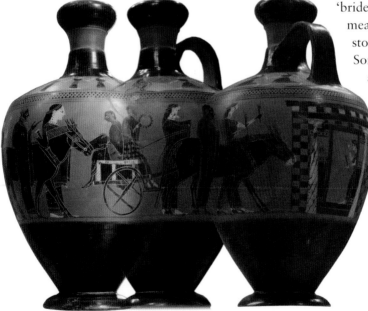

Song of Songs 3:6–11 may be describing a wedding procession. This Greek oil flask shows a bride and groom seated in a cart. The first attendant holds torches to lead the way while two more flank the donkeys. They are heading to the bridgroom's house (550–530 BC).

[*kallah*], 'bride,' as a term of affection for a woman who was not in fact one's bride."[5]

Munro argues that "in the course of the description of the garden, the emphasis changes from an evocation of the woman's virginal purity to the promise of life which she holds forth."[6] The Old Testament emphasis on the importance of a bride's virginity prior to marriage suggests that celebrating a sexual encounter outside the context of marriage would be unlikely in Hebrew culture and in the Bible. Thus it is plausible to see 3:6–11 as a description of their wedding, 4:1–15 as their private conversation after their marriage, the last part of 4:16 as her invitation to make love to her, and 5:1 as the consummation of their relationship.

Another relevant point that goes beyond what this section or the book itself explicitly teaches seems appropriate to affirm as well. It is obvious from the experiences of life, from empirical studies about relationships, and from wisdom material such as the early chapters of Proverbs that marriage does not guarantee the kind of relationship described in the Song. Even in the proper context, the love, mutuality, respect, delight, and praise that the book affirms must be cultivated and practiced in order for men and women to function in the ways that are seen here. Good relationships do not consist of a few bursts of fireworks like those described in the Song but must continue to develop over time if they are to reach the mature love that is the real goal.

Perhaps a digression from the text could focus on how people can be more intentional in recognizing that one's spouse is a good gift from God and letting him or her know that. While these verses focus on the lover's delight in his beloved's physical attributes and their physical intimacy, it should be recognized that a person's beauty often lies in realms other than the physical, as Proverbs 31:30 makes clear. It is important to be disabused of the idea that beauty consists only in superficial things like physical attributes and includes character as well. It is also important to emphasize the error in supposing that sex is the ultimate goal of every relationship between a man and a woman.

What Is So Special about Your Beloved?

Big Idea *The woman's hesitation leads to frustrated desire and single-minded pursuit.*

Understanding the Text

The Text in Context

The woman's speech (5:2–8) is followed by two units of dialogue between her and the daughters of Jerusalem (5:9–16 and 6:1–3). Like Song of Songs 2:8–3:5, this section recounts an experience where the woman was dreaming at night about her absent lover. Her distress over his absence prompted her to seek him in the city, where she encountered the city watchmen and the daughters of Jerusalem. Both sections include an account of the man standing outside her house/door, desiring to be present with her. Differences exist in the role of the daughters of Jerusalem and in the response of the watchmen. Both sections include the woman's affirmation of the couple's mutual commitment (2:16 and 6:3), and many similarities exist in wording. This section also contains a *wasf*, a poem in which the woman praises her lover's body, beginning with his head and ending with his feet.[1] Typically, the poetic medium creates ambiguity in terms of whether the woman is describing something that actually took place or is metaphorically describing feelings and emotions that are commonly experienced in relationships. The woman's hesitation in responding to him results in separation, followed by her diligent search for him. She ends the section with a statement reflecting her confidence about their mutual commitment.

Historical and Cultural Background

A Sumerian poem describes the marriage of the deity Dumuzi to the goddess Inanna. The poem describes their marriage in terms of Inanna "opening the door of her house" to Dumuzi.[2] Jacobsen says that the "opening of the door by the bride to the bridegroom counted as the formal act that concluded a Sumerian marriage."[3] An Egyptian love poem in which a boy complains that he was kept outside of the girl's house perhaps provides a more relevant parallel:

> As for what she—(my) sister—did to
> me,
>   should I keep silent to her?

She left me standing at the door of her
	house
	while she went inside,
and did not say to me "Welcome!"
	but blocked her ears in *my* night.[4]

Parallels have been noted between this section in the Song and themes like the "excluded lover" or the "laments at the door" in Greek and Latin poetry, where lovers are prevented from gaining access to their beloved. Murphy says, "There is no reason to doubt that the biblical Song is indebted, at least indirectly, to older traditions of Near Eastern love poetry. Nor need one quarrel with the likelihood that some of these antecedent traditions had specifically sacral significance."[5] Israel, however, set this common language in a context informed by its unique theological and moral perspective. There are other thematic similarities between the Song and other love poetry. Things like anxiety over an absent lover or frustration over being denied entrance to the place where one's lover is are such common experiences in human love relationships that they can likely be accounted for simply on that basis.

Interpretive Insights

5:2 *I slept but my heart was awake.* This expression leaves it uncertain

whether this is an actual experience or a dream.

My beloved is knocking. The text gives no reason for the man's appearance, except to find respite from the uncomfortable conditions of the evening. The word "open" occurs three times in the passage (5:2, 5, 6), each time without an object. Exum observes that "its erotic suggestiveness [is] heightened by the absence of the direct object."[6]

5:3 *taken off my robe.* "Robe" is sometimes used of an undergarment and possibly indicates that the woman was wearing nothing else, perhaps another sexually suggestive statement.

5:4 *thrust his hand through the latch-opening.* This describes his attempt to open the door from the outside. His persistence has apparently increased her desire for him and prompted her to respond to his request. (See the sidebar, as well as the more detailed description in *ZIBBCOT*, 2:130–31.)

5:5 *my hands dripped with myrrh.* Myrrh was often associated with love or lovemaking and suggests that romantic passions have been

"I slept but my heart was awake" (5:2). This Egyptian figurine of a woman asleep on her bed may have been placed in a tomb as a magical object to ensure success in love in the afterlife (1550–1295 BC).

aroused. As Bergant notes, the poetic form "allows the poet to be sexually suggestive without being erotically explicit."[7]

5:6 *he was gone. My heart sank.* Munro says, "The effect of her delay is destructive beyond all her imaginings."[8] The woman's distress at his absence ("my heart sank") caused her to seek him immediately despite the risk of wandering through city streets late at night.

5:7 *The watchmen . . . beat me.* Perhaps the watchmen beat her because they assumed that no woman except a prostitute would be alone in the city at such a late hour. Middle Assyrian Law (ca. 1200 BC) indicates that a prostitute should be beaten with a club and have asphalt poured over her head. Her clothing was taken away from her as well. As Keel notes, "Even if Israel's practice were less brutal, the Assyrian background helps explain the rough treatment of the woman and, above all, the fact that they took away her mantle."[9]

5:9 *How is your beloved better than others . . . ?* The woman responds to this question by the daughters of Jerusalem with a poem celebrating her beloved's worth and noble virtues. Her description would probably provide little help in recognizing him but reveals how she views him. This man is too wonderful for her not to pursue him and do whatever is necessary to protect their relationship; he is too valuable to lose.

5:10 *radiant and ruddy.* These terms probably describe an appearance indicative of health, prosperity, or success. By comparing him with precious metals and rare and beautiful stones, she is likely affirming that, in her eyes, he is spectacular; he is truly "one in a million."

5:11–16 The woman's words bring to mind statues of deities from Mesopotamia and Egypt meant to inspire awe in those seeing them.[10] She is affirming the spectacular nature of this man. He has taken on larger-than-life qualities in her eyes. His strength is impressive; his beauty breathtaking; his worth immense. According to Exum, "Like gold, the man is rare, precious, and desired for his worth and beauty."[11]

5:12 *doves by the water streams, washed in milk, mounted like jewels.* She describes his eyes as he has described hers in 1:15 and 4:1, adding "by the water streams," perhaps to suggest peace and tranquility. Keel argues that she is describing a basin with doves sitting around the rim.[12] The basin full of milk would represent abundance, and white doves were particularly revered. Keel says that this would "emphasize the freshness, radiance, and happiness characteristic of eyes that proclaim love."[13]

5:13 *like lilies dripping with myrrh.* The connection between myrrh and lovemaking in the Song makes it likely that she is thinking about his kisses. Bergant says, "The man's lips are said to drip myrrh, a resin with intoxicating qualities that always carry erotic meaning in the Song. . . . The man's lips are extolled . . . for the enchantment that kissing them can generate."[14] Keel argues that the flower is the lotus and says, "The metaphor expresses not the form or the color of the lips but the enlivening effect of their kisses. . . . The man's kisses are like life-giving amulets."[15]

5:14 *lapis lazuli.* This beautiful blue stone (from the northeastern part of what is today Afghanistan) was highly prized in the ancient world. It was being mined there as early as the third millennium BC.

5:15 *Lebanon, choice as its cedars.* Cedar from Lebanon was valued by kings for their building projects and was used in constructing the temple in Jerusalem as well as David's and Solomon's palaces. Its aromatic quality makes it resistant to dry rot and damage from insects, and it was renowned for its strength. The metaphor affirms the man's magnificent and breathtaking appearance as well as his strength.

5:16 *His mouth is sweetness itself.* Using words similar to those he uses of her in 4:11, she reiterates the delight that she finds, possibly in his words, but more likely in his sweet kisses.

he is altogether lovely. In 4:7 he describes her as "altogether beautiful," and here she makes a similar point, using a different word, which normally emphasizes "the attractiveness of an object, with some emphasis on the value of the object."[16]

She is probably standing, with hands on her hips, as she emphatically says to the daughters of Jerusalem, "This is what my beloved is like! This is why he is so special! Now do you see why I cannot let anything undermine this relationship?" Fox says, "She speaks in triumphant satisfaction, as if her magnificent verbal creation has irrefutably answered the girls' skepticism."[17]

6:1–2 *to his garden ... to browse ... and to gather lilies.* The women's inquiry about where the woman's beloved has gone is not unexpected, since they want to search for her lover, but her response is surprising because it implies that she now knows where he is. This is poetry, and the logic of other genres is not to be expected. Her reply picks up on a number of expressions used earlier in the book. The woman herself is likely the garden, and she knows that he can be found with her, grazing and gathering lotus flowers, terms that imply intimacy (see the commentary on Song 2:16).

6:3 *I am my beloved's and my beloved is mine.* Her reflection about her lover has reaffirmed his immense worth to her and reminded her of a central reality in their relationship.

Theological Insights

The relationship in the Song has been characterized by mutual respect, praise, delight, and desire, but as the present section makes clear, the path of true love is not always smooth. The woman's hesitancy in responding to the man's request and his impatience in leaving prematurely create a problem, but she persistently seeks her lover despite personal inconvenience and risk. Her portrayal of him to the daughters of Jerusalem reveals much about their relationship, as she describes the beauty,

The woman says the appearance of her beloved is "like Lebanon, choice as its cedars" (5:15). Shown here is a large, stately cedar of Lebanon.

Ancient Locks

The statement of 5:4 about the lover thrusting his hand through the latch opening is perhaps explicated by an understanding of door locks in antiquity. By 1000 BC locks like this one were often used in the Near East:

> The mechanism consists of a key and a lock. The key is simply a bit of wood with small pins, usually of brass. These pins enter small holes in the bolt and lift similar pins in the lock. The pins of the key push the lock pins out of the holes, and the bolt can be moved aside and the door opened. When leaving the building, the bolt is slid across the door jamb, and the pins fall into the grooves in the bolt. To unlock, the key is slid into the opening in the bolt and lifted up, which moves the bolt-pins out of the way.[a]

It seems likely that the lover was attempting to lift the pins by reaching into the opening, and the woman was stirred by his efforts to be with her.

A replica of an ancient Egyptian pin-tumbler lock with key inserted.

[a] Mara Bishop and Amanda Payne Burton, "Tumbler Lock, Egypt, Iraq, Greece, 1000 BCE," Smith College History of Science, Museum of Ancient Inventions, http://www.smith.edu/hsc/museum/ancient _inventions/hsc09b.htm.

priceless qualities, and great worth that she finds in this unique man. The section also affirms the importance of the couple's commitment to each other. Her feelings about him are reciprocated, and this assures her that their relationship is intact.

Teaching the Text

The thin narrative thread makes it difficult to reconstruct the details of the story, and many details remain unclear, though several themes clearly should be emphasized. The first theme is the need to promptly respond to the needs and desires of one's mate despite distractions and inconveniences. Patience and understanding are needed virtues in relationships and are part of the mutuality that is essential in relationships of every sort. Often signals are not as overt as pounding on the locked door and asking that it be opened, but few qualities are more important in a relationship than the sensitivity to recognize needs and desires of a partner on the basis of subtle clues—sometimes even before the other person is consciously aware of them.

Second, it is important to recognize the degree to which the beloved values her lover, and he values her. Recognizing the great worth of another is facilitated by focused reflection on a person's good qualities; regularly praising another contributes significantly to a growing appreciation for that person.

A third theme is the idea that the sort of relationship described in this poem is built on a foundation of commitment, something that is difficult to understand in our culture where contracts, agreements, and commitments of virtually every kind are viewed as revocable. What is needed is a mind-set that takes one's words and promises seriously and recognizes the importance of honesty and integrity. It is important to regularly affirm our commitment to the one we love and to live it out in ways that build the kind of trust and confidence that will sustain the relationship in times of difficulty and struggle. The application of these principles has the power to move many marginal marriages (and other relationships as well) in the direction of the one depicted in the

Song, where husbands and wives, in the loving eyes of their spouses, take on the larger-than-life dimensions that we see in these poems. Such relationships, characterized by respect and praise, create a context where passion and delight can flourish and where others can see lived out before them aspects of God's love for his people. God is honored, and we find great delight in relationships that function according to God's design.

Illustrating the Text

Delayed response to a lover's needs can result in relational separation.

Literature: ***Gone with the Wind*, by Margaret Mitchell.** Both novels and movies sometimes set a stage on which a man is interested in a woman (or vice versa) but she is reluctant, despite his gallantry, compelling attributes, and obvious interest. Not until the plot turns, revealing the man facing some danger or having finally lost his devotion, does she realize what she could have had; then *she* pursues *him*. One of the most famous examples is the novel *Gone with the Wind* (1936). In this Civil War romance, the willful heroine, Scarlett O'Hara, is pursued by the dashing Rhett Butler. Only at the story's conclusion, when Rhett, now her husband, is finally weary of trying to win her love and leaves, does Scarlett realize what she has lost.

Lovers must express fully and specifically how much they value each other.

Poetry: Poets, on occasion, recognize that genuine beauty is found in more substantial qualities than appearance. "Sonnet XIV," one of the *Sonnets from the Portugese* by Elizabeth Barret Browning, shows this. "Amoretti," by Edmund Spenser, affirms the point well:

> Men call you fair, and you do credit it,
> For that yourself ye daily such do see:
> But the true fair, that is the gentle wit
> And virtuous mind, is much more
>   praised of me.
> For all the rest, however fair it be,
> Shall turn to naught and lose that glorious hue;
> But only that is permanent and free
> From frail corruption that doth flesh
>   ensue.
> That is true beauty; that doth argue you
> To be divine, and born of heavenly
>   seed;
> Derived from that fair Spirit, from
>   whom all true
> And perfect beauty did at first proceed:
>   He only fair, and what he fair hath
>   made;
>   All other fair, like flowers, untimely
>   fade.[18]

Song of Songs 5:2–6:3

The Spectacular Delights of Love

Big Idea *Regular and repetitive praise contributes significantly to the delights of love.*

Understanding the Text

The Text in Context

This section begins with another poem praising the woman's beauty and describing its effect on the man. It is perhaps his response to her fears about their separation and assures her that he remains irrevocably committed to her. He is overwhelmed by her spectacular beauty, which prompts women, from queens to ordinary citizens, to praise her and call her blessed. Song of Songs 6:4–10 is a small subunit that begins and ends with the same Hebrew phrase (NIV: "majestic as troops" [v. 4]; "majestic as the stars" [v. 10]). The man praises his beloved in 7:1–9 in perhaps the most erotic poem in the book, and the woman responds in 7:10–13 by inviting him to join her in the country, where she will give him her love.

Historical and Cultural Background

Ancient Near Eastern texts often see erotic associations with apples, pomegranates, vines, gardens, nuts, and mandrakes, as does the Song. A boy in Egypt compares his girl with the rising of a star and praises her beauty in a way that resembles the Song.[1] The metaphor of the man being captured by her hair is also found in an Egyptian poem that says,

> With her hair she lassos me,
> with her eye she pulls (me) in,
> with her thighs she binds,
> with her seal she sets the brand.[2]

Interpretive Insights

6:4 *as beautiful as Tirzah . . . Jerusalem.* Tirzah was the capital of the northern kingdom for about fifty years. Excavations there have revealed significant building during the time of Solomon,[3] suggesting that it was "a city renowned for its beauty and strength."[4] Jerusalem was located on a hill surrounded on three sides by valleys and

In 6:1 the woman's loveliness is likened to Jerusalem and Tirzah, royal cities of the monarchial period. This comparison may be due to elegant architectural features such as the Proto-Aeolic capital (top of a column) that graced palaces and public buildings during this time. Shown here is a Proto-Aeolic capital from Ramat Rachel, where it was once part of a seventh-century BC palace. The carving on the capital may represent a palm tree or the tree-of-life motif common in Assyrian reliefs, images of fertility and life.

would have been an impressive sight. This woman's stunning beauty creates in the man the same feelings of awe produced when one sees a splendid city like Tirzah or Jerusalem.

as majestic as troops. The Hebrew word translated as "majestic" also appears in Habakkuk 1:7 (NIV: "feared"), and its use there suggests that her beauty leaves him awestruck, as would seeing a powerful army on the move.

6:8–9 *Sixty queens . . . and eighty concubines.* "Sixty" and "eighty" are probably figures for a large number. Keel suggests that these are categories of women associated with the royal court.[5] The use of the plural "queens" is unusual because a king would normally have only one queen, but the word probably includes all the king's wives. Concubines were wives of secondary rank. Keel suggests that the "young women" were "young girls at court, daughters who provide various services, gaining in turn an education that will enable them to marry well."[6] Walton has argued that these were women in the harem who had not yet had children.[7] This woman's qualities surpass even the elite women in society, and even they are forced to acknowledge her excellence.

6:10 *like the dawn, fair as the moon, bright as the sun.* The man compares her to the dawn, the sun, the moon, and the stars of the heavens, all of which inspired such awe in the ancient world that they were deified by Israel's neighbors.[8] As Garrett says, "While the woman receives extravagant, hyperbolic praise, she is not divinized (nor is this a hymn in praise of a goddess)."[9]

6:11 *grove of nut trees . . . vines . . . pomegranates.* The woman probably went to the nut orchard to check on the new spring growth, but as Pope points out,

in ancient Near Eastern mythology, nuts were thought to possess both magical and sexual properties,[10] and the same is true with vines and pomegranates in the Song. Bergant says, "Whatever the exact meaning of this reference may be, its exotic and erotic character is unmistakable."[11] The woman will echo these words in 7:12.

6:12 *my desire set me among the royal chariots.* The Hebrew text of this verse is obscure, to the extent that translations are little more than guesses.

6:13 *come back, O Shulammite.* The Hebrew word for "Shulammite" looks like a feminine form of "Solomon." It may be related to the word *shalom* and mean something like "perfect one." It could be another way of saying that the man finds no blemish in her (cf. 4:7; 5:2). On the lips of the friends, it may reflect sarcasm.

the dance of Mahanaim. Jacob camped at Mahanaim on his return from Aram, but we know nothing that would explain this reference or a dance related to the place.

7:1–9a The man again praises the woman's beauty, and his desire to enjoy the delights found in her is clear. While the author intends to communicate something specific about the features he describes, "the poem is not primarily visually descriptive, but rather the emotive response of the lover towards the beauty of his girl."[12]

7:1 *your sandaled feet.* Feet are not normally considered erotic or stimulating, but in the man's view every part of her body is beautiful. An account in the Apocrypha relates how Judith assassinates a general sent by Nebuchadnezzar against Jerusalem, and how his fascination with her feet contributed to his demise. According to Judith 16:9, "Her sandals caught his eyes, and her beauty captivated his mind. The sword cut through his neck" (NAB). His fascination with her feet proves fatal.

O prince's daughter! Song of Songs 1 suggests that the young woman is from the ordinary citizenry rather than from the country's elite, so "prince's daughter" probably means "noble woman" and reflects how the lover sees her.

Your graceful legs. "Graceful legs" is a paraphrase of the Hebrew term, meaning "curved or rounded thighs,"[13] which are as superbly crafted as beautifully designed jewelry.

7:2 *navel . . . waist . . . encircled by lilies.* Keel argues that "navel" is a euphemism for the vulva, while "waist" refers to the "womb," and concludes that the metaphors focus on the life-giving and sustaining powers of the woman. Wheat and wine represent nourishment and sustenance, and Keel sees the image of these things surrounded by lotus flowers (NIV: "lilies") as a powerful symbol of regeneration and life.[14] Thus the man is praising the woman for her ability to bring refreshment and new life to him and to bring children into the world.

7:4–5 *neck is like an ivory tower.* He likely praises her elegant and exquisite beauty and the delicate workmanship reflected in the smoothness of her neck. He could also be describing a beautiful and valuable ivory necklace that adorns her neck.

eyes are the pools of Heshbon. Keel notes that the pools in Heshbon attracted many from the desert who came to drink and refresh themselves. He says, "The beloved's eyes have the same effect . . . on her lover."[15]

like the tower of Lebanon . . . like Mount Carmel. The metaphors for the woman's nose and head perhaps describe something dominating and impressive. They may also reflect the value of products from Lebanon and Carmel.

Your hair is like royal tapestry. The Hebrew says literally, "your hair is like purple," but the comparison probably does not relate to color. The dye used to produce this color was obtained from a certain shellfish, and because it was so expensive, its use was limited to royalty and the very rich. "A king" (not "the king," as in the NIV) likely refers to her lover, who is captivated by her luxuriant hair.

7:6 *beautiful . . . delights.* Verse 6 ends with the same words with which the subsection began in verse 1 ("How beautiful") and introduces the next subunit, which describes his intention to enjoy these delights to the full.

7:7 *Your stature is like that of the palm.* The woman is tall and stately like the date palm, which sometimes reaches a height of eighty to a hundred feet. Keel says that the focus of the metaphor is "the beloved's abundant endowment with 'fruits'" and points to iconographic evidence relating the palm to the tree of life. He also says that "the palm was again and again closely connected with important goddesses."[16]

like clusters of fruit. Her breasts are like sweet dates, and he wants to taste and kiss them.

7:8–9a *I will take hold of its fruit.* According to Hess, the man's description of her "provide[s] a feast of sensuality."[17]

7:9b–10 *May the wine go straight to my beloved.* This is likely spoken by the woman since "my beloved" is her special term for him.

flowing gently over lips and teeth. The NIV's translation of the end of verse 9 reflects the change of a single letter in the Hebrew text, which many conclude does not make sense. Hess argues that the present text, as reflected in the NASB translation ("flowing gently through the lips of those who fall asleep"), "may suggest the collapse into sleep that comes after the frenzy of lovemaking."[18]

I belong to my beloved. She affirms her fundamental commitment to him, and elsewhere (2:16; 6:3; and likely 8:6) his commitment to her is affirmed in similar terms. She recognizes his strong sexual desire for her, and as the following verses make clear, the desire is mutual.

7:11–13 *to see if the vines have budded.* Springtime, gardens, budding plants, pomegranates, and vineyards are regularly associated with love in the Song and combine to create a picture of the spectacular delights the couple anticipate sharing together.

mandrakes send out their fragrance. Mandrakes have a long root similar to a potato and have long been used in folk medicine and as an aphrodisiac.

"The mandrakes send out their fragrance" (7:13). Mandrake plants produced yellow-orange fruit that yield the pleasing aroma mentioned here. They were part of cultivated gardens in ancient Egypt. This painting from the Tomb of Nebamun (fourteenth century BC) shows a beautiful garden where date palms, sycamore figs, and mandrake plants ring a pool containing fish and lotus plants.

Theological Insights

Love poetry is an unlikely vehicle for communicating or constructing theology, though sometimes connections with other passages make it likely that important theological issues are being addressed. The word for "desire" in 7:10 occurs elsewhere in the Bible only in Genesis 3:16 and 4:7. The Genesis passages are in contexts dealing with the consequences of the fall, and each uses almost identical language involving desire and ruling over. The Genesis 3 and Song passages use the word "desire" in contexts involving male-female relationships, though the tenor of the passages is different. Genesis 3:16 describes the consequence of Adam and Eve's disobedience for the woman and reflects a significant change in the one-flesh relationship. The harmonious and cooperative relationship designed to bless and facilitate full human function now involves fallen creatures, who are proud and self-centered. God's declaration in Genesis 3:16 begins by describing increased pain and risk in pregnancy and childbirth. It is difficult to imagine that "desire" is not related in some way to that aspect of the judgment, and this suggests that sexual desire is at least a part of the picture.

The desire is also related to the man's rule (a conclusion supported by the parallel in Gen. 4:7), and the verse suggests that human depravity both undermines the woman's response to the man and negatively impacts the way the man relates to his wife. Pride, selfishness, competition, and domination replace the cooperative, loving relationship that reflects God's order.

Song of Songs describes a relationship rooted in the couple's mutual desire and exclusive commitment to each other ("I am my beloved's and my beloved is mine," 6:3). Song of Songs 7:10 focuses on the man's desire for the woman, rather than her desire for him as in Genesis 3:16, and the things that characterize the relationship in the Song are very different from those implied in Genesis 3:16. There her desire for him is related to fallen man's ruling over her, and this leads to disastrous consequences for both women and men, as the history culminating in Genesis 6 makes clear. The inversion that we see between Genesis 3 and Song of Songs 7 likely has to do with Yahweh's order and how the man and woman relate to each other throughout the Song. The implication is that even in a fallen world people functioning in relationships according to God's order can avoid much of the chaos and disaster that result from human rebellion against God and disregard for his order. (See also the "Additional Insights" section after this unit.)

Teaching the Text

Many of the expressions used to praise the woman in this section occur throughout the book, and this suggests one important teaching point. Gledhill says,

> The language of love bears repeating. Relationships are oiled and progress more smoothly with a little bit of praise. It is not self-serving flattery, but a genuine desire to compliment the other. And it is often surprising how a small word of praise goes such a long way in energizing and establishing a relationship. If someone praises you, you are not likely to forget it readily. A certain amount of self-esteem, corroborated by a partner, does wonders for the system.[19]

It is important that the praise be regular rather than limited to special occasions or as something done to gain special favors. For this to become a regular habit, it will have to be intentionally cultivated.

This section also emphasizes the importance of an unconditional and single-minded commitment to one's beloved. It is the commitment reflected in Shakespeare's words: "Love is not love which alters when it alteration finds."[20] House and Durham observe, "According to God's Word, to be righteously married is to dance with the one who brought you, whether you arrived there through pre-arrangement or through romance."[21] This kind of commitment can be undermined in many ways. It can be eroded by looking at other people and imagining what life with them would be like or admiring their appearance or qualities and wishing one's spouse were more like that. It can be diluted through romance novels or movies that encourage an unhealthy focus on appearance or passion, and this, persisted in over time, can stimulate destructive lust. The distractions of life can cause us to take the one we love for granted. The kind of commitment that we see in the Song places limits on other relationships and determines what we do, where we go, and even the nature of our conversations with others, especially those of the opposite sex.

Illustrating the Text

Lovers see their beloved's beauty and attributes as greater than any other's.

Literature: *Romeo and Juliet*, by William Shakespeare. This tragedy, written early in Shakespeare's career, is a familiar and intense story about star-crossed young lovers. The following words spoken by Romeo to Juliet in act 1 reflect the truth of the principle above.

> O, she doth teach the torches to burn bright!
> It seems she hangs upon the cheek of night
> As a rich jewel in an Ethiop's ear—
> Beauty too rich for use, for earth too dear!
> So shows a snowy dove trooping with crows
> As yonder lady o'er her fellows shows.
> The measure done, I'll watch her place of stand
> And, touching hers, make blessed my rude hand.
> Did my heart love till now? Forswear it, sight!
> For I ne'er saw true beauty till this night. (act 1, scene 5)

Lovers must make an unconditional and single-minded commitment to each other.

Quote: *Adam Bede*, by George Eliot. "What greater thing is there for two human souls, than to feel that they are joined for life—to strengthen each other in all labour, to rest on each other in all sorrow, to minister to each other in all pain, to be one with each other in silent unspeakable memories at the moment of the last parting?"[22]

Poetry: "Let Me Not to the Marriage of True Minds," by William Shakespeare. In this well-known sonnet, Shakespeare describes true love as a fixed, unchanging, unshakable mark that does not admit impediments, that remains stable through every storm, and that outlasts the changes that time brings to the human face and body.

> Let me not to the marriage of true minds
> Admit impediments. Love is not love
> Which alters when it alteration finds,
> Or bends with the remover to remove:
> O no! it is an ever-fixed mark
> That looks on tempests and is never shaken;
> It is the star to every wandering bark,
> Whose worth's unknown, although his height be taken.
> Love's not Time's fool, though rosy lips and cheeks
> Within his bending sickle's compass come:
> Love alters not with his brief hours and weeks,
> But bears it out even to the edge of doom.
> If this be error and upon me proved,
> I never writ, nor no man ever loved.[23]

Song of Songs 6:4–7:13

Relationships That Reflect Yahweh's Order | Moving beyond Song of Songs

While some have suggested that Song of Songs reveals a way to regain paradise and return to Eden, Gledhill points out that the consequences of the fall on humanity make this impossible, either theologically or morally.

> Man and woman were expelled from the garden for their rebellion, for their insubordination in refusing to accept their creaturely status as dependent upon their Creator. This rebellion against their Maker not only fractured their relationship with him, but their relationship to each other and to their environment was also irreversibly disrupted.[1]

The consequences of the fall were too far-reaching for human beings to repair the damage and construct a path back to Eden. As Gledhill says, "This is simply because our sexuality, our wills, our minds have all been affected by the fall. To pretend that they have not been is to live in a fool's paradise of self-delusion."[2]

Even as we assent to this reality, Song of Songs also alerts us to another dimension of living in a fallen world. The Song shows us a man and a woman relating to each other in ways that are not adversarial, combative, or self-serving but reflect valuing another person as a lover—and as another person made in God's image. It shows two people expressing their love and gratitude to each other for that person's contribution to the other's life. We likely see a relationship operating according to Yahweh's order and observe the benefits and delight that result. It is a relationship characterized by praise, honor, valuing, and respect, and it is set in a context of mutual commitment. It is also a relationship that is in process, and it is perhaps legitimate to infer that we are seeing more than just romantic passion and fireworks. The actions and attitudes depicted here, persisted in over time, are likely a key to developing the love and trust that is characteristic of

The author of Song of Songs uses garden imagery to describe both a beautiful meeting place and the delights that await the couple as they anticipate being together. One of the plants included in the garden descriptions is the pomegranate. Shown here is a bush in bloom with several fruits starting to grow.

mature and healthy relationships. Since most marriages in Israel did not begin with love and romantic passion but were arranged, it may well be that what the Song shows us is particularly significant in moving a relationship—however it began or wherever it presently is—toward the goal that reflects God's purpose in the one-flesh relationship. This picture stands in strong contrast with the dysfunctional, manipulative, and abusive relationships that history reveals and that popular culture sets before us as normative.

A psychologist was asked after a presentation on marriage at a church, "What are the things that are necessary for a successful Christian marriage?" He answered, "The same things that are necessary for a successful non-Christian marriage." His point was that the curse in Genesis 3:16 does not describe the inevitable reality of marriage after the fall, and people who are not Christians can still live according to God's order. They can live with some degree of wisdom; they can respect others and treat them with kindness and civility. One does not have to be a religious person to be faithful to a spouse or to live with integrity and honesty in that relationship. Nor does being a Christian guarantee that a person will possess these virtues and live them out in his or her relationships. Relationships that function according to Yahweh's order can, to a large degree, experience the delight and blessing that God designed into the one-flesh relationship and that we see depicted in Song of Songs. While people who live according to Yahweh's order do not return to Eden and paradise, they do put themselves into a position to experience more fully the relational blessings that God desires for humanity. They also avoid much of the chaos and many of the difficulties that result from rejecting God's instruction and living in ways that are incongruent with his order.

Paul's advice to husbands and wives in Ephesians 5:21–33 is set in a radically different context—that of the character transformation that results from regeneration—but he includes many of the attitudes and practices depicted in the Song. The broader context for his instruction for marriage has to do with values and behaviors that should characterize every relationship of believers, and these include such things as using words that build up and give grace to those who hear them (4:29); avoiding bitterness, wrath, and anger (4:31); showing forgiveness and kindness to one another (4:32); avoiding sexual immorality (5:3–5); and submitting to one another out of reverence for Christ (5:21). That such attitudes and behaviors are expected in the relationship between a husband and a wife is evident from Paul's exhortation for a husband to love his wife with the same kind of sacrificial love that Christ demonstrated toward the church—a love that is not selfish but focuses on the well-being and best interests of the other person. It is a love that reflects the kind of humility that is seen in the incarnation (Phil. 2:5). Such love is content to serve the other rather than demanding that the other serve oneself. Such environments create a context where relationships can flourish and move closer to that which the one-flesh relationship was meant to be.

The Awesome Power of Love

Big Idea *Love is characterized by awesome power and fierce persistence.*

Understanding the Text

The Text in Context

This entire section lacks thematic coherence. It is likely that Song of Songs 8:1–4 belongs in the previous section, since the warning in verse 4 has previously ended sections. But given 8:1–4's lack of clear connection with the previous section, I will discuss these verses in this final section. Verses 1–4 describe the woman's frustration over social constraints about expressing their love in public. Verses 6–7 represent the climax of the book's teaching and deal with the power and nature of true love. Verses 8–10 describe a conflict with the woman's brothers regarding her maturity and readiness for a romantic relationship. Verses 11–12 contrast Solomon's "vineyard"[1] with the couple's relationship. Verses 13–14 end the book but leave the story open ended as the woman sends the man away but then calls him back to her as she did in 2:17. According to Exum this structure reflects "a design that makes the Song, in effect, a poem without beginning or end. Like the love it celebrates, the Song of Songs strives to be ongoing, never-ending."[2]

Historical and Cultural Background

Creation in the ancient Near East was often described as a struggle between the forces of order and chaos, and while those metaphors do not play a significant role in the Genesis accounts, other passages (allusions in Job, a few psalms, and Isaiah) make it clear that these stories were known to the biblical authors. The sea, the flood, deep waters, and darkness were deified in ancient Near Eastern mythology and represented forces of chaos that had the power to extinguish organized human society and the cosmos. Ancient creation accounts often focus on bringing order, purpose, and function to disorder rather than creating that which did not exist before, and these ideas perhaps provide a background for some of the metaphors used in this section.

Interpretive Insights

8:1 *like a brother . . . I would kiss you.* Kissing one's brother in public was apparently acceptable, while kissing a lover—or even a spouse—was not. "Sister" was used earlier as a term of endearment (e.g., 4:9–12; 5:1), but here "brother" refers to a blood relative.

8:2 *she who has taught me.* The Hebrew form is ambiguous (it could be translated either "she taught me" or "you taught me"), and it is unclear who did the teaching and what was taught. Perhaps this was general knowledge, including information about love and romance that a mother would teach a daughter.

I would give you spiced wine. The woman imagines giving her lover spiced wine and the nectar of her pomegranates, with its erotic associations, likely as a prelude to intimacy.

8:4 *Do not arouse or awaken love.* Munro says one purpose of the Song is to warn young women "that love is not to be meddled with. . . . If the Song evokes the experience of love in order to demonstrate its power, . . . it is in order to protect these young women lest they open themselves to love too soon."[3] (See also the commentary on Song 2:7.)

8:5 *Who is this . . . ?* Previously, the warning to the daughters of Jerusalem was followed by the appearance of the beloved (or Solomon's sedan chair). This time it is followed by the woman with her beloved.

I roused you . . . your mother conceived you. "Roused" and "conceived" have strong sexual connotations, and the woman is likely reflecting back on the time when their love was first stirred.

Ecclesiastes 8:1 seems to indicate that it was not socially acceptable for lovers to be seen kissing in public. This clay plaque from ancient Iran shows a couple kissing (third century BC to first century AD).

8:6 *like a seal over your heart . . . on your arm.* Seal impressions were used to indicate ownership of material, and, on correspondence, indicated that a document was authentic and came with the sender's authority. Longman says that "she wants him to willingly give himself to her."[4] Putting her seal on his heart may reflect the personal and private nature of their commitment, while her seal on his arm represents a public declaration of it.

its jealousy unyielding as the grave. Carr says, "When death summons, each one answers, so too, when love calls, that call is irresistible."[5] "Jealousy" ("its" is not in the Hebrew) is a synonym for "love," and Yahweh's jealousy for Israel likely defines what is involved here. Israel had the assurance of God's passionate commitment to it, but he also required its exclusive commitment to him—Israel was to have no other gods before him. As Garrett says, "Those who passionately love are passionately possessive. . . . Exclusivity is not of itself

Song of Songs 8:1–14

corrupt or oppressive. . . . The term [jealousy] refers to a proper possessiveness in the setting of a wholesome relationship. Rightly experienced by healthy souls, this exclusivity is part of the glory of love and further indicates the seriousness of entering this relationship."[6]

It burns like blazing fire, like a mighty flame. Love burns with an intensity that not even a flood of waters can extinguish (v. 7). The expression "mighty flame" ends with a shortened form of the name Yahweh, and some translate the phrase "flame of the Lord" (so ESV; see NIV footnote). It is also possible that "flame of Yahweh" is a term for lightning, an appropriate parallel to "blazing fire" in the previous line.

8:7 *Many waters cannot quench love.* Love resists the most formidable obstacles that can confront a couple. In view of the mythological allusions that likely lie in the background, the author may be suggesting that love can resist even those forces that want to plunge the world into chaos and disrupt life as God intended it. Estes says, "As 7:10 alludes to love as a partial triumph over the curse on humanity, so also 8:6–7 perhaps suggests that in God's design love functions to counteract the destructive effects of chaos that threaten to extinguish life."[7]

If one were to give all the wealth of one's house. The kind of passion for another person described in the Song is a gift. It cannot be bought or sold, and every attempt to do so will be received with contempt.

8:8 *We have a little sister.* The woman's brothers think their little sister is too immature for marriage and want to guard her chastity. She and her lover vigorously disagree (v. 10).

8:9 *If she is a wall . . . If she is a door.* A wall is meant to keep people out and probably represents chaste behavior. If the brothers see prudent behavior, they will reinforce her inaccessibility and enhance her beauty with towers of silver. A door lets people in, and if they see inappropriate behavior, they will nail the door shut with cedar boards to protect her virtue.

8:10 *I am a wall, and my breasts are like towers.* The woman insists that she is sexually mature and that her virtue is intact. She may also be asserting her right to make her own decisions about love and romance.

like one bringing contentment. The word for "bringing" can also mean "finding," and both meanings may be intended here. Her lover agrees that she is sufficiently mature to bring well-being and contentment to him, but in their relationship she will also find peace/contentment. Bringing and finding *shalom* may well be a goal of the seeking and finding seen throughout the book.

8:11–12 *Solomon had a vineyard in Baal Hamon.* Verse 11 probably refers to an actual vineyard that Solomon placed into the care of managers, perhaps like an arrangement between an owner and a tenant farmer. In the light of verse 12, it is possible that Solomon's great "holdings in women" are also in view. We do not know of a place named Baal Hamon, but the name means "Master of great wealth" and could even mean "Master (or husband) of a multitude." Presumably, each tenant had to pay Solomon a "thousand shekels" for the use of the vineyard and then received "two hundred" shekels in compensation for the work.

my own vineyard is mine to give. The meaning of "vineyard" changes in verse

According to 8:12, tenant farmers tended and harvested the grapes in Solomon's vineyards. This ancient Egyptian painting from the Tomb of Nakht shows grapes being gathered (Valley of the Nobles, Thebes, Egypt, Eighteenth Dynasty, ca. 1567–1320 BC).

8:14 *Come away . . . on the spice-laden mountains.* She responds to his request to hear her voice (v. 13) by inviting him to join her. The reference to "spice-laden mountains" is probably an allusion to her breasts, as representative of all her charms and the delight they will bring him. The Song ends without finality or closure, and, as Bergant says, "As incomplete as this may sound, it is also quite true of authentic love. Human love knows no definitive consummation, no absolute fulfillment. Loving relationships are never complete; they are always ongoing, always reaching for more. Regardless of the quality or frequency of lovemaking, there is always a measure of yearning present."[10]

Theological Insights

God's work in creation involved bringing order and purpose to the world. As Walton says, "God made everything just right and set it up to function properly within his purposes. . . . He demonstrates his power and sovereignty by bringing the cosmos into conformity with his purposes."[11] Understanding and living according to God's order decreases disharmony and reduces the adverse consequences that come from disregarding God and his wisdom. While the consequences of the fall and human depravity are broad and extensive, this section suggests that men and women functioning in relationships characterized by love, with its consequent

12, where the vineyard becomes the woman herself, including her body and sexuality, which she freely gives to the man she loves. The verse likely contrasts a relationship based on love and self-giving for the benefit of the other with the king's affairs (commercial and also harem related), which were managed by others and brought him benefits (income and physical pleasure). This understanding leaves no exact correspondence at the figurative level with the thousand and two hundred shekels, but as Exum says, "Because Solomon's vineyard [v. 11] operates on two levels, literal and metaphorical, whereas the man's [v. 12] is clearly metaphorical (the woman), one should perhaps not expect the correspondences between the two vineyards to work completely."[8] The woman's comments reflect the mutuality of the relationship as seen throughout the poem and celebrate the value of her vineyard over everything Solomon owns. The verse reinforces the idea that love cannot be bought or coerced and affirms the freedom of the woman to make choices about her sexuality on the basis of love rather than having them dictated to her. Gledhill aptly titles verses 11–12, "A vineyard not for hire."[9]

behaviors and attitudes, can minimize the negative relational outcomes implied in Genesis 3:16—outcomes that are particularly evident in relationships where wealth and power enable men to buy and sell others and use them as things for their own pleasure.

Teaching the Text

It is easy for people to become so enamored with the delight of romance and the desire for intimacy that they try to force commitment through sex or some other means. People destroy marriages to pursue excitement and passion, only to discover that they were pursuing a mirage. They discover, too late, the pain, disaster, and even legal and social consequences that come from pursuing a path contrary to God's order. For all the healing and transforming power of love, romance, and sex, they can also be destructive forces of chaos unless constrained by God's order. Understanding that there is much more to love between a man and a woman than sex equips men and women to plumb the depths of the one-flesh relationship and to receive and give help to one another in ways that reflect God's design.

Few people in Western cultures find themselves subject to power, money, and other such forces in the ways that were common in the ancient Near East, but fallen human beings still manage to manipulate and exploit others. Gledhill talks about the man who is constantly showering gifts on a woman in order to win her affections, who gives her gifts instead of giving himself, or the woman who "can 'sell' her favors to her lover in order to extort from him a greater prize, of security or material advantage or marriage."[12] The same things can happen after people are married.

It is important to develop the habit of living according to God's order in relationships. Honor, respect, and behaving in ways that reflect a deep desire for another's well-being are essential virtues. We must practice the kind of love that God commends in 1 Corinthians 13:4–6,[13] and we need to remember the paradigm for loving one's spouse set forth in Ephesians 5:21–33. In so doing we demonstrate to those around us the nature of God's love for his people.

Last, it is important to understand that relationships do not come to us fully developed, and they continue to change throughout our lives. They can become deeper and more intimate, and the passion and delight can continue to grow, or they can become more distant and strained, but they will not stay the same. Consequently, we must be intentional and focused on our relationships and be willing to adjust as changing circumstances require.

Illustrating the Text

Love is as strong as death.

Poetry: *Sonnets from the Portuguese*, by Elizabeth Barrett Browning. The central claim of the Song is that love is as strong as death (8:6). One of Browning's sonnets ("Sonnet XXVII") captures this idea and reflects her experience. Suffering from ill health, she believed death was imminent. Then her life was turned upside down by her relationship with Robert Browning, convincing her of love's strength in providing a blissful life.

Elizabeth Barrett Browning (1806–61)

My own Belovèd, who hast lifted me
From this drear flat of earth where I
    was thrown,
And, in betwixt the languid ringlets,
    blown
A life-breath, till the forehead
    hopefully
Shines out again, as all the angels see,
Before thy saving kiss! My own, my
    own,
Who camest to me when the world was
    gone,
And I who looked for only God, found
    thee!
I find thee; I am safe, and strong, and
    glad.
As one who stands in dewless asphodel,
Looks backward on the tedious time
    he had

In the upper life,—so I, with
    bosom-swell,
Make witness, here, between the good
    and bad,
That Love, as strong as Death, retrieves
    as well.[14]

Many waters cannot quench love.

Poetry: "To My Dear and Loving Husband," by Anne Bradstreet. Bradstreet (1612–72) was New England's first published poet. In this poem addressed to her husband, she echoes the words of Song of Songs 8:7.

If ever two were one, then surely we.
If ever man were lov'd by wife, then
    thee.
If ever wife was happy in a man,
Compare with me, ye women, if you
    can.
I prize thy love more than whole Mines
    of gold,
Or all the riches that the East doth
    hold.
My love is such that Rivers cannot
    quench,
Nor ought but love from thee give
    recompense.
Thy love is such I can in no way repay;
The heavens reward thee manifold I
    pray.
Then while we live, in love lets so
    persevere,
That when we live no more, we may
    live ever.[15]

Love and the Choices We Make

The mystery of romance and passion is affirmed in the Song, but it is also important to recognize that our choices go a long way toward determining the direction and depth of our relationships. We can choose words that encourage and uplift or words that tear down and humiliate. We can choose to honor or demean; we can choose to praise our partners in ways that stimulate them to grow in love and godliness. We can focus on the ways in which our spouse is a good gift to us, or we can constantly criticize and complain. We also make choices at work, in ministry, and in social settings that reinforce our faithfulness, or we can make choices that put that in jeopardy. Doing the things we see lived out in the Song will not guarantee that our relationships will be characterized by a similar kind of passion and delight, but failing to do them will often leave us bogged down in a relational morass that falls far short of the potential described in

The woman tells her lover to "place me like a seal over your heart, like a seal on your arm" (8:6). Stamp seals were carved with a design or inscription unique to the owner. They were used to make impressions in soft clay bullae (clay molded around a cord) or clay tablets (shown here) to authenticate the sender or owner (Hittite tablet, 1470 BC).

the Song. We must choose to follow God's order, we must be intentional and focused to cultivate behaviors that do not come naturally to us, and we must practice these skills until they become sustainable habits.

While the central teaching of the Song has to do with the power of love and passion, the book also recognizes the importance of commitment in relationships. This is suggested by the affirmation "my beloved belongs to me and I belong to him," which occurs three times in the book (2:16; 6:3; and 7:10),[1] and perhaps by her request that he set her like a seal on his heart and arm. Sometimes passion and commitment pull people in very different directions and profoundly test the will and the choices that people make. Two examples illustrate the dilemma posed by choices that sometimes must be made in the realm of relationships.

A column in the *Chicago Tribune* presents the following case study:

Michael said Elizabeth was the love of his life, but he wound up marrying Karen because of a silly fight. He never loved Karen the way he loved Elizabeth—he thought that "crazy in love" feeling happens only once—but he and Karen had a pretty good marriage and three children. And then he met Kelsey, who was "Elizabeth reincarnated." He felt "crazy in love" again, and this time he didn't want to blow it. He left his wife for Kelsey. Is he a fool? Or a wise man?[2]

The readers who responded to this story were divided on the answer. Several commended Michael for his courage in pursuing passion and love, with one expressing her hope that one day she might muster the courage to do the same thing. Another said that if Michael had stayed with his wife and family he would have cheated himself and Kelsey out of their great love and Karen out of her chance for one. Another also concluded that Michael did the right thing, something that most people lack the courage to do. She said, "So many people remain in marriage for the wrong reasons: children, security, comfort or the fear of the unknown." For these readers passion obviously trumps commitment. Other readers concluded that commitment, responsibility, and integrity are higher values than passion.

A second example comes from an article in *Parade* magazine about Betty Schimmel, a Jewish girl who grew up in Hungary before World War II. She fell in love with a young man named Richie, and they planned to marry. She survived a Nazi concentration camp and after the war tried desperately, but unsuccessfully,

to learn what happened to her fiancé, so she concluded that he had not survived the war. Several years later she married Otto, a man with whom she was not in love but who wanted to marry her even under those conditions. They came to the United States and had several children. More than twenty years later she returned to Hungary for a visit and by chance saw Richie, who happened to be in Budapest for a scientific conference. They still had strong feelings for each other, and he begged her to leave her husband and marry him. The passion was obviously still there, but after a long and difficult struggle, she chose to stay with her husband and family. She said, "For the first time, I allowed myself to love [Otto] for himself." As she reflected on the experience, she concluded, "Over the years, I've had my share of second thoughts. But looking back, after celebrating 50 years of marriage and enjoying all our children and grandchildren, I know I made the right decision. I had once a young love . . . and that was my love for Richie. Then I was fortunate enough to have a mature love, and that was my love for Otto."[3]

The love that Song of Songs 8:6–7 says is stronger than death and that cannot be extinguished by a flood of water consists of far more than romantic love or the "crazy in love" kind of love. It grows and matures over time as people choose to think and act in ways that reflect their faithful love for a spouse. Such behavior often ignites the spark of passion, but whether or not that occurs, such actions, persisted in over time, make for relationships that truly honor God.

Notes

Introduction to Ecclesiastes

1. Pronounced *Ko-heh'-leth*.
2. Some would argue that the book of Ecclesiastes as we have it now has been modified by scribes who were more orthodox than Qoheleth and that Qoheleth himself may well have either questioned the existence of God or held a very different view of God's nature from the view that appears elsewhere in biblical literature.
3. Kushner, *When Bad Things Happen*, 134.
4. Kushner, *When Bad Things Happen*, 148.
5. This theological topic is known as "theodicy," which is defined by *Merriam-Webster's Collegiate Dictionary* (11th ed.) as the "defense of God's goodness and omnipotence in view of the existence of evil."
6. Brueggemann, *Psalms*, 9.
7. Von Rad, *Wisdom in Israel*, 101.
8. Goldingay, *Songs from a Strange Land*, 35.
9. Bartholomew, *Ecclesiastes*, 93.
10. Hill and Walton, *Survey*, 460.

Ecclesiastes 1:1–11

1. George, *Epic of Gilgamesh*, xiii.
2. Kovacs, *Epic of Gilgamesh*, xvii.
3. Van der Toorn, "Echoes of Gilgamesh," 511.
4. See Eccles. 1:3; 2:11, 13; 3:9, 19; 5:16; 6:8, 11; and 7:11, 12.
5. L. Ryken, *Bible as Literature*, 95–96.
6. Kidner, *Message of Ecclesiastes*, 28.
7. Garrett, *Proverbs, Ecclesiastes, Song of Songs*, 287.

Ecclesiastes 1:12–2:11

1. See Eccles. 1:14, 17; 2:1, 11, 15, 17, 19, 21, 23, and 26.
2. Seow, *Ecclesiastes*, 144.
3. For a more detailed discussion, see Longman, *Book of Ecclesiastes*, 17–22, and the additional references there.
4. Kidner, *Message of Ecclesiastes*, 31. Others reach the same conclusion based on the object of his study. Eaton

(*Ecclesiastes*, 62) says, "*All that is done under heaven* shows that the total resources of a limited world-view are the object of the study; the vertical aspect is not yet in view."
5. Goldingay, "'Salvation History' Perspective," 200.
6. Bartholomew, *Ecclesiastes*, 124.
7. Longman, *Book of Ecclesiastes*, 35.
8. Provan, *Ecclesiastes, Song of Songs*, 69–70.
9. For example, spoil taken by soldiers in battle, land assigned to people after the conquest, or an inheritance.
10. Fox, *Time to Tear Down*, 110.
11. Crenshaw, *Old Testament Wisdom*, 18.
12. Crenshaw, *Old Testament Wisdom*, 19.
13. Verheij, "Paradise Retried," 114.
14. Whybray, "Qoheleth as a Theologian," 261.
15. Kushner, *All You've Ever Wanted*, 16.
16. Cited by P. Ryken, *Ecclesiastes*, 39.

Ecclesiastes 2:12–26

1. Kovacs, *Epic of Gilgamesh*, 96.
2. Kovacs, *Epic of Gilgamesh*, 85.
3. Kidner, *Message of Ecclesiastes*, 34.
4. Murphy, *Ecclesiastes*, 27.
5. Ogden and Zogbo, *Handbook on Ecclesiastes*, 83.
6. Crenshaw, *Ecclesiastes*, 91.
7. Goldingay, "'Salvation History' Perspective," 199.
8. Certainly he did not know what the New Testament would later reveal about the topic.
9. Seow, *Ecclesiastes*, 156.
10. Brown, *Ecclesiastes*, 37.
11. Buchanan, "Road to Emmaus," 56.
12. Buchanan, "Road to Emmaus," 57.
13. Brown, *Ecclesiastes*, 38.

Ecclesiastes 3:1–15

1. Provan, *Ecclesiastes, Song of Songs*, 90.
2. Krüger, *Qoheleth*, 88.
3. Kidner, *Message of Ecclesiastes*, 39, italics in original.

4. Garrett, *Proverbs, Ecclesiastes, Song of Songs*, 299.

5. Longman, *Book of Ecclesiastes*, 124.

6. Seow, *Ecclesiastes*, 174.

7. Seow, *Ecclesiastes*, 174.

8. Bartholomew, *Ecclesiastes*, 170, italics in original.

9. Provan, *Ecclesiastes, Song of Songs*, 91.

10. Murphy, *Ecclesiastes*, 114.

Additional Insights, pages 32–33

1. Kidner, *Genesis*, 63.

2. Von Rad, *Genesis*, 89.

3. Von Rad, *Genesis*, 97.

4. Allen, *Spiritual Theology*, 7.

Ecclesiastes 3:16–4:3

1. For example, time and God's control of it (3:1–17), death (2:14–16, 18–21), advantage (1:3–11; 2:3–11; 3:9), human inability to know and control life (1:12–18; 2:22–26; 3:11), and the exhortation to enjoy (2:24–25; 3:12–13).

2. A translation of the edict can be found in Kramer, *Sumerians*, 317–21.

3. Numerous examples can be found in Fensham, "Widow, Orphan, and the Poor," 129–39.

4. Provan, *Ecclesiastes, Song of Songs*, 93.

5. Bartholomew, *Ecclesiastes*, 179.

6. Seow, *Ecclesiastes*, 187.

7. http://boston.com/news/packages/jfkjr/plane_globe.htm.

Additional Insights, pages 40–41

1. Murphy, *Ecclesiastes*, 36.

2. Farmer, *Who Knows*, 162.

Ecclesiastes 4:4–16

1. So Seow, *Ecclesiastes*, 186.

2. Krüger, *Qoheleth*, 94–101.

3. Quoted in Seow, *Ecclesiastes*, 180.

4. See Fox, *Time to Tear Down*, 222.

5. Brown, *Ecclesiastes*, 51.

6. Farmer, *Who Knows*, 165.

7. This is the title of a book by Eugene Peterson. The words are taken from Friedrich Nietzsche: "The essential thing 'in heaven and earth' is . . . that there should be long obedience in the same direction; there thereby results, and has always resulted in the long run, something which has made life worth living" (Nietzsche, *Beyond Good and Evil*, trans. by Helen Zimmern [New York: Macmillan, 1907], section 188; see Peterson, *Long Obedience*, 17).

8. Kidner, *Message of Ecclesiastes*, 52.

9. For example, the destructive nature of idleness, the self-sufficient individual who does not behave wisely in relationships, and the speed with which political fortunes can change.

10. Hoekema, *Created in God's Image*, 76–78.

11. For example, Rom. 12:2; 1 Pet. 1:14; 1 John 2:15, 16; Isa. 52:11; 2 Cor. 6:14–18; along with many warnings throughout the Prophets.

12. Peterson, *Long Obedience*, 11.

13. Kidner, *Psalms 1–72*, 100.

14. Provan, *Ecclesiastes, Song of Songs*, 106.

15. Howard Halpern, "What Defines the 'Successful' Woman," On Your Own, *Los Angeles Times*, May 7, 1989.

16. John Steinbeck, *The Pearl* (New York: Bantam Books, 1967), 30.

Ecclesiastes 5:1–9

1. See the commentary on Eccles. 3:16–4:3, and examples in Fensham, "Widow, Orphan, and the Poor."

2. Petersen, "Tax, Taxing," 603–6.

3. Seow, *Ecclesiastes*, 195.

4. For example, the dreams of Joseph, Pharaoh, or Nebuchadnezzar.

5. Walton, Matthews, and Chavalas, *IVP Bible Backgrounds Commentary*, 572.

6. John Walton, personal communication, December 20, 2011.

7. Bartholomew, *Ecclesiastes*, 216.

8. Longman, *Book of Ecclesiastes*, 156.

9. Garrett, *Proverbs, Ecclesiastes, Song of Songs*, 312.

10. Matthew Saltmarsh, "Going After Government Looters," *New York Times*, June 11, 2010, http://www.nytimes.com/2010/06/12/business/global/12iht-assets12.html?pagewanted=all&_r=0.

Ecclesiastes 5:10–6:9

1. See Gianto, "Human Destiny"; see also Garrett, "Ecclesiastes," *ZIBBCOT* 5:511.

2. Gianto, "Human Destiny," 478.

3. Daniel Gilbert, *Stumbling on Happiness* (New York: Vintage, 2007), 239. He includes references to the most significant studies on this topic.

4. Kamano, *Cosmology and Character*, 149.

5. P. Ryken, *Ecclesiastes*, 129.

6. George Herbert, "The Pulley," in *George Herbert and the Seventeenth-Century Religious Poets*, ed. Mario A. Di Cesare (New York: W. W. Norton, 1978), 57.

Ecclesiastes 6:10–7:14

1. Walton argues that in Genesis God's naming actually brings things into existence insofar as their function is concerned, and if this is the case it further affirms God's sovereignty over creation (*Genesis*, 86–87).

2. Seow, *Ecclesiastes*, 230.

3. Provan, *Ecclesiastes, Song of Songs*, 134.

4. Provan, *Ecclesiastes, Song of Songs*, 134.

5. Murphy, *Ecclesiastes*, 64–65.

6. See Bartholomew, *Ecclesiastes*, 251–52.

7. William Ernest Henley, "Invictus," in *Modern British Poetry*, ed. Louis Untermeyer (New York: Harcourt, Brace and Howe, 1920), 10.

8. Elisabeth Elliot, *In the Shadow of the Almighty* (New York: Harper, 1958), 15, 19.

Additional Insights, pages 68–69

1. For example, see Curtis, "Learning Truth," 113–28.

2. Miller, *Symbol and Rhetoric*, 160–61.

3. Miller, *Symbol and Rhetoric*, 166.
4. Ogden, *Qoheleth*, 110–11.
5. Vawter, "Intimations of Immortality," 163.
6. Fox, *Time to Tear Down*, 25–26.

Ecclesiastes 7:15–29

1. Lambert, *Babylonian Wisdom Literature*, 10–11.
2. Kramer, *Sumerians*, 125.
3. Estes, *Handbook*, 346.
4. Seow, *Ecclesiastes*, 267.
5. Gordis, *Koheleth*, 277.
6. Many argue that "fear of God" in Ecclesiastes has a different meaning than it does elsewhere in the Old Testament. See comment above on 3:14.
7. Garrett, *Proverbs, Ecclesiastes, Song of Songs*, 324.
8. Seow, *Ecclesiastes*, 271.
9. Seow, *Ecclesiastes*, 270.
10. Estes, *Handbook*, 350.
11. Provan, *Ecclesiastes, Song of Songs*, 150.
12. Provan, *Ecclesiastes, Song of Songs*, 151.
13. Provan, *Ecclesiastes, Song of Songs*, 151.

Additional Insights, pages 76–77

1. So Murphy, *Ecclesiastes*, 76–77; Ogden and Zogbo, *Handbook on Ecclesiastes*, 272–73.

Ecclesiastes 8:1–17

1. Lichtheim, *Ancient Egyptian Literature*, 2:143.
2. See Pritchard, *Ancient Near Eastern Texts*, 428–29, ll. 95–110.
3. Provan, *Ecclesiastes, Song of Songs*, 168.
4. Goldingay, "'Salvation History' Perspective," 200.
5. L. E. Maxwell, *Crowded to Christ* (Grand Rapids: Eerdmans, 1955), 37.
6. See P. Ryken, *Ecclesiastes*, 181, 189.

Ecclesiastes 9:1–18

1. Lichtheim, *Ancient Egyptian Literature*, 1:193; for the text of a song, see 196–97.
2. George, *Epic of Gilgamesh*, 124.
3. Kidner, *Message of Ecclesiastes*, 80.
4. Kidner, *Message of Ecclesiastes*, 81.
5. Provan, *Ecclesiastes, Song of Songs*, 193.
6. Estes, *Handbook*, 357.
7. Ogden, *Qoheleth*, 159.
8. Farmer, *Who Knows*, 183.
9. Farmer, *Who Knows*, 185.

Additional Insights, pages 90–91

1. Ogden, *Qoheleth*, 157.
2. Farmer, *Who Knows*, 185.
3. Longman, *Book of Ecclesiastes*, 223.

Ecclesiastes 10:1–20

1. Seow, *Ecclesiastes*, 325.
2. Shupak, "Admonitions," 93.
3. Fox, *Time to Tear Down*, 306, italics in original.

4. The word is used to describe Solomon when he becomes king (1 Kings 3:7).
5. Murphy, *Ecclesiastes*, 105.
6. Kenneth Grahame, *The Wind in the Willows* (London: Folio Society, 1997), 96.
7. Hans Christian Andersen, "The Emperor's New Clothes," in *The Arbuthnot Anthology of Children's Literature*, vol. 2, *Time for Fairy Tales*, ed. Zena Sutherland, May Hill Arbuthnot, et al., rev. ed. (Glenview, IL: Scott, Foresman, 1961), 368.
8. Michael Glenny and Norman Stone, *The Other Russia: The Experience of Exile* (New York: Viking, 1990).

Ecclesiastes 11:1–12:8

1. Translations of these passages can be found in Seow, *Ecclesiastes*, 373–75.
2. Lichtheim, *Ancient Egyptian Literature*, 1:193.
3. Seow, *Ecclesiates*, 348.
4. Provan, *Ecclesiastes, Song of Songs*, 213.
5. Walton, *Genesis*, 38–109.
6. Ogden, *Qoheleth*, 224.
7. Seow, *Ecclesiastes*, 371, italics in original.

Additional Insights, pages 104–5

1. Fox, "Aging and Death," 55.
2. Estes, *Handbook*, 375.
3. Farmer, *Who Knows*, 193–94.
4. Bartholomew, *Ecclesiastes*, 353.

Ecclesiastes 12:9–14

1. Seow, *Ecclesiastes*, 392. For a translation of the text, see Lichtheim, *Ancient Egyptian Literature*, 1:59–60.
2. Estes, *Handbook*, 381.
3. Garrett, *Proverbs, Ecclesiastes, Song of Songs*, 345.
4. Nancy M. Tischler, *All Things in the Bible: An Encyclopedia of the Biblical World* (Westport, CT: Greenwood, 2006), 250–51.
5. Tosefta (on Parah 4:1), cited by T. A. Perry, *Dialogues with Kohelet* (State College: Penn State Press, 1993), 40.
6. This description is taken from Bruce and Laurel Aulie, prayer letter, September 29, 2001.

Introduction to Song of Songs

1. With the possible exception of 8:6.
2. Clues like those regularly found in *Pilgrim's Progress*, by John Bunyan.
3. John Walton, personal correspondence, December 29, 2011.
4. Deere, "Song of Songs," 2.
5. First Kings 4:32 says that Solomon "spoke three thousand proverbs and his songs numbered a thousand and five."
6. Pope summarizes opinions about the date of the book (*Song of Songs*, 22–33). It is clear that many who dismiss the significance of the references to Solomon still date the book to the Solomonic era. Clearly these scholars do not see the linguistic evidence as precluding such a date.
7. Hess, *Song of Songs*, 19.
8. Gledhill, *Message*, 28.

9. Estes, "Song of Songs," 292.
10. Gledhill, *Message*, 29.
11. L. Ryken, *Literature of the Bible*, 121.
12. Exum, *Song of Songs*, 10.
13. Gledhill, *Message*, 30.
14. Exum, *Song of Songs*, 7–8.

Song of Songs 1:1–2:7

1. See Lapinkivi, *Sumerian Sacred Marriage*, 1–14, 241–48.
2. Exum, *Song of Songs*, 104.
3. Hess, *Song of Songs*, 60.
4. Exum, *Song of Songs*, 109.
5. Pope, *Song of Songs*, 338–39.
6. Bergant, *Song of Songs*, 19.
7. The perfume is likely nard—a fragrant, exotic, and expensive oil from the Himalayan region of India.
8. Keel, *Song of Songs*, 78–80.
9. Keel, *Song of Songs*, 80.
10. Carpenter and Grisanti, "דֶּגֶל," 920.
11. See Pope, *Song of Songs*, 375–77.
12. Gordis, *Song of Songs*, 38, italics in original.
13. White, *Language of Love*, 105.
14. Longman, *Song of Songs*, 115.
15. Hubbard, *Ecclesiastes, Song of Solomon*, 288.
16. For the view that the admonition is a call not to disturb the couple until their lovemaking is complete and a critique of the view advocated here, see Gault, "Admonition."
17. H. A. Ironside, *Addresses on the Song of Solomon* (New York: Loizeaux Brothers, Bible Truth Depot, 1933), 30.
18. Elizabeth Barrett Browning, "Sonnet I," in *Sonnets from the Portuguese* (Portland, ME: Thomas B. Mosher, 1910), 3.

Song of Songs 2:8–3:5

1. Fox, *Song of Songs*, 66–68.
2. Examples of such common themes and metaphors can be found throughout Fox, *Song of Songs*, and Munro, *Spikenard and Saffron*.
3. Bergant, *Song of Songs*, 30.
4. Bergant, *Song of Songs*, 32.
5. Hess, *Song of Songs*, 100.
6. Campbell, *Ruth*, 64.
7. Much as we see the farmer doing in Isa. 28:23–29.
8. Hess, *Song of Songs*, 101.
9. John Boyle O'Reilly, "A White Rose," in *The Oxford Book of English Verse: 1250–1918*, ed. Arthur Quiller-Couch (London: Oxford University Press, 1919), 831.
10. Lewis Smedes, *Sex for Christians* (Grand Rapids: Eerdmans, 1976), 38–39.

Additional Insights, pages 132–33

1. Bergant, *Song of Songs*, 33.
2. Gledhill, *Message*, 128–29.

Song of Songs 3:6–5:1

1. Van der Toorn, "Significance of the Veil," 330.
2. Van der Toorn, "Significance of the Veil," 332.

3. Bergant, *Song of Songs*, 44.
4. Keel, *Song of Songs*, 143–47.
5. Keel, *Song of Songs*, 147 (see also the figures on pp. 60, 90).
6. The likely meaning of the word the NIV translates as "lilies."
7. Keel, *Song of Songs*, 147–51.
8. Keel, *Song of Songs*, 151.
9. See, for example, Wiseman, "Mesopotamian Gardens," 137–44; and Fox, *Song of Songs*, 283–87.
10. Munro, *Spikenard and Saffron*, 107.
11. Exum, *Song of Songs*, 157.
12. Bloch and Bloch, *Song of Songs*, 35.
13. See John Gottman, *Why Marriages Succeed or Fail* (New York: Simon & Schuster, 1995).
14. Elizabeth Barrett Browning, "Sonnet XXI," in *Sonnets from the Portuguese* (Portland, ME: Thomas B. Mosher, 1910), 23.

Additional Insights, pages 140–41

1. Posner, "Marriage: Marriage Ceremony," 565.
2. Posner, "Marriage: Marriage Ceremony," 565.
3. Munro, *Spikenard and Saffron*, 53.
4. Van der Toorn, "Significance of the Veil," 331.
5. Garrett, *Song of Songs*, 193.
6. Munro, *Spikenard and Saffron*, 108.

Song of Songs 5:2–6:3

1. For more on *wasfs*, see the "Historical and Cultural Background" section in the unit on Song 3:6–5:1.
2. For a discussion of the controversy associated with the Sumerian sacred marriage texts and their possible relevance to Song of Songs, see Lapinkivi, *Sumerian Sacred Marriage*, 1–14, 241–48.
3. Jacobsen, *Harps That Once . . .* , 19.
4. Fox, *Song of Songs*, 75, italics in original.
5. Murphy, *Song of Songs*, 97.
6. Exum, *Song of Songs*, 192.
7. Bergant, *Song of Songs*, 63.
8. Munro, *Spikenard and Saffron*, 129.
9. Keel, *Song of Songs*, 195.
10. For example, Nebuchadnezzar's image in Daniel 2.
11. Exum, *Song of Songs*, 204.
12. According to Keel, such examples date back to at least 2000 BC (*Song of Songs*, 199–201).
13. Keel, *Song of Songs*, 201.
14. Bergant, *Song of Songs*, 71.
15. Keel, *Song of Songs*, 201–2.
16. Talley, "חמד," 168.
17. Fox, *Song of Songs*, 149.
18. Edmund Spenser, "Amoretti," in *English Poetry* (1170–1892), selected by John Matthews Manley (Boston: Ginn, 1907), 90.

Song of Songs 6:4–7:13

1. Fox, *Song of Songs*, 52–55.
2. Fox, *Song of Songs*, 73.
3. See Garrett, "Song of Songs," *ZIBBCOT* 5:528.

4. Hess, *Song of Songs*, 200.

5. Keel, *Song of Songs*, 218.

6. Keel, *Song of Songs*, 218.

7. Walton, "עֲלוּמִים," 415–19.

8. For examples of this, see Keel, *Song of Songs*, 220–21.

9. Garrett, *Song of Songs*, 229.

10. Pope, *Song of Songs*, 574–79.

11. Bergant, *Song of Songs*, 79.

12. Gledhill, *Message*, 205.

13. Or perhaps hips or buttocks.

14. Keel, *Song of Songs*, 78–80, 114–15, 234–35.

15. Keel, *Song of Songs*, 236.

16. Keel, *Song of Songs*, 242.

17. Hess, *Song of Songs*, 222.

18. Hess, *Song of Songs*, 223.

19. Gledhill, *Message*, 192–93.

20. Sonnet 116 ("Let Me Not to the Marriage of True Minds"). See the "Illustrating the Text" section in this unit.

21. House and Durham, *Living Wisely*, 72.

22. George Eliot, *Adam Bede*, in *The Best-Known Novels of George Eliot* (New York: Random House, n.d.), 386. "George Eliot" is the pen name of Mary Ann Evans (1819–80).

23. William Shakespeare, "Let Me Not to the Marriage of True Minds," in *Great Sonnets*, ed. Paul Negri (New York: Dover, 1994), 15.

Additional Insights, pages 154–55

1. Gledhill, *Message*, 188.

2. Gledhill, *Message*, 189.

Song of Songs 8:1–14

1. The term likely refers both to an actual vineyard and is a figure for his harem.

2. Exum, *Song of Songs*, 13.

3. Munro, *Spikenard and Saffron*, 147.

4. Longman, *Song of Songs*, 210.

5. Carr, *Song of Solomon*, 170.

6. Garrett, *Song of Songs*, 256–57.

7. Estes, *Handbook*, 436.

8. Exum, *Song of Songs*, 261.

9. Gledhill, *Message*, 238.

10. Bergant, *Song of Songs*, 105.

11. Walton, *Genesis*, 91.

12. Gledhill, *Message*, 241.

13. The love described in 1 Cor. 13:4–6 is "patient and kind; [it] does not envy or boast; it is not arrogant or rude. It does not insist on its own way; it is not irritable or resentful; it does not rejoice at wrongdoing, but rejoices with the truth" (ESV).

14. Elizabeth Barrett Browning, "Sonnet XXVII," in *Sonnets from the Portuguese* (Portland, ME: Thomas B. Mosher, 1910), 29.

15. Anne Bradstreet, "To My Dear and Loving Husband," in *The American Tradition in Literature*, ed. Sculley Bradley et al., 4th ed. (New York: Grosset & Dunlap, 1978), 24.

Additional Insights, pages 162–63

1. It is interesting to note that this is the one phrase from Song of Songs that is used in Jewish wedding ceremonies today.

2. Cheryl Lavin, "Crazy in Love, or Just Crazy? Readers Check In," Tales from the Front, *Chicago Tribune*, July 18, 1993, http://articles.chicagotribune.com/1993-07-18/features/9307180255_1_crazy-love-wrong-reasons.

3. Joyce Gabriel, "It Was the Hardest Choice of My Life," *Parade*, July 30, 2000, 9. The full story is told in Joyce Gabriel and Betty Schimmel, *To See You Again: A True Story of Love in a Time of War* (New York: Plume, 2000).

Bibliography

Recommended Resources

Bartholomew, Craig G. *Ecclesiastes*. Grand Rapids: Baker Academic, 2009.

Bergant, Dianne. *The Song of Songs*. Berit Olam. Collegeville, MN: Liturgical Press, 2001.

Exum, J. Cheryl. *Song of Songs*. Old Testament Library. Louisville: Westminster John Knox, 2005.

Gledhill, Tom. *The Message of the Song of Songs*. Bible Speaks Today. Downers Grove, IL: InterVarsity, 1994.

Hess, Richard. *Song of Songs*. Baker Commentary on the Old Testament Wisdom and Psalms. Grand Rapids: Baker Academic, 2005.

Longman, Tremper, III. *The Book of Ecclesiastes*. New International Commentary on the Old Testament. Grand Rapids: Eerdmans, 1998.

———. *Song of Songs*. New International Commentary on the Old Testament. Grand Rapids: Eerdmans, 2001.

Ryken, Philip Graham. *Ecclesiastes: Why Everything Matters*. Preaching the Word. Wheaton: Crossway, 2010.

Seow, C. L. *Ecclesiastes*. Anchor Bible 18C. New York: Doubleday, 1997.

Select Bibliography

Allen, Diogenes. *Spiritual Theology*. Boston: Cowley Publications, 1997.

Barton, George A. *The Book of Ecclesiastes*. International Critical Commentary. Edinburgh: T&T Clark, 1908.

Bloch, Chana, and Ariel Bloch. *The Song of Songs*. New York: Modern Library, 2006.

Brown, William. *Ecclesiastes*. Interpretation. Louisville: Westminster John Knox, 2000.

Brueggemann, Walter. *The Psalms and the Life of Faith*. Minneapolis: Fortress, 1995.

Buchanan, Mark. "Stuck on the Road to Emmaus." *Christianity Today* 43, no. 8 (July 12, 1999): 55–57.

Campbell, Edward F. *Ruth*. Anchor Bible 7. New York: Doubleday, 1975.

Carpenter, Eugene, and Michael A. Grisanti. "דָּגֵל." In *New International Dictionary of Old Testament Theology and Exegesis*, edited by Willem VanGemeren, 1:919–20. Grand Rapids: Zondervan, 1997.

Carr, G. Lloyd. *The Song of Solomon*. Tyndale Old Testament Commentaries. Downers Grove, IL: InterVarsity, 1984.

Coogan, Michael D. *A Reader of Ancient Near Eastern Texts: Sources for the Study of the Old Testament*. New York: Oxford University Press, 2012.

Crenshaw, James. *Ecclesiastes*. Old Testament Library. Philadelphia: Westminster, 1987.

———. *Old Testament Wisdom*. Atlanta: John Knox, 1981.

Curtis, Edward. "Learning Truth from the Sages." *Christian Education Journal* 2 (2005): 113–28.

Deere, Jack. "The Meaning of the Song of Songs: An Historical and Exegetical Inquiry." ThD diss., Dallas Theological Seminary, 1984.

Eaton, Michael A. *Ecclesiastes*. Tyndale Old Testament Commentary. Downers Grove, IL: InterVarsity, 1983.

Estes, Daniel. *Handbook on the Wisdom Books and Psalms*. Grand Rapids: Baker Academic, 2005.

———. "Song of Songs." In *Ecclesiastes and the Song of Songs*, by Daniel Estes and Daniel Fredericks, 265–444. Apollos Old Testament Commentary. Downers Grove, IL: InterVarsity, 2010.

Falk, Marcia. *Love Lyrics from the Bible*. Sheffield: Almond, 1982.

Farmer, Kathleen. *Who Knows What Is Good? A Commentary on the Books of Proverbs and Ecclesiastes*. International Theological Commentary. Grand Rapids: Eerdmans, 1991.

Fensham, Charles. "Widow, Orphan, and the Poor in Ancient Near Eastern Legal and Wisdom Literature." *Journal of Near Eastern Studies* 21 (1962): 129–39.

Fox, Michael V. "Aging and Death in Qoheleth 12." *Journal for the Study of the Old Testament* 42 (1988): 55–77.

———. *The Song of Songs and the Ancient Egyptian Love Songs*. Madison: University of Wisconsin Press, 1985.

———. *A Time to Tear Down and a Time to Build Up*. Grand Rapids: Eerdmans, 1999.

Garrett, Duane. "Ecclesiastes." In *Zondervan Illustrated Bible Backgrounds Commentary: Old Testament*, edited by John H. Walton, 5:504–17. Grand Rapids: Zondervan, 2009.

———. *Proverbs, Ecclesiastes, Song of Songs*. New American Commentary. Nashville: Broadman, 1993.

———. *Song of Songs*. In *Song of Songs, Lamentations*, by Duane Garrett and Paul R. House, 1–265. Word Biblical Commentary 23B. Nashville: Thomas Nelson, 2004.

———. "Song of Songs." In *Zondervan Illustrated Bible Backgrounds Commentary: Old Testament*, edited by John H. Walton, 5:518–33. Grand Rapids: Zondervan, 2009.

Gault, Brian. "An Admonition against 'Rousing Love': The Meaning of the Enigmatic Refrain in Song of Songs." *Bulletin for Biblical Research* 20 (2010): 161–84.

George, Andrew. *The Epic of Gilgamesh*. New York: Barnes & Noble, 1999.

Gianto, Augustinus. "Human Destiny in Emar and Qohelet." In *Qohelet in the Context of Wisdom*, edited by A. Schoors, 473–79. Bibliotheca Ephemeridum Theologicarum Lovaniensium 136. Leuven: Leuven University Press, 1998.

Ginsburg, Christian David. *The Song of Songs and Coheleth*. 1857. Reprint, New York: KTAV, 1970.

Glickman, S. Craig. *A Song for Lovers*. Downers Grove, IL: InterVarsity, 1976.

Goldingay, John. "The 'Salvation History' Perspective and the 'Wisdom' Perspective within the Context of Biblical Theology." *Evangelical Quarterly* 51 (1979): 194–204.

———. *Songs from a Strange Land: Psalms 42–51*. Downers Grove, IL: InterVarsity, 1978.

Gordis, Robert. *Koheleth—The Man and His World*. New York: Schocken, 1951.

———. *The Song of Songs and Lamentations*. Rev. ed. New York: KTAV, 1958.

Greenstein, Edward. "Sages with a Sense of Humor: The Babylonian Dialogue between a Master and His Servant and the Book of Qoheleth." In *Wisdom Literature in Mesopotamia and Israel*, edited by Richard J. Clifford, 55–65. Society of Biblical Literature Symposium Series 36. Atlanta: Society of Biblical Literature, 2007.

Greidanus, Sidney. *Preaching Christ from Ecclesiastes*. Grand Rapids: Eerdmans, 2010.

Gunn, Battiscombe G. *The Instruction of Ptah-Hotep and the Instruction of Ke'Gemni: The Oldest Books in the World*. Reprint of the 1909 edition, Project Gutenberg, 2009. http://www.gutenberg.org/files/30508/30508-h/30508-h.htm.

Hengstenberg, E. W. *Commentary on the Book of Ecclesiastes*. 1869. Reprint, Minneapolis: James & Klock, 1977.

Hill, Andrew, and John Walton. *A Survey of the Old Testament*. 3rd ed. Grand Rapids: Zondervan, 2009.

Hoekema, Anthony. *Created in God's Image*. Grand Rapids: Eerdmans, 1986.

House, Wayne, and Kenneth Durham. *Living Wisely in a Foolish World*. Grand Rapids: Kregel, 1997.

Hubbard, David. *Ecclesiastes, Song of Solomon*. Communicator's Commentary. Dallas: Word, 1991.

Jacobsen, Thorkild. *The Harps That Once . . . : Sumerian Poetry in Translation*. New Haven: Yale University Press, 1987.

———. *The Treasures of Darkness*. New Haven: Yale University Press, 1976.

Kaiser, Walter C., Jr. *Ecclesiastes: Total Life*. Chicago: Moody, 1979.

Kamano, Naoto. *Cosmology and Character: Qoheleth's Pedagogy from a Rhetorical-Critical Perspective*. New York: Walter de Gruyter, 2002.

Keel, Othmar. *Gods, Goddesses, and Images of God in Ancient Israel*. Translated by Thomas H. Trapp. Minneapolis: Fortress, 1998.

———. *The Song of Songs*. Translated by Frederick J. Gaiser. Continental Commentary. Minneapolis: Fortress, 1994.

Kidner, Derek. *Genesis*. Tyndale Old Testament Commentaries. Downers Grove, IL: InterVarsity, 1967.

———. *The Message of Ecclesiastes*. The Bible Speaks Today. Downers Grove, IL: InterVarsity, 1976.

———. *Psalms 1–72*. Tyndale Old Testament Commentaries. Downers Grove, IL: InterVarsity, 1973.

Kinlaw, Dennis. "Song of Songs." In *The Expositor's Bible Commentary*, edited by Frank E. Gaebelein, 5:1199–1244. Grand Rapids: Zondervan, 1991.

Kovacs, Maureen Gallery. *The Epic of Gilgamesh*. Stanford, CA: Stanford University Press, 1989.

Kramer, Samuel Noah. *The Sumerians*. Chicago: University of Chicago Press, 1963.

Krüger, Thomas. *Qoheleth: A Commentary*. Translated by O. C. Dean. Hermeneia. Minneapolis: Fortress, 2004.

Kushner, Harold S. *When All You've Ever Wanted Isn't Enough*. New York: Pocket, 1986.

———. *When Bad Things Happen to Good People*. New York: Schocken, 1981.

Lambert, W. G. *Babylonian Wisdom Literature*. Oxford: Clarendon, 1960.

Lapinkivi, Pirjo. *The Sumerian Sacred Marriage in the Light of Comparative Evidence*. The Neo-Assyrian Text Corpus Project 15. Helsinki: University of Helsinki Press, 2004.

Lichtheim, Miriam. *Ancient Egyptian Literature*. 3 vols. Berkeley: University of California Press, 1975–80.

Limburg, James. *Encountering Ecclesiastes*. Grand Rapids: Eerdmans, 2006.

Lohfink, Norbert. *Qohelet*. Translated by Sean McEvenue. Continental Commentaries. Minneapolis: Fortress, 2003.

Longman, Tremper, III, and Peter Enns, eds. *Dictionary of the Old Testament: Wisdom, Poetry, and Writings*. Downers Grove, IL: IVP Academic, 2008.

Meyers, Jeffrey. *A Table in the Mist: Meditations on Ecclesiastes*. Monroe, LA: Athanasius, 2006.

Miller, Douglas B. *Symbol and Rhetoric in Ecclesiastes*. Atlanta: Society of Biblical Literature, 2002.

Munro, Jill M. *Spikenard and Saffron: A Study of the Poetic Language of the Song of Songs*. Journal for the Study of the Old Testament Supplement Series 203. Sheffield: Sheffield Academic Press, 1995.

Murphy, Roland E. *Ecclesiastes*. Word Biblical Commentary 23A. Waco: Word, 1992.

———. *Proverbs*. Word Biblical Commentary 22. Nashville: Thomas Nelson, 1998.

———. *The Song of Songs*. Hermeneia. Minneapolis: Fortress, 1990.

Ogden, Graham S. *Qoheleth*. 2nd ed. Sheffield: Sheffield Phoenix, 2007.

Ogden, Graham S., and Lynell Zogbo. *A Handbook on Ecclesiastes*. New York: United Bible Societies, 1997.

Perry, T. A. *Dialogues with Qohelet*. State College: Penn State Press, 1993.

Petersen, L. M. "Tax, Taxing." In *The Zondervan Pictorial Encyclopedia of the Bible*, edited by Merrill C. Tenney, 5:603–6. Grand Rapids: Zondervan, 1975.

Peterson, Eugene. *A Long Obedience in the Same Direction: Discipleship in an Instant Society*. Downers Grove, IL: InterVarsity, 1980.

Pope, Marvin. *Song of Songs*. Anchor Bible 7C. Garden City, NY: Doubleday, 1977.

Posner, Raphael. "Marriage: Marriage Ceremony." In *Encyclopaedia Judaica*, edited by Fred Skolnik and Michael Berenbaum, 2nd ed., 13:565–68. New York: Macmillan Reference USA, 2007.

Pritchard, James B. *Ancient Near Eastern Texts Relating to the Old Testament*. 3rd ed. with supplement. Princeton: Princeton University Press, 1969.

Provan, Iain. *Ecclesiastes, Song of Songs*. NIV Application Commentary. Grand Rapids: Zondervan, 2001.

Rad, Gerhard von. *Genesis*. Translated by John H. Marks. Old Testament Library. Philadelphia: Westminster, 1972.

———. *Wisdom in Israel*. Translated by James D. Martin. Nashville: Abingdon, 1972.

Rowley, H. H. "The Interpretation of the Song of Songs." In *The Servant of the Lord and Other Essays on the Old Testament*, 2nd rev. ed., 195–245. Oxford: Blackwell, 1965.

Ryken, Leland. *How to Read the Bible as Literature*. Grand Rapids: Zondervan, 1984.

———. *The Literature of the Bible*. Grand Rapids: Zondervan, 1974.

Short, Robert L. *A Time to Be Born—A Time to Die*. New York: Harper & Row, 1973.

Shupak, Nili. "The Admonitions of an Egyptian Sage: The Admonitions of Ipuwer (1.42)." In *The Context of Scripture*, edited by William Hallo and K. Lawson Younger, 1:93–98. Leiden: Brill, 1997.

Talley, David. "חמד." In *New International Dictionary of Old Testament Theology & Exegesis*, edited by Willem VanGemeren, 2:167–69. Grand Rapids: Zondervan, 1997.

Trible, Phyllis. *God and the Rhetoric of Sexuality*. Overtures to Biblical Theology. Philadelphia: Fortress, 1978.

Van der Toorn, Karel. "Echoes of Gilgamesh in the Book of Qohelet? A Reassessment of the Intellectual Sources of Qohelet." In *Veenhof Anniversary Volume*, edited by W. H. van Soldt, 503–14. Leiden: Nederlands Instituut voor het Nabije Oosten, 2001.

———. "The Significance of the Veil in the Ancient Near East." In *Pomegranates and Golden Bells*, edited by David P. Wright, David Noel Freedman, and Avi Hurvitz, 327–40. Winona Lake, IN: Eisenbrauns, 1995.

VanGemeren, Willem, ed. *New International Dictionary of Old Testament Theology & Exegesis*. 5 vols. Grand Rapids: Zondervan, 1997.

Vawter, Bruce. "Intimations of Immortality and the Old Testament." *Journal of Biblical Literature* 91 (1972): 158–71.

Verheij, Arian. "Paradise Retried: On Qohelet 2:4–6." *Journal for the Study of the Old Testament* 50 (1991): 113–15.

Walton, John H. "עֲלוּמִים." In *New International Dictionary of Old Testament Theology & Exegesis*, edited by Willem VanGemeren, 2:167–69. Grand Rapids: Zondervan, 1997.

———. *Genesis*. NIV Application Commentary. Grand Rapids: Zondervan, 2001.

Walton, John, Victor Matthews, and Mark Chavalas. *The IVP Bible Backgrounds Commentary*. Downers Grove, IL: InterVarsity, 2000.

White, John. *A Study of the Language of Love in the Song of Songs and Ancient Egyptian Poetry*. SBL Dissertation Series 38. Missoula, MT: Scholars Press, 1975.

Whybray, R. N. *Ecclesiastes*. New Century Bible Commentary. Grand Rapids: Eerdmans, 1989.

———. "Qoheleth as a Theologian." In *Qohelet in the Context of Wisdom*, edited by A. Schoors, 239–65. Bibliotheca Ephemeridum Theologicarum Lovaniensium 136. Leuven: Leuven University Press, 1998.

Wiersbe, Warren. *Be Satisfied: Looking for the Answer to the Meaning of Life*. Old Testament Commentary. Wheaton: Victor, 1990.

Wiseman, Donald. "Mesopotamian Gardens." *Anatolian Studies* 33 (1983): 137–44.

Wright, J. Stafford. "Ecclesiastes." In *The Expositor's Bible Commentary*, edited by Frank E. Gaebelein, 5:1135–97. Grand Rapids: Zondervan, 1991.

Zuck, Roy B., ed. *Reflecting with Solomon: Selected Studies on the Book of Ecclesiastes*. Grand Rapids: Baker, 1994.

Image Credits

Unless otherwise indicated, photos, illustrations, and maps are copyright © Baker Photo Archive.

The Baker Photo Archive acknowledges the permission of the following institutions and individuals.

Photos on pages 74, 101, 116 © Baker Photo Archive. Courtesy of the Aegyptisches Museum, Berlin, Germany.

Photos on pages 18, 26–27, 36, 46, 66, 73, 82, 88, 122, 132, 151 © Baker Photo Archive. Courtesy of the British Museum, London, England.

Photo on page 94 © Baker Photo Archive. Courtesy of the Eretz Israel Museum, Tel Aviv, Israel.

Photo on page 5 © Baker Photo Archive. Courtesy of the Jordanian Ministry of Antiquities and the Amman Archaeological Museum.

Photos on pages 34, 55, 63, 70, 80, 124 © Baker Photo Archive. Courtesy of the Musée du Louvre; Autorisation de photographer et de filmer. Louvre, Paris, France.

Photos on pages 9, 14, 21, 40, 52 © Baker Photo Archive. Courtesy of the Oriental Institute Museum, Chicago. Inscription on page 14 quoted from museum sign.

Photo on page 106 © Baker Photo Archive. Courtesy of the Pergamon Museum, Berlin.

Photos on pages 1, 29, 114 © Baker Photo Archive. Courtesy of the Turkish Ministry of Antiquities and the Istanbul Archaeological Museum.

Photos on pages 3, 50 © Baker Photo Archive. Courtesy of the Vatican Museum.

Additional image credits

Photo on page 93 © Dr. James C. Martin and the Israel Museum. Collection of the Israel Museum, Jerusalem, and courtesy of the Israel Antiquities Authority, exhibited at the Israel Museum, Jerusalem.

Photo on page 7 © Dr. James C. Martin and the Israel Museum. Collection of the Israel Museum, Jerusalem, and courtesy of the Israel Antiquities Authority, exhibited at the Rockefeller Museum, Jerusalem.

Photo on page 86 © Ealdgyth. Courtesy of the British Museum, London, England / Wikimedia Commons, CC-by-sa-3.0.

Photo on page 134 © Egyptian National Museum, Cairo, Egypt / The Bridgeman Art Library.

Photo on page 12 © HoremWeb / Wikimedia Commons, CC-by-sa-3.0.

Photo on page 32 © Jebulon / Wikimedia Commons.

Photo on page 145 © Jerzy Strzelecki / Wikimedia Commons, CC-by-sa-3.0.

Photo on page 154 © Kim Walton.

Photos on pages 56, 102 © Kim Walton. Courtesy of the British Museum, London, England.

Photo on page 157 © Kim Walton. Courtesy of the Israel Museum, Jerusalem, and courtesy of the Israel Antiquities Authority.

Photo on page 118 © Kim Walton. Courtesy of the Musée du Louvre; Autorisation de photographer et de filmer. Louvre, Paris, France.

Photos on pages 111, 140, 143 © Kim Walton. Courtesy of the Metropolitan Museum of Art, New York.

Photo on page 79 © Kim Walton. Courtesy of the Papyrus Collection, Neues Museum, Berlin, Germany.

Photo on page 162 © Kim Walton. Courtesy of the Pergamon Museum, Berlin, Germany.

Photo on page 25 © Library of Congress, Prints & Photographs Division [LC-USZ62-109888].

Photo on page 161 © Library of Congress, Prints & Photographs Division [LC-DIG-ggbain-03571].

Contributors

General Editors
Mark L. Strauss
John H. Walton

Associate Editor, Illustrating the Text
Rosalie de Rosset

Series Development
Jack Kuhatschek
Brian Vos

Project Editor
James Korsmo

Interior Design
Brian Brunsting

Visual Content
Kim Walton

Cover Direction
Paula Gibson
Michael Cook

Image Credits

Index